ACROSS THE ROOF OF THE WORLD

Photogravure by Emery Walker from a photograph

ACROSS THE ROOF
OF THE WORLD

A RECORD OF SPORT AND TRAVEL
THROUGH KASHMIR, GILGIT, HUNZA,
THE PAMIRS, CHINESE TURKISTAN,
MONGOLIA AND SIBERIA

BY

LIEUT. P T ETHERTON,
F.R.G S F Z S.

39TH GARHWAL RIFLES (INDIAN ARMY)

Travel is conquest
—ARAB PROVERB

WITH MAP AND ILLUSTRATIONS

NEW YORK
FREDERICK A STOKES COMPANY
PUBLISHERS

TO THE

𝔐emory

OF

MY MOTHER

THE FIRST INTIMATION OF WHOSE ILLNESS AND DEATH
I RECEIVED ON REACHING THE TRANS-SIBERIAN RAIL-
WAY, AND TO WHOSE DEEP AND ABIDING INTEREST IN
THE EXPEDITION I OWE SO MUCH

255903

CONTENTS.

——◆——

LIST OF ILLUSTRATIONS.

—◆—

PREFACE.

THE following narrative constitutes an account of a Trans-Asiatic journey of nearly four thousand miles which led me from India through Kashmir, Gilgit, Hunza, and over the Pamirs (the Roof of the World), thence through Chinese Tartary, Mongolia, and Siberia, to the Trans-Siberian Railway, a journey to the successful completion of which considerable doubt had been expressed prior to my departure, since it had never previously been essayed

The book lays no claim to being other than a plain record of a year's wanderings in the lesser known parts of Central Asia for the purposes of sport and travel

An expedition of this nature cannot but be interesting and instructive from whatever point of view it is regarded, since it affords some of the finest shooting in the world, leads amongst strange and fascinating tribes of nomads, and takes one through countries which ancient associations have invested with a halo of romance, and have, more particularly in recent years, given rise to questions of deep political import

It has been asked what are the possibilities of the journey across Asia from India to Siberia being accomplished in the future by means of the railway On such a question I would not venture to legislate, since it is essentially one for the engineer rather than the wandering sportsman From my own observations, however, such an undertaking seems impracticable, for the lofty mountain ranges to be crossed and the many stupendous physical obstacles to over-come appear to me to present insurmountable difficulties. Never-theless, it may be that in the years which are to come the engineering skill and indomitable perseverance displayed by the nations of the West will triumph and a Trans-Asiatic railway eventuate

Of the illustrations contained in the book, one hundred and twenty are from my own photographs, and for the remaining ten I owe thanks to Captain Ronald Cheape, 1st King's Dragoon Guards

In connection with my arrangements for the expedition from its inception to its final conclusion I am indebted to many for much ready and willing assistance   Foremost in this respect I would beg His Excellency Sir Arthur Nicolson, then His Majesty's Ambassador at St Petersburg, to accept grateful thanks for much kindly interest shown me when frostbitten near the Siberian frontier, and to his representations thereon to the Russian Government on my behalf

I am under a deep sense of obligation to Colonel Sir Francis Younghusband, K C I E, late British Resident in Kashmir, for invaluable assistance rendered me prior to the start

To all the British Officials met with I would tender my cordial thanks and particularly to Captain A R B Shuttleworth, Indian Army, then acting as His Britannic Majesty's Consul in Chinese Turkistan   I am sensible of much sympathetic interest and ever-ready help he afforded me during my trek through Kashgaria—and afterwards

It is, too, a pleasing task to place on record my grateful recognition of much kindness and courtesy exhibited by Russian and Chinese Officials, especially by the Russian authorities at Zaisan, that far distant outpost of the Czar's Empire on the borders of Siberia and Mongolia   To them I owe a debt of gratitude for their care and attention, both to myself and my orderly, when suffering from severe frostbite

Finally, I cannot close this Preface without a tribute of praise to my Garhwali Orderly, Rifleman Gyan Sing Pharswan, who accompanied me throughout the journey, and was the only man to compass the entire route with me from start to finish

P T ETHERION

January 1911

CHAPTER I

THE subject of Central Asia has ever been an absorbing one from a political point of view, whilst from its sporting aspect it is none the less interesting since there is found such shooting as rarely falls to the lot of man   Foremost in this latter connection, and skirting the northern boundaries of our Indian Empire, are the Pamirs, that vast, mountainous region fitly termed the " Roof of the World, ' lying as it does at an average elevation of 13,000 feet. Here, amidst the wide, open valleys and formidable leads, forming the principal features of these bleak uplands, is the home of the *Ovis poli*, the largest and finest of all the wild sheep.   Many hundreds of miles further north lie the Thian Shan, a grand chain of mountains running east and west, dividing Kashgaria from the Ili Valley and Northern Turkistan, the habitat of the Asiatic wapiti and the big Turkistan ibex. There also are found Asiatic roe-deer, *Ovis karelini*, red, and black bear, while on the plains to the northward gazelle are encountered of a type peculiar to Central Asia   Continuing the onward march across the wind-swept plains of Northern Turkistan and the desolate Mongolian steppes, one reaches the Great Altai Mountains, the haunt of the true *Ovis ammon*, another species of wild sheep.   The immense distances separating these shooting grounds constitute in themselves an obstacle that requires all the energy and experience of the sportsman to overcome, whilst the route through wild and little-known countries, amongst strange races of nomads, and over ground but seldom trodden by man, is sufficient to put his patience and endurance to the severest test.

Across the Roof of the World

It had been a long-cherished desire of mine to undertake a big-game shooting expedition into Central Asia, a scheme as bold as it was comprehensive, since it included the Pamirs, the Thian Shan, and the Great Altai Mountains, thence through Siberia to the Trans-Siberian Railway. Such a journey, embracing as it does so vast and varied a field, necessitates a considerable amount of preparation and forethought, and might well appal the most enthusiastic shikari The idea first took definite shape in Chitral, in 1906-7 where my regiment was then stationed as garrison of the most northerly outpost of the Indian Empire. During 12 months spent there I first experienced that fascination for the lands which lay beyond, that desire to penetrate into the heart of Asia culminating in the Trans-Asiatic journey the following pages endeavour to describe.

I fully appreciated the difficulties, and realised it would be a hard proposition, so with a view to rendering the chances of success as favourable as possible I devoted much time and care to the necessary preparations I did not, however, believe the enterprise to be beyond the power of accomplishment, for I had had the good fortune to gain much of that experience in various parts of the world so necessary to one who would venture into the unknown, travel off the beaten track, and penetrate regions where man is still in the most primitive state

The spring of 1909 saw my preparations completed and everything ready for the great trek The fundamental principle underlying success in such an expedition is the thoroughness of one's arrangements, or "bundobast," as it is known in India I therefore go somewhat fully into the question of outfit and personnel, in the hope that the outcome of my experience may be of use to future travellers in the composition of their caravan, prefacing my remarks with some account of the formalities necessary to obtain the requisite sanction of the Government of India, and as to the passports needed to enable one to enter and travel in Russian and Chinese territory.

An application must first be submitted to the Government

of India, if the applicant is resident in India, or to the Foreign Office if in England   The application should set forth in detail the nature of the proposed journey and the objects thereof, the route it is intended to follow, the strength and composition of the caravan, and details respecting arms and ammunition to be taken.   The sanction of Government having been obtained it then becomes necessary to apply for a Chinese passport, which for those serving in India is obtained through His Britannic Majesty's Minister at Pekin, and at home through the Foreign Office   Passports to travel in Russian territory, other than Russian Turkistan, for which the special permission of the Governor-General of Russian Turkistan is required, are obtained through the Foreign Office in London.

These preliminary steps, of necessity, take some time so that the applications should be lodged at least six months before the date on which it is proposed to start

In my own case permission was duly accorded, and I then applied to the British Minister at Pekin for a Chinese passport, which was readily procured for me, and forwarded without delay. The matter of leave of absence from my regiment was also satisfactorily arranged and then it only remained for me to fix the date of my departure.

My watchword for the expedition was "mobility," as I knew that if I set out encumbered with anything beyond the necessary kit my prospects of achieving the object in view would be seriously jeopardised.   Everything was cut down as low as possible in order to facilitate rapid marching, and the covering of the vast distances separating the shooting grounds so as to reach them as nearly as possible at the right seasons. I appreciated that those distances would necessitate much hard marching, though I never realised it would be as severe and trying as actually proved to be the case

With regard to stores I think it a mistake to carry too many, as they greatly hamper a traveller's movements and render any attempt at mobility futile.   A number of things, such as rice, flour. meat, vegetables and salt, can generally be obtained *en route*, so that a sufficient supply of only a limited number of articles need be taken   During the summer fruit of sorts is always available, and dried apricots can be found in most of the native villages. Articles essential to be taken right through the journey would comprise —Butter, jam, baking powder, tea and a few luxuries, which entirely depend on one's personal idiosyncrasies.

My own " through " list consisted of the following :—Butter, pearl barley, jam. baking powder, cornflour, Bird's custard powder, assorted soups in squares cocoa, vermicelli, dried tinned fruits, red currant jelly, Bovril, and saxin, the tabloid form of sugar which enables one to carry in an infinitesimal space a quantity sufficient to last a whole year.   As vegetables are not always procurable a quantity of compressed should be taken

I had originally intended taking some tins of Army rations, but cut them out at the last minute to save weight, a decision I afterwards on many occasions regretted.   They form an appetising meal, and often when trekking across the Pamirs or over the bleak Mongolian steppes, where only yak or camel dung is available as fuel and the low temperature and intense cold render cooking operations a matter of extreme difficulty, this form of ready-cooked food, which only needs heating, would have proved an inestimable boon.   A useful item is some whisky or brandy, a small quantity of which might be taken more as a medicine than a luxury.

The purchase of stores should be left until arrival at Srinagar in Kashmir, the great fitting-out place for all expeditions into Tibet and Chinese Turkistan, as here one finds a large number of shops where anything can be purchased from a pin to an anchor   Moreover, one saves the carriage into Kashmir, and the Customs duties on imported goods, Kashmir being a native state with Customs, rules and regulations of its own

When travelling within the boundaries of the Chinese Empire it is usual to give presents to the Chinese officials in return for the

4

sheep, fruit, rice, and other articles which they offer, so that a supply of gifts suitable for this purpose is essential. Those most preferred would appear to be liqueurs and crystallised fruits, especially the former, ever welcome to the Celestial. I therefore provided myself with an assortment of good liqueurs, together with some boxes and bottles of crystallised fruits, all of which were productive of the best results. For the minor officials I took some good shikar knives and one or two odds and ends, though for these people hard cash is at once the best and easiest way out of the difficulty.

I had heard much as to the advisability of being equipped with an ample medicine chest calculated to cure all the ills to which flesh is heir, but decided to limit myself to a supply of only the indispensable drugs, the use of which does not demand any great display of medical skill, I being, moreover, a firm believer in the old adage that a little knowledge is a dangerous thing. Certainly I had many opportunities afforded me of achieving distinction as a medico amongst the nomad tribes of Kirghiz, Kalmuk, and the primitive Mongols. As an instance, my services were once requisitioned by a deputation of three nomads to cure an elderly dame, who, from the graphic description they afforded me of her ailments, I diagnosed to be subject to epileptic fits One of them, in his anxiety that I should fully appreciate the old lady's symptoms, by way of illustration threw himself on the ground and proceeded to writhe and tumble about, whilst the other two attempted to foam at the mouth In the end I told them the patient should be kept as quiet as possible, and that the case was not one in which my personal attendance would serve any useful purpose, nor would I advise administering any of the potions at my disposal. The fact is I was at a loss to know what to do and was right glad when they withdrew I shifted my camp the next day, and what ultimately happened to the old lady I did not hear.

My list of medical comforts consisted only of cascara sagrada, quinine, phenacetin, chlorodyne, permanganate of potash, Eno's

Fruit Salt, pills of various kinds, and vaseline, together with a number of dressings, and some spare lint and medicated wool.

The whole of the foregoing require to be packed in yak-dans, and a list of the contents of each kept so as to avoid a prolonged chase for anything which may be required, a proceeding which generally necessitates the opening of every yak-dan, the requisite article seldom being forthcoming until the last box has been undone   This unhappy state of affairs can be obviated by tabulating the contents as above   Yak-dans are procurable in Srinagar at prices varying from 12 to 18 rupees per pair, the figure mainly depending on the relative acumen of vendor and purchaser   They are leather covered and wonderfully strong, as indeed they need to be to withstand the constant knocking about   Another form of portable box is the "kilta," a wicker-work article which soon goes to pieces, and is therefore not to be recommended for a long journey

In regard to the question of tents and outfit, the former should combine strength and lightness, the seams and component parts calling for particular attention   My own tent, which was 7 feet square and 6½ feet high inside, was made of milleraincd khaki drill by the Elgin Mills Company of Cawnpore, and comprised inner and outer fly bathroom and verandah, the weight complete being only 55 lbs   In the front I had two latticed windows, which permitted of the tent being closed, an advantage when travelling in the wilds of Central Asia, where the whole population usually turns out to gaze at the strange antics of the Feringhi and watch his every movement, as though he were out for their especial benefit and delectation

For camp furniture, i e , bed, table, chair and bath, I do not think the X pattern articles can be improved upon, as they are rapidly put together and seldom break, which is a consideration, especially amongst Oriental servants, who seem to regard everything as armour-plated   As to bedding camel-hair blankets are excellent, being both light and exceedingly warm

6

A moderately thick cottonwool mattress to roll up easily is also required, and mosquito curtains are an absolute necessity. A strong Wolseley valise should be taken for the above, the straps of which must be stout enough to withstand an unlimited amount of rough treatment

Cooking utensils should be of aluminium, which is by far the best material, as it is extremely light. and does not require tinning like the native copper article, from the use of which one stands a reasonable chance of being poisoned. Aluminium screw-top jars to fit one into the other are also very handy for jam, butter, and similar articles.

The list of miscellaneous articles required comprises, amongst others, good shikar knives, skinning knives and whetstone, blue snow spectacles, ink tabloids and note paper, travelling ink bottle, a fountain pen, envelopes, diary, housewife, files, candle lantern with talc slides, riding saddle and girths, bridle, a powerful pair of field glasses, a telescope, camera and plates, or films, developing outfit, and sundry odds and ends which suggest themselves when making out one's lists

Then there is the most important matter of arms and ammunition, concerning which a considerable diversity of opinion exists Not being an authority on the subject I do not propose to do more than state the composition of my own battery. For big game I used a 404 Jeffery-Mauser rifle firing the ordinary soft-nosed split bullets supplied by the makers, a rifle that gave me entire satisfaction, as it combines lightness with great accuracy and striking power Two rifles are essential in case of accidents, my second being a ·303 carbine firing the ordinary sporting bullets made by Kynoch's A double-barrelled hammerless gun and 750 cartridges for same, made up of 300 No. 6, 200 No. 4, 100 No. 2, 150 Nos 9 and 12 for small birds, completed my arms and ammunition. For maintaining one's weapons in sound condition, a sufficient quantity of the best rifle oil must be taken, as also pull-throughs, spare gauze for same and flannelette.

7

When on the march time passes rapidly enough, but the hours in camp and after return from the day's sport are apt to hang rather heavily, so a supply of readable books that will bear perusal several times over should be taken. My library consisted of about a dozen volumes of sporting, military and general interest

With regard to the matter of expense, this is a subject on which I refrain from advising, since so much depends on one's personal tastes and inclinations, and the manner in which a hold is maintained on the purse strings, as also the successful frustration of the wiles and stratagems of the wicked to snare the unwary traveller.

A vexed question is that of servants, a really good one being difficult to obtain, the majority of those in Srinagar being more than average scoundrels against whom a stranger needs to exercise considerable caution   In addition to my Garhwali orderly, I engaged a man to act as cook and go right through He was a native of Baltistan and had served some time with a brother officer who was good enough to arrange for him to accompany me   Unfortunately he did not prove a success, and I had to dispense with his services in Gilgit, where, however, I had the luck to engage an excellent man, in the person of Piroz Zaman, a Kanjuti, who served me well and faithfully during my march through Hunza, and across the Pamirs to Yarkand and Kashgar

My permanent staff, therefore, consisted of the orderly and cook, with a third man to act as helper and make himself generally useful, whilst others were engaged from time to time to accompany the expedition for certain stages, an arrangement which I found to work very well   The composition of the caravan of necessity changes according as means of transport vary in different parts of the country traversed

In an expedition to Central Asia the problem of securing a suitable interpreter is a difficult one   There are a good many men in Kashgar and Yarkand who can speak both Hindustani

8

and Persian and have served with well-known travellers, but from what I could glean they had little else to recommend them, their main object in life apparently being to get the better of the inexperienced stranger.

Fortunately I knew Hindustani, Persian, and Pushtu, the second of which languages I found to be useful in Southern Chinese Turkistan amongst the educated Mahommedan population, and on the Pamirs, where the nomad Kirghiz possess an acquaintance with Persian, in addition to their own tongue. This obviated to a considerable extent the interpreter difficulty, and enabled me to convey my orders direct and not through the medium of another, who generally manages to pass on one's remarks in a mutilated form.

The matter of money and its exchange at points throughout the journey are less embarrassing than might be imagined. Indian money is accepted on the Pamirs, and for one's financial needs beyond it can be converted into Chinese money at the current rate of exchange   The latter is mostly in the form of parchment notes, though silver coin is also obtainable   This coin has again to be changed in Ili owing to the variation in the face value.   Russian roubles are acceptable practically throughout Central Asia, more especially in the Thian Shan, and as there are branches of the Russo-Chinese Bank at Kashgar and Kulja, no difficulty would be experienced financially if arrangements are made with the latter.

CHAPTER II.

ACROSS THE HIMALAYAS TO GILGIT.

LANSDOWNE, the starting point of the expedition, is situated amongst the foothills of the Himalayas in the British district of Garhwal, at an elevation of 6,000 feet. The nearest railway station is Kotdwara about 130 miles north-west of Bareilly, and

LANSDOWNE.

there is a cart road, 26 miles long, connecting it with Lansdowne, while the bridle path for horse and foot traffic only is eight miles shorter. Lansdowne was first constituted a permanent cantonment in 1887, during the Viceroyalty of the late Marquis of Dufferin and Ava. The garrison now consists of two battalions of Garhwalis and two of Gurkhas.

10

Lansdowne is a picturesque little station crowning the summit of a well-wooded ridge which overlooks the plains to the south, whilst to the north it commands a superb view of the main range of the Himalayas, that stupendous natural barrier between Tibet and Hindustan

The province of Garhwal contains within its limits some 20 peaks exceeding a height of 20,000 feet, including Nanda Devi (25,660 feet), the highest mountain in British territory outside Kashmir, Trisul (23,409 feet), and many others of almost equal magnitude. On a clear day the panorama of this grand chain of mountains from the ridge and the gardens surrounding the Mess of the 39th Garhwal Rifles is hardly to be surpassed in the world.

The Garhwalis, who are short in stature but of sturdy build, are recruited from these mountain fastnesses, and with the military training, coupled with their own mountaineering and natural fighting qualities, form a fine combatant unit. Formerly a great many of them were enlisted in Gurkha regiments and contributed a by no means insignificant share to the honours borne by some of the more famous of those units It was not until 1887 that Lord Roberts, then commanding in India, conceived the happy idea of forming all the Garhwalis, then serving in Gurkha regiments, into one battalion, and the experiment met with such success that a second battalion was raised in 1901 The Garhwali, though he in many respects resembles the Gurkha in his qualities as a soldier, is of a distinct race and not to be tribally confounded with the latter

Great interest was taken in the expedition by my regiment, hopes being expressed that I might meet with a full success, and still further swell the splendid collection of trophies adorning the mess walls

At my own urgent request my Commanding Officer arranged that I should take a Garhwali orderly, a rifleman from the regiment, and when this became known amongst the men great keenness was displayed for the honour of selection I decided to limit it to my own Double Company, from which there were 40 volunteers. The nature and extent of the journey were fully explained, and that the route would take us through wild and little-known parts of Asia, whilst the successful accomplishment of the undertaking was also pointed out as being by no means assured. Their ardour was not, however, in the least degree damped, the love of adventure and a journey into the unknown appealing strongly to them.

After careful examination a man was chosen to fill the coveted post. Rifleman Giyan Sing, the hero in question, followed my fortunes right through, being the only man to complete the entire journey with me from start to finish. His experiences throughout so extensive a field of travel, and the marvels they brought in their wake, culminating with our arrival in London, the hub of the mightiest Empire the world has ever seen, were indeed a revelation to him. Until we reached Flushing, $11\frac{1}{2}$ months after leaving Landsowne, he had never set eyes upon the sea, whilst the area of vast London, the wonders of tube railways, the ceaseless stream of people encountered in the streets, and numerous other astounding sights left upon him a profound and lasting impression.

For several weeks prior to my departure from Lansdowne I was busily occupied with the final preparations. All was ready, however, on March 8th, when I sent off my kit in charge of the orderly, with instructions to await my arrival at Srinagar. A week later, on the 15th, accompanied by the good wishes of the regiment, I left myself, cycling down the hill road which leads from Lansdowne to the railway branch station at Kotdwara. Coasting along the narrow and winding track a feeling of keenest joy took possession of me as I pondered over the possibilities of the future, and the chances of record heads in those happy hunting grounds far away in the heart of Asia. The realisation of a long-cherished dream was at hand. The great trek had commenced.

From Kotdwara a branch line leads to Najibabad, on the main

Calcutta-Peshawar railway route, whence the Punjab Mail took me on to Rawalpindi. Here a tonga service runs to Murree and Srinagar, the mail tonga leaving after the arrival of the train, but

RIFLEMAN GIYAN SING.

on this occasion the driver was induced to tarry the while I discussed a hasty meal in the railway hotel. A tonga is a low, two-horsed vehicle, strongly built, and capable of withstanding much,

13

always a recommendation in this land where most things suffer
from rough usage.

Another mode of conveyance peculiar to the Shiny East, and
in great evidence on the Kashmir road, is the " ekka," a small,
clumsily built cart with a low covered-in top having the appearance of a dome perched on two wheels. An ekka will carry a
considerable amount of kit, but to sit in it with any comfort
is a matter of some difficulty, unless one is an expert at
contortions and can roll up like a hedgehog. Loading up the
light luggage I stepped aboard the tonga, the driver cracked

his whip, and we
were off at a rattling
pace towards the
hills, changing horses
every few miles. For
the first 16 miles or
so the road lies across
the level plain until
the foothills are
reached. Thence en-
sues a steady climb
along a well-made
road through a vista
of pleasant valleys,

CHANGING TONGAS ON THE ROAD TO SRINAGAR.

and forests of tower-
ing deodar and fir.

As we ascended, the air became keener, the aspect of the
scene changed, and beyond Tret snow was encountered, whilst
anon we would pass gangs of coolies hard at work repairing the
road. Late in the afternoon we ran into Murree, a well-known
hot-weather station and sanatorium, commanding magnificent
views over the Himalayas, whilst to the south, as far as the eye
could reach, stretched the vast plains of the Punjab. I stayed
the night at Chamber's Hotel, the only hostelry then open, all
the bungalows at this early season of the year being empty.

Snow lay deep in the streets, and at nightfall the air became bitterly cold so that I was glad of the warming influence of a cheery blaze, a change from the hot and arid plains through which we had coursed in the morning

At dinner I met two senior officers of the Northumberland Fusiliers the famous Fighting Fifth, and we foregathered and discussed, amongst other topics, my journey into the wilds of Central Asia, and the prospects of a fine bag on the Pamirs and in the far-distant Thian Shan

The following morning dawned clear and frosty and I was away by 10 o'clock, downhill to the Jhelum, the road winding and turning as only mountain roads can. The way was reported to be open, though snow was met with in great quantities, but not sufficiently to bar our progress   In places where it had accumulated to any considerable depth we alighted, the tonga was hauled through the obstruction, and the onward run resumed

The drive from Murree to Kohala is a very fine one, lying through grand mountain scenery on one side lofty, forest-covered slopes, on the other sheer precipices rising from the banks of the Jhelum, the Hydaspes of the ancients.

The distances between stages average about eight miles, the changing of horses being rapidly effected without any of the annoying delays which are the rule and not the exception when one is posting in Russia   There an hour is quick work for this, often as much as two hours elapsing before fresh horses are produced, a proceeding scarcely calculated to improve the energetic Britisher's temper.

On the Kashmir road the stages consist of a small shelter for the men detailed to look after the animals, and stables for the latter   A syce, or groom, accompanies each tonga to the next stage, hanging on behind, and on arrival leads the relieved pair back

It is a 34-mile run to Kohala on the banks of the Jhelum, which marks the frontier between the territories of the Maharajah of Kashmir and British India   There is a dak bungalow here and also a custom house, duty being leviable on certain specified articles.

From Kohala the road assumes an upward gradient, and the scenery partakes more of a cultivated nature, the slopes being well-grown and the artistically built-up terraces irrigated by tiny canals   In the distance one catches sight of giant snow-capped ranges, beneath which stretch thickly wooded forests whose dark green colour lends enchantment to the view, forming a fine background and standing out sharply against the pale blue sky.

At Dulai I halted for tiffin and then journeyed on another 23 miles to Garhi, stopping the night in the dak bungalow, having done 62 miles from Murree   These dak bungalows are very comfortable, being well-appointed and with a good staff of servants, as indeed are all the post houses on this road, the Kashmir state authorities leaving nothing undone in their efforts to meet modern requirements, and the demands of the ever-increasing annual influx into Kashmir from India.   I left Garhi at 8 a m. the next morning, and drove to Uri where I lunched   On the way there we passed several breaks in the road due to the heavy snow-fall of the winter, at one point the way being completely blocked by a huge avalanche of rock and stone   It there became necessary to change tongas, one being in waiting with fresh horses on the far side of the rock slide so no delay was occasioned.   Past Uri we came into a good many snow drifts which required careful negotiation, but nothing untoward occurred, and we rolled into Baramula soon after six, putting up at the dak bungalow by the river side

From Baramula it is a run of 30 miles to Srinagar, through an avenue of poplars, imparting a pleasing aspect to the route which lies through a broad and open stretch of country

Some four miles outside Srinagar I had my first experience of the importunity of the Kashmiri servant, in the person of a shikari who aspired to the honour of being guide, philosopher, and friend to the expedition   This gentleman pulled up my

16

tonga, flourishing a letter in his hand, which on inspection I found
to be addressed to me in a hand unmistakably that of the local
babu's. But I had been there before and was not to be so easily
trapped. With a face as immovable as the Egyptian sphinx I
informed him that the Sahib was coming behind and that the
best course he could adopt would be to press on to meet him,
which he did, setting off up the road at a pace calculated to

"THE WAY WAS BLOCKED BY A HUGE AVALANCHE OF
ROCK AND STONE."

win renown on the racing track. Thus relieved I drove on into
Srinagar to the Chenar Bagh, so called from the chenar trees
which cover the grassy patches by the water's edge, where I
found my camp pitched, Giyani and the cook having arrived a
few days before.

Rain was falling fast, and the threatening rise in the river
indicated a possible retreat from the garden to higher and less

dangerous ground   The Chenar Bagh was quite empty when I arrived, the influx of visitors from India not having yet commenced   The weather was cold and dull, whilst towards the ranges of mountains to the north, dark, gloomy clouds filled the air, boding ill for the passage of the Gilgit route, and the crossing of the Tragbal and Burzil Passes

I had much to do in Srinagar concerning the final arrangements for the onward march of the expedition, and the obtaining of "parwanas," or permits, enabling me to procure coolies and supplies on the way from Bandipur to Gilgit

There are in Srinagar, as elsewhere, a number of gentry whose chief aim in life seems to be to get to windward of the stranger, so that a certain amount of enquiry is advisable before placing orders   The morning after my arrival, word having gone forth that I was located in the Chenar Bagh, numbers of rascals swooped down like vultures, full of that hope which ever buoys up the Oriental spirit when any rupees are to be made, thinking to find an easy prey   Their tenacity was extraordinary, and though I was bored by their persistence I secretly admired their ambition   The river fronting my camp was thronged with "shikaras," long canoes resembling somewhat the gondolas of Venice, laden with wares of divers sorts which their owners extolled with a volubility that declined to be curbed   On the shore were gathered all the rogues and rascals of Srinagar, tailors, bootmakers, outfitters of every description, all eager to do business, and being particularly anxious that the Sahib should understand they were there entirely for his welfare and that for them to state anything but the truth would be something quite foreign to their nature

However, their importunities were unavailing, and when I had enjoyed the play long enough proceeded to pass them out, in which work I was ably supported by my Garhwali orderly, who thoroughly appreciated the fun

One of the best and most reliable outfitters in Srinagar, and from whom everything needful can be had, is Mian Mahomed, well known to many Indian officers. I procured practically all my stores and other articles from him. Many travellers bring things with them from India ; this is a great mistake, since all one requires can be obtained locally, the selection of shops in Srinagar being extensive, and from them everything requisite for an expedition can be purchased.

Srinagar has been styled the City of the Sun, which did not strike me as being a particularly appropriate title, for though the

A WATERWAY IN SRINAGAR.

main waterway is picturesque and reminds one of Venice, an excursion into the many side streets and alleys quickly dispels the idea, the surroundings and general aspect of dirt and squalor being of a marked order. The river is spanned by several bridges of native construction, and from a gondola one can step into shops or residences in much the same way as in Venice.

The day of arrival I dined with the Assistant Resident, who, acting on instructions received from Colonel Sir Francis Young-

husband, K C I E , the Resident in Kashmir, was good enough
to furnish me with the necessary permits for coolies and supplies
on the Gilgit route

Owing to the very unsettled weather, prospects of getting
through to Gilgit were far from cheering, while reports had
come down that numerous avalanches had occurred, blocking
the road and rendering it impassable even to the hardy post
runners   I had experienced great difficulty in obtaining permission from the Government of India to proceed by the Gilgit
route so early in the season, as it is not considered open until
May 15th, on account of the danger from avalanches and snow-
slides, a danger which is by no means exaggerated

The track winds through narrow and precipitous ravines and
valleys, and across two high passes, a journey involving many
perils to those who would essay the undertaking in March.
Thanks, however, to the assistance afforded me by Sir Francis
Younghusband, all difficulties in connection with the necessary
permission were surmounted and I boarded my houseboat on
the evening of the 29th and set sail for Bandipur, which lies on
the other side of the Woolar Lake   All night we glided silently
on, propelled by three or four Kashmiri boatmen, through the
main waterway of Srinagar and out into the open valley, and
skirting the shore of the lake reached Bandipur on the afternoon
of the following day.   From the lake a magnificent view of forest-
clad mountain presents itself, the valleys and ravines therein
being noted ground for that fine stag the " barasingh "

On disembarking at Bandipur my goods and chattels were
spread out upon the shore, forming such an imposing array that
the natives must have thought I was a Whiteley come to provide.
Grouped around my belongings were a number of coolies in
readiness to transport them to Gurai, where they would be relieved
by others in accordance with arrangements made by the Governor
of Kashmir   When the signal was given to load up and march
for Tragbal, the first stage from Bandipur, it was quite amusing
to watch the efforts of these sturdy varlets to secure the lightest

burden   One of the loads was a small oblong box containing
rifle and shot gun cartridges, which looked light and enticing,
but proved to be a great sell when lifted, for it weighed some
80 lbs.   To see the coolies at every stage eyeing that box and then
rushing to secure such a seeming featherweight afforded me much
amusement, not lessened by the looks of disgust and disappointment which followed.

The Gilgit route is an engineering feat of a high order, and was
constructed during Colonel Durand's term of office as Political
Agent in Gilgit in 1889   Prior to this period communication
between Gilgit and Kashmir was maintained over a rough track
quite impassable for any but coolie transport, and often obliterated
entirely by tremendous avalanches which sweep down carrying
all before them   The only means by which supplies could be
conveyed into the country was on the backs of coolies, alone
requiring an organisation of considerable magnitude   The
country between Kashmir and Gilgit is to a very large extent
unproductive, so that all the stores and impedimenta of a thousand
and one kinds had to be imported

During the construction of the road large gangs of coolies of
many different tribes and castes were employed, the management
of whom called for a display of that tact and administrative
ability in which our frontier officials excel   The road averages
some ten or a dozen feet in width, and during the summer months,
when the route is open and free from snow, a transport service
is maintained from Srinagar to Chalt, two marches beyond
Gilgit   The open season extends from May 15th to about the
middle of October, after which traffic is discontinued and the
mail services are kept up by post runners, who daily risk their
lives amongst the dark ravines and steep valleys of the Gilgit
route

After leaving Bandipur the road rises rapidly, in a succession
of zigzags, to the summit of the Tragbal Pass   I and the coolies
followed the short cut which leads straight up the hillside, a long
and exceedingly stiff climb, rendered all the more so by the

melting snow and the consequent slush which covered the ground, and on which one constantly slipped and fell. Below the summit of the Tragbal is a bungalow, a rough construction, but a welcome shelter nevertheless, and of which we were glad to avail ourselves.

Tragbal lies in a forest of towering deodars which afford an ample quantity of fuel, and as the shades of night closed in blazing fires turned the otherwise cheerless log hut into one of warmth and comfort, gathering round which all forgot the inclemency of the

CROSSING THE TRAGBAL PASS.

weather. The last coolie arrived at a quarter to nine, the tiring climb of 4,000 feet in eight miles having severely taxed their powers.

I started just after daylight on the 31st to ascend the Tragbal Pass, which lies at an altitude of 11,900 feet above sea level. The day was fine, though a fairly strong wind was blowing. On the northern side of the pass there commences a steep descent through deep, soft snow, in which the only evidence of path or track was that made by the footsteps of the post runners and my own party. This descent continues for some considerable distance until the Zudkusu Valley is reached, one of the most dangerous parts of the Gilgit route.

Here the path lies through a narrow ravine whose sides are so precipitous that it seems impossible the snow could remain there at all. It is said the vibration of the air caused by speaking is sufficient to bring down an avalanche, so being undesirous of qualifying for an early grave we kept a discreet silence, girding up our loins ready to lower all previous sprinting records.

I camped that night in the bungalow at Gurai, now completely buried in snow, entrance to it having to be effected by burrowing through the white layer hardened by continual frost. It was of vital importance to start early in the mornings before the sun could gain sufficient power to act on the snow and bring it down in avalanches. During the night it, of course, freezes hard, but should the day be fine the hot sun loosens the outer layers from the precipitous cliffs, sending them down in irresistible slides.

So I set out the next morning at four o'clock in the hope of doing a long march and getting over some of the worst parts of the road before the sun should bring down avalanches from the steep ravine sides through which our way now led. The going was heavy in the extreme and in places all trace of the path had been completely obliterated by avalanches necessitating a laborious climb over these obstructions with the ever-present possibility of starting them afresh. The road was everywhere blocked by these avalanches, many of which, coming down as we pushed on through the ravines, threatened to engulf and sweep us away in their deadly embrace.

Gurais was reached in the late afternoon, but I decided to push on to Dudgee, which lay some six miles further up the valley. So, halting only for a cup of tea and to change coolies, resumed the onward march through a mighty ravine which was simply one mass of avalanches. Ever and anon they would come crashing down, inspiring a feeling of awe as one realised how powerless man is against the mighty works of nature.

We reached a bad part of the road at eight o'clock, and one that required daylight for its successful negotiation, the waning light and the rapid advance of darkness rendering the task of getting over the difficult terrain one of extreme danger. On the desolate slopes the gaunt deodar and chir stood outlined against the sky, sombre and forbidding, the only note of colour in this

A RAVINE IN THE GILGIT VALLEY SHOWING THE TRACKS OF
THE EXPEDITION.

gloomy wilderness. There was a small telegraph hut here used by those whose duty it is to repair the line when broken by avalanches or landslides. Before arrival at this haven of refuge we passed an avalanche that occupied twenty minutes in crossing, sufficient proof that we were playing touch and go with a dangerous enemy. The structure in question was just a rough log hut, with one room, in which my orderly proceeded to light a fire and drive me

out with the pungent fumes inseparable from damp wood The
last coolie arrived at nine o'clock, and, after depositing his load
inside the hut, joined his comrades who had found accommodation in a tiny village below   The wind blew a regular nor'-
easter so that we were compelled to have the door shut, which
made matters worse, for Giyani blew vigorously at the fire and
raised enough smoke and dust to bury the expedition.   He
however, seemed to thoroughly enjoy it, shaking with subdued
laughter at my attempts to avoid the dense fumes by burrowing beneath the blankets   Dinner that night was a smoky
performance, but I was too elated at being well on the way to
happy hunting grounds to grumble at trifles

I was off again the next morning at six o'clock, halting
for a brief meal at Pachwari, some miles up the valley   The
going was particularly bad, through deep, soft snow, into
which one sank to the knees at every step, making progress as
slow as it was exhausting.   The track, a mere footpath worn by
the post runners, led us over steep slopes and beneath towering
heights covered with a thick layer of snow ever ready to descend
and swallow up all within its pitiless grasp   Over this ticklish
bit of ground we slowly wended our way, myself and Giyani
leading, the coolies following in single file.   We had reached
a point in the valley where the ground sloped up to our left
at an alarming angle   Beneath us to our right flowed the river,
its banks encrusted with snow and ice, forming in places arched
bridges over which one could cross to the opposite side. It was late
in the day, the sun had been shining for several hours through a
cloudless sky, loosening the upper layers of snow and causing
intermittent avalanches, the noise of which reverberated throughout the valley. Suddenly a huge avalanche came thundering down
just as we were passing, cutting off myself and the orderly from
the coolies following behind.   It was a great rush for safety as the
immense white mass came hurtling on in one irresistible sweep,
bringing in its wake rocks, trees, and débris of all descriptions
Luckily the coolies were able to take shelter under the lee of a

depression in the hillside, whilst I and Gyani were just fortunate enough to get beyond it in time to avoid being carried away

No power on earth can resist the onslaught of an avalanche as it crashes downward, gathering bulk as it goes, and sweeping onward with an ever-increasing impetus Such perils as these are daily encountered by the hardy post runners who maintain communication with the distant frontier post of Gilgit during the hard and inexorable winter. Theirs, indeed, is a hazardous task, carrying His Majesty's mail through the snows of the Himalayas, risking life hourly in the tremendous ravines and narrow neks of this wild and rugged land There is no honour and glory attached to this onerous calling, only an ever-present danger from the swift and awe-inspiring avalanche, which knows no obstacle and spares no man Should the post runner be engulfed he passes from mortal ken, unknown, unhonoured and unsung

A few hours before I passed through these dreaded ravines two of the post runners had been overwhelmed by an avalanche and buried alive As I stood by the spot I could not help pondering on their dreadful death, swallowed up as they were in the merciless avalanche with no warning of the fate that was to overtake them. Beneath the snowy pall the bodies would rest until spring, when the warming influence of the sun would melt the snow and disclose the victims thus entombed

Apart from the avalanches there are other and equally perilous risks to run on this road in winter In places one crosses from bank to bank by means of snow bridges, which are simply masses of snow and drift ice that have fallen into the river and, becoming jammed, have frozen solid, forming a natural bridge beneath which the water rushes and roars with terrific force One such bridge we had to pass on the afternoon of our narrow escape from being carried away in the avalanche. It was a thin arch of frozen snow, and the only way by which the opposite bank could be reached Just as we gained the middle it collapsed and threw us into the water, a foaming torrent, dashing and splashing over the rocks and boulders which formed the river bed Gyani, with an agility worthy of an acrobat, balanced himself momentarily on a boulder in mid-stream and then, with a frantic leap, and struggling against the current, reached the opposite bank, whilst I followed suit. Fortunately the coolies were able to find a safe crossing lower down, thus obviating the risk of loss of life and baggage which passages of these turbulent mountain streams engender.

Towards six o'clock we reached Minimerg, a telegraph station manned by two European telegraphists, good fellows, who welcomed me as the only visitor they had known for many months,

MINIMERG.

cut off as they are from the outside world, and hemmed in by the icy grip of winter which does not relax its grasp until well on into May. The telegraph line runs from Kashmir to Gilgit and thence to Chitral viâ the Shandur Pass and Mastuj.

Till now the weather had been fine and clear, and prospects of a successful crossing of the formidable Burzil Pass, which lay some ten miles ahead, were correspondingly brighter. I spent an enjoyable evening in the company of the two telegraph officials, who were more than kind and hospitable to the stranger within their gates.

27

Across the Roof of the World.

Next morning I started the coolies off before daylight, and left myself about an hour later. The way led through a narrow valley, at that season of the year draped in snow many feet in depth, its sides covered with the lofty pines which constitute the principal feature in the landscape at these high altitudes.

Past Burzil Chauki, five miles beyond Minimerg, the road assumes an ever-increasing gradient and the ravine becomes wilder and more rugged until one nears the summit, when a long stretch of down has to be crossed, swept by winds and snowstorms during the winter with a fury nothing can resist.

THE TELEGRAPH STATION AT MINIMERG BURIED IN SNOW.

The summit of the Burzil lies at an elevation of 13,500 feet, and marks the border line between Kashmir, with its fertile plains, and the more desolate and arid country of Astor and Gilgit. The pass has ever possessed a sinister reputation for the storms inseparably associated with it, and though it is quite passable for men and animals in the summer, the passage of it during the long winter months is an undertaking attended by the gravest danger. Many lives have been lost in the crossing

A SUMMER VIEW OF THE VALLEY LEADING TO THE BURZIL PASS.

of this dreaded pass, months afterwards, when the snow has melted and the ground somewhat cleared, the bodies being re-covered. A stone hut has been built on the summit to afford shelter to travellers and mail runners when overtaken by storms. The view therefrom is dreary and depressing in the extreme, being nothing but snow-covered wastes, and with range upon range of mountains all wrapped in the same white mantle.

I halted on the summit some twenty minutes to permit the coolies to overtake me, but as they did not appear I decided to push on to Chillum Chauki, down the valley on the Gilgit side. The sun, shining brilliantly, had softened the upper layers of snow, making the going arduous and exhausting to a degree, and

COOLIES NEAR THE SUMMIT OF THE BURZIL PASS.

though the sky was cloudless the air was keen and sharp, whilst every now and again a cold blast would sweep down from the mountains, whirling up the powdery snow into fitful eddies.

Five miles below the summit I reached the post runner's shelter, known as Sirdar Kothi, the only sign of habitation on the desolate, treeless plain—five miles of ploughing and blundering through knee-deep snow.

I halted the night at Chillum Chauki, after another two hours' further struggling through the interminable snow, finding there a fairly plentiful supply of firewood, which, when kindled, imparted a cheerful aspect to the gloomy surroundings. The coolies dropped in one after the other up till nine o'clock, but the one carrying my Wolseley valise with the bedding failed to appear, nor did he show himself during the night, causing me a certain amount of disquietude lest he might have been caught in an avalanche and buried alive At daybreak a post runner passed the hut and informed me he had met the coolie on the far side of the pass the previous night. The latter had explained matters by stating he had reached the summit of the pass alone, the other coolies being ahead, and as there was then a strong wind still blowing had turned back, retracing his steps to Burzil Chauki His dull mind was apparently unable to appreciate the fact that it was just as easy to go on to Sirdar Kothi as to retire the way he had come, since both spots are equidistant from the summit, besides which he would have saved himself the labour of another cross-ing However, the Oriental is a strange creature, and it is at times difficult to fathom his ideas and appreciate his weird idiosyncrasies. I was therefore deprived for two nights of the wherewithal to obtain much needed rest, though my cheery little orderly insisted on my sharing his blankets, and would indeed have preferred had I taken them all

I left Chillum at six in the morning, and pushed on to Kharam, where I was fortunate enough to engage ponies for the march on to Astor It is all down hill to Gudai, a 16-mile march, through alternate forests and rocky cliffs looming dark and sombre, their upper reaches clothed sparsely with fir and pine Beyond Gudai, where I stayed for tiffin, we emerged from snow into a warmer clime as welcome as it was cheery Being desirous of reaching Gurikot, some little distance this side of Astor, that night, I decided to push ahead, so continued march-ing till 9 p m , putting up in the Engineer s bungalow The following morning I moved on to Astor, a well-known sporting centre of the Gilgit Agency, and the scene of former fighting in the days before our suzerainty was asserted

The chief feature of interest there is the markhor shooting obtainable in the nullahs   The variety found is the Astor markhor (*Capra falconeri typica*), whose horns assume the open spiral shape, and are much sought after by sportsmen   A certain number of permits are granted annually, the shooting season being divided into two periods, and a limit fixed as to the number of heads to be shot

One of the most difficult stretches of the Gilgit road is met with after leaving Astor ; it conducts up to and over the famous Hattu Pir   The actual distance from Astor to Gilgit is five marches, and very stiff marches they are   There are now rest-houses all the way, so that one need not camp as was formerly the case   I had engaged fresh ponies in Astor and sent forward the baggage the same day, intending to overtake it in the afternoon, after lunching with the telegraph officials there, whose cordial invitation I had gladly accepted

Once beyond Astor the scenery underwent a marked change   I had crossed the dividing line between the pine-clad slopes and snowy solitudes of the Himalayas, and was confronted with the mighty Hindu Kush, a land bare and arid, but withal a gladsome change from the wintry wastes traversed for the last week

From Astor to Dashkin the road leads through gorges, and then by a zigzag path up over gravel-strewn hills, the Astor River flowing many hundreds of feet below   The scenery is strikingly impressive, and one feels that admiration which asserts itself when confronted with some of Nature's grandest works.

After Dashkin a weary march ensued to Doyen, partly through forest, where the snow, hidden from the sun's rays, lies thick, not melting until late in the year. The ponies sank into it at every step, plunging wildly about on the narrow path, unable to find a solid footing in the treacherous ground

I know no more laborious task than that of forcing a way through deep, soft snow, which, yielding to the pressure of the

33   D

feet, causes one to sink into it knee-deep, and often to the waist, a mode of progression most exhausting to even the hardy hill-men, and rendering abortive any attempt at rapid marching.

At Doyen I again secured another change of ponies to take the baggage on to Bunji, some 19 miles away. The road over the Hattu Pir is severe and trying, especially in the summer It crosses the watershed of the Indus and Astor Rivers at an altitude of 10,000 feet, from the summit of which there is an almost sheer drop of nigh on 7,000 feet to Ramghat, the confluence of the above-mentioned rivers. For several miles it is a constant succession of steep zigzags cut out of the black rock and gravel, with never a sign of tree or bush, nor a drop of water to temper the toils of this realistic Hades.

In former days the ascent of the Hattu Pir was attended with a heavy mortality in men and baggage animals, for no proper road existed, only the merest track, up which the wretched coolies had to struggle, over shale and loose rocks, along ledges and by yawning precipices. Years ago, when the Kashmir State authorities were at perpetual warfare with the turbulent tribes, large numbers of coolies were impressed for service with the Kashmir forces, and the lack of organisation, together with the treatment to which they were subjected told heavily, few surviving the horrors of the Gilgit road

At the foot of the Hattu Pir lies Ramghat, on the banks of the Astor River, the latter spanned by a substantial bridge Beyond Ramghat a two-hour march over a sandy and other-wise desolate plain took me into Bunji, where there is a good dak bungalow

Since Gilgit and the district have come under our control, British officers are attached to the Imperial Service troops garrisoning Gilgit to act as Inspecting Officers and supervise the training on progressive lines. In the Agency there are two such officers. one of whom resides at Bunji, and the other at Gilgit, and they have at their command some of the best shooting obtainable within the limits of trans-India In the nullahs

34

around Bunji and Gilgit is found that fine goat, the markhor, whilst ibex, urial, and bear flourish in goodly numbers   In winter, duck-shooting is to be had, and chikor, the hill partridge, is found on the gravel slopes and fans of the valley

It is 34 miles from Bunji to Gilgit, just too long a march to be done comfortably in one day, so I made two out of it, camping the night at Safed Pari, where is another passable roadside bungalow, situated out in a wilderness of rock and sand

The Gilgit Valley is shut in by high mountains, rendering it hot in summer, and, since warmer weather was now setting in, I moved out from Safed Pari at the unearthly hour of three in the morning, reaching Gilgit shortly before nine   When passing through Astor I had received a letter from the Political Agent in Gilgit inviting me to be the guest of the Agency during my stay there, an invitation I gratefully accepted. I found a large marquee pitched for my accommodation in a shady garden surrounding the bungalow of the surgeon, Captain Taylor, I M S , most comfortably furnished and spread with carpets, in which pleasant camp I spent ten days, a welcome change after the hardships of the journey from Kashmir

CHAPTER III.

Through the Hunza Valley

Gilgit lies to the north-west of Kashmir, and was constituted a Political Agency in 1889   Within the limits of this Agency are included Hunza and Nagar, the northern boundaries of which strike the point where three empires meet   The distance from Srinagar is over 200 miles, but since the construction of the military road it has, so far as the summer months are concerned, been shorn of many of its difficulties   It is a lonely sojourn in this distant spot, and the long winter cuts one off from communication with the outer world, often for two or three weeks at a stretch   But it has its compensating advantages, for few sporting localities rival the deep ravines and precipitous slopes which are the dominant note of this trans-frontier possession

On the afternoon of my arrival I witnessed a game of polo by native teams in company with the Political Agent, Major A B Dew, and his charming wife   Polo is the national game of the Gilgitis, and, judging from the number of players, the ground on which it is played, and the general devil-may-care manner in which everyone dashes about, death ought to exercise a prominent part in it   The players consist of about ten a side, usually captained by the local king, or some other equally important individual   From the point of view of first-class polo the game can scarcely be called a success, but the participants seem to thoroughly enjoy it, paying scant attention to such details as crossing and other fouls, the while careering up and down the ground, barging into members of the opposing team and generally making a fast and truly furious game of it   It usually lasts two hours or more and the same ponies are used all through

At this season of the year Gilgit was looking its best, all the trees being in full bloom, the orchards and numerous gardens presenting a picturesque spectacle. My ten days there were fully occupied with making arrangements for the onward march to the Chinese frontier, replenishing my supplies, and gaining all available information as to the poli ground on the Pamirs, and the best nullahs.

A SNOW LEOPARD.

One day Sher Mahomed, formerly British Native Agent at Tashkurghan in Sarikol, called. He told me a great deal about the Pamirs and the country round Yarkand and Kashgar, and was one of the best-educated Indians it has been my good fortune to meet.

Prior to my arrival in Gilgit a fine specimen of the snow leopard had been brought in and was, at the time of my visit, confined in a wire cage. Owing, however, to its savage nature it had to be shot, and this was done immediately after I had photographed it.

In the afternoons tennis was generally in vogue in the gardens belonging to the Political Agent, the tennis court having been considerably improved and the grounds artistically laid out under the able supervision of Mrs. Dew. Time passed pleasantly enough during my stay, the last "stand easy" I should be able to indulge in for some time to come.

"THE TRACK HANGS ON TO THE MOUNTAIN SIDE."

On the morning of April 20th I sent off the baggage in charge of Giyani, and after lunch, having bid farewell to the genial residents of Gilgit, whose kindness and hospitality I had enjoyed to the full, started myself, riding to Nomal, the first march out from Gilgit, where I stayed the night. The road runs along the right bank of the Kanjut River over sandy reaches and through precipitous rock gorges, and in Nomal village leads amongst leafy lanes and orchards, the trees being then in full bloom.

From Nomal to Chalt the road crosses some very bad "parris," the worst of which is the Chaichar Parri, a former outpost to the Hunza-Nagar Valley, and a position of great natural strength. A path has been made along a sheer precipice several hundred feet above the river bed, altogether a grim-looking spot, but typical of the country to be traversed in the Kanjut Valley. The track hangs on to the mountain side, hollowed out

A VIEW OF MOUNT RAKAPUSHI BEYOND CHALT.

of the solid rock, and viewed from beyond the "parri" looks as though not even a goat could maintain a footing there.

Beyond Chalt one passes the famous heights of Nilt, stormed during the Hunza expedition of 1891, and on which the ruins of the old fort still stand. Some distance out of Chalt a magnificent view is to be had of Mount Rakapushi, towering

39

up 26,670 feet, and dominating the whole valley, truly a stupendous spectacle

We had rather an exciting incident on the march from Chalt, just before crossing to the left bank of the Kanjut River Giyani was mounted on a little hill pony, which, judging from its antics and the gyrations it commenced to perform, must have made him wish he were on his native hillsides rather than on the back of a creature spending most of its time going sideways and performing a two-step on its hind legs. Beyond the rest-house there is a large stretch of open ground, on reaching which Giyani's steed went off like a rocket. He hung on manfully, until the saddle slipped round and dislodged him, the pony bolting and defying all efforts at recapture Fortunately Giyani was not hurt, and having mounted another and quieter charger we proceeded on our way, the last view of the runaway revealing an energetic pursuit by sundry Kanjutis endeavouring to corner him on the slopes high up above the river

I had arranged to stay the night in the Political Officer's camp at Phakai, so, taking Giyani with necessary kit, and sending the remainder on by the direct route to Hunza, followed the path to Phakai, a laborious climb, over many zigzags, on to a plateau where I found Major Dew's camp in a delightful orchard, commanding a superb view of Mount Rakapushi and the Hunza Valley towards the north The Major had just come down from Hunza, and in order to render the streams passable had had some temporary bridges constructed, the dismantling of which he at once ordered to be delayed until I had passed This act of thoughtfulness saved me a long journey round and was the means of considerably shortening the distance to Hunza I spent a very pleasant evening in this camp, listening to the Major's stories of the making of frontiers, and the onerous work our officials are called upon to perform in these outposts of Empire

Next morning I started, after breakfasting with Major and Mrs Dew, on the road to Hunza, involving a steep descent

"CAMP WAS IN A DELIGHTFUL ORCHARD."

to the river, and a climb up to the polo ground over tiers of cultivated land, to the Political Officer's bungalow placed at my disposal.

The approach to Baltit, the capital of Hunza, is very fine,
lying through terraced fields watered by irrigation channels, the
valley being shut in on either side by gigantic mountains. The
village stands on an eminence at the mouth of a grand gorge.
Behind the castle, forming the residence of the Mir, or Raja, of

"THE MIR'S CASTLE IS SITUATED AT THE MOUTH OF A GRAND GORGE."

Hunza, the mountains rise to an enormous height, whilst
towards the river it is a scene of orchards, now in the full glory
of spring blossoms. The houses are built tier upon tier, and the
castle of the Mir, which is reached through a number of steep
and tortuous passages, crowns the summit.

Hunza commands one of the routes to the Pamirs and Central
Asia, and in this respect occupies a position of considerable
importance.

The passes to the east of the Hunza, or Kanjut Valley lead into the Raskum Daria, and on to the great highway of trade between Ladakh and Chinese Turkistan. In former days raids on caravans using this route were of frequent occurrence, and formed the main source of income to the rulers and people of Hunza. The Kanjutis, taking full advantage of the inaccessible nature of their mountain fastnesses, would cross into the Raskum Valley, rob passing caravans, and dispose of the captives as slaves to the

"THE HUNZA VALLEY IS SHUT IN BY GIGANTIC MOUNTAINS."

Chinese. The natural consequence of these raids was that entire valleys on the Turkistan side were depopulated, and the name of Kanjut became a byword amongst travellers. This state of affairs terminated with the subjugation of Hunza brought about by the expedition of 1891.

The Kanjutis are much akin to the Chitralis, being a fine race of people with fair complexions. They are splendid mountaineers,

possessing great powers of endurance and have ever enjoyed a
fine reputation for bravery, while former struggles with their
neighbours of Nagar, and their raiding exploits, testify to the
warlike qualities possessed by them to a marked degree

On the afternoon of my arrival, the Mir of Hunza, accompanied by his little son, Wazir Humayun, and the native Political
Assistant, called on me. We had a long conversation, the Mir
speaking fluent Hindustani, and proving himself an entertaining
man. He had already visited India, and expressed admiration
of all he had seen there, more particularly the splendidly trained
Indian native army. He enquired as to the latest developments
in this world of wonders, and when I informed him that flying
was becoming an established fact, and that ships were being
made to sail in the air, he was very keen on having one to explore
the skies. Tea was served during the visit, his son, a pretty
bright-eyed boy revelling in the delights of a bottle of crystallised fruits I produced for his delectation. In the courtyard
outside the Mir had his bodyguard drawn up for my inspection,
a score of strapping cheery ruffians, dressed in dark uniforms
with red fezzes. The commander of this ferocious-looking squad
was a tall swarthy fellow of most determined mien, wearing the
full dress tunic of an officer of the Bedfordshire Regiment but
as to how he had acquired it did not transpire. Armed with a
long sword, and a revolver stuck in his belt, he seemed altogether
an individual of whom to beware. The men of the bodyguard
carried old muskets, and impressed me as constituting fine
material for the fighting line.

Later in the afternoon I returned the Mir's call, accompanied
by Giyani, looking very spic and span. I was received at the
foot of the steps leading to the royal apartments by the Mir and
Wazir Humayun. These steps led up through a trap-door in
the roof, whence we passed into the reception room, the balconied
windows commanding magnificent views of the Hunza Valley
and of Mount Rakapushi. The rooms were spread with rugs
and carpets, while the walls were hung with portraits of well-

known people, such as King Edward VII, the Russian Generals Kuropatkin, Linievitch, the Aga Khan and others. Some of the portraits were upside down, which did not seem to worry the Mir in the least. However, as the portrait of the King-Emperor hung correctly I did not worry either.

During tea the Mir discussed the Russo-Japanese War and other topics, displaying a considerable knowledge of current

THE MIR OF HUNZA AND HIS BODYGUARD.

events. He was much interested in my smart little Garhwali orderly, and the latter's sturdy appearance and fine physique drew forth fresh encomiums on the Indian Army, greatly pleasing Giyani, who beamed with delight. After tea I took a photograph of the Mir with his little son, surrounded by the bodyguard, and then, taking leave, returned to my quarters.

I was very fortunate in Hunza in engaging an excellent man

to replace the one who had accompanied me from Lansdowne
in the capacity of cook, but whose general incompetency for the
billet had occasioned his discharge here   Piroz Zaman, the new
incumbent, was a big broad-shouldered giant, a typical Kanjuti,
and an excellent fellow in every way.   He had been with one or
two travellers before, and in my service acquitted himself admirably, and at the same time was thoroughly straightforward
and honest, and knew a certain amount of Turki   The Mir
was kind enough to arrange for him to accompany me as far
as I might wish, in which Piroz Zaman readily acquiesced,
expressing his willingness to remain with me throughout my
wanderings.

I decided to resume the march to the Pamirs the next day,
and, in accordance with arrangements made by the native
Political Assistant, coolies were in readiness soon after daybreak

As far as Hunza there is a fairly good road, passable for
laden animals, but beyond coolies have to be utilised, for the
going is exceedingly rough, over huge parris and through
tremendous gorges, in addition to which the river has constantly
to be forded.   The Mir sent a trusty henchman as guide,
philosopher and friend, he journeying with me as far as Misgar,
near the foot of the passes leading on to the Taghdumbash, to
make necessary arrangements and render me any assistance I
might need   I intended to double-march to Gulmit by changing
coolies half way at a village called Atabad, so sent them off at
8 o'clock in charge of Giyani   The Mir was good enough to come
and see me off, wishing me *bon voyage* and much luck amongst
the poli.   The weather was now glorious, and the radiant bloom
of the Hunza orchards imparted a sense of peace and content,
delighting the eye with its fragrant beauty.

The Hunza Valley, like most of those in the Hindu Kush, is
exceedingly rocky, except where the villages are situated   Here
one notes patches of apricot trees and cultivation, but towards
the north the country is nothing but a stony waste, shut in by

tremendously high mountains, which in many places rise sheer from the water's edge, towering up thousands of feet, their summits capped by eternal snow. The sun has scant opportunity to show itself in these dark and gloomy canyons, some of the villages only getting an hour or so of sunshine during even the long days of summer.

Just below the village of Atabad, a few miles out of Hunza, I halted on a sandy stretch by the river to change coolies.

"THE RIVER HAD TO BE FORDED A NUMBER OF TIMES."

From here on to Gulmit, a good 20-mile march from Hunza, the river had to be forded a number of times, but as the guide sent by the Mir knew the way it did not occasion more than the usual blundering and stumbling over hidden boulders lying along the bed. Luckily the weather was not yet warm enough to melt the snow in sufficient quantities to render the fords impassable, which is the case during summer, when the volume of water from the snows above turn the river into a roaring toirent nothing can face, let alone cioss in safety

At Gulmit I camped in a fine orchaid above the right bank of the river, and was the recipient of presents of fruit fiom the lumbardar in charge of the village. The Mir of Hunza has a summer residence here, rather a pretty place, commanding a fine view of the suirounding country and the mountains across the river to the east

The following day I again double-marched to Khaibar, a distance of 18 miles, halting at Pasu, half way, for tiffin, which the indefatigable Piro served in a glorious oichard whilst the coolie relief was being arranged Just before reaching Pasu there is a big moraine to cross, foimed by the deposit of a great glacier that year by year continues its steady advance, the solid walls of ice piesenting an imposing spectacle

The village haid by possessed a ieputation in former days by reason of its being located near the entrance to the famous Shimshal Ravine, the route followed by raiding parties of Kanjutis into the Raskum Valley This nullah is on the left bank a little distance above the village, and certainly has all the appearance of rough going The pass itself, which lies at an elevation of about 14,000 feet, presents no difficulties, but on the Hunza side for a distance of several miles it becomes impracticable foi laden animals on account of the iocks and boulders with which the nullah is stiewn.

CHAPTER IV

ON THE PAMIRS

THREE miles out of Pasu I crossed the mighty Batur glacier, one that completely fills the nullah in which it is situated and by its advance threatens to block up the Kanjut Valley Year by year it creeps steadily onward, nothing being capable of stemming its irresistible march The crossing took some considerable time, the surface being much broken and hummocky, with here and there crevasses of a forbidding nature The towering heights enclosing the valley on either side are in keeping with its erstwhile reputation for brigandage

A man I met in the village of Khaibar told me of the stirring times they enjoyed in the days when raiding of caravans in Chinese territory was the leading pursuit On one occasion he accompanied a party bent on waylaying a rich caravan, the raiders returning laden with booty and several thousand head of cattle and sheep, with a numerous band of slaves, who were disposed of to the Chinese at high prices

Beyond the Batur glacier is a fair path along the valley, in places one being able to canter and make up for lost time At Khaibar I camped in a field below the village, at the mouth of a grand gorge, the sides rising precipitously from the water's edge. Here all movement is a matter of the utmost difficulty, but in places the dark and narrow gorge widens, forming small stretches occupied by Kanjuti villages The aspect of these gorges is sombre and majestic, impressing one with a feeling of awe, and compelling the admiration of my Garhwali orderly, who remarked that even the mountains of his very mountainous land did not come up to the Hunza Valley in the immensity of its sublime grandeur.

There are a few houses in Khaibar village, the inhabitants of which must lead a dull and gloomy life, shut in as they are by the mountains and practically cut off from the outside world. But then the Oriental is differently constituted to his Western brother.

THE MIGHTY CANYONS OF THE KANJUT RIVER.

Later in the Ili Su I met some Tajik villagers who had never gone beyond their own rocky fastnesses and knew nothing of the Taghdumbash Pamir, 20 miles away, or of the country further down the nullah. Such characteristics are inexplicable to the European, and especially to the energetic Anglo-Saxon; the desire to explore and push into the unknown being innate in our race. As Rudyard Kipling has aptly expressed it, "East is East and West is West, and ne'er the twain shall meet."

Across the Roof of the World.

The coolies were off before six the next morning, marching through gorges along the river bed, a wild and desolate country. There was a great deal of fording to be done, the water being swift, icy, and deep, necessitating careful negotiating. The summer route is over parri spurs and along narrow ledges in the face of the cliffs, formed by placing ladders of brushwood on stakes driven into the rock and then covered with earth and

CHANGING COOLIES IN THE KANJUT VALLEY.

stones, a rickety and nerve-trying roadway, ever ready to collapse and throw the traveller into the seething torrent.

At the little village of Gircha I obtained another relief of coolies, during which Piro served tiffin in an old disused temple, prepared for the occasion by the lumbardar, so that my surroundings had an element of holiness as well as antiquity.

Beyond Gircha it is an arduous march to Misgar, over huge parris, ever up and down and through numerous fords in the Kanjut River, deep and often difficult. On the way I met an envoy of the Mir of Hunza returning from Yarkand, whither he had been to present gold dust the annual tribute paid by the Mir to the Chinese Government, to whom the former has owed nominal allegiance for centuries. The envoy and his party were bringing presents in return, probably of greater value than those taken to Yarkand, and spoke of the good time they had had in Chinese territory, where they had been well received by the Celestial authorities. The envoy told me the Kilik Pass was closed on account of the depth of snow, and that he and his followers had crossed by the Mintaka. This was unwelcome news to me, as the Mintaka, being further to the east, would necessitate a detour and result in a much longer trek to the poli ground.

I arrived at Misgar at half-past three in the afternoon, the last coolie coming in at six, not a bad performance considering the nature of the road and the constant succession of rocks and boulders over which one has to scramble.

Misgar is the last inhabited village in the Kanjut Valley, and lies at an elevation of 10,200 feet. It is situated on the left bank of the river, here flowing in a deep chasm in the centre of the valley, a steep and zigzag path conducting to the higher ground where the village stands. There are no trees here and wood is brought up from the river banks lower down the valley, where the willow jungle gives the villagers their firewood supply. It is a desolate windy spot, and the general aspect of bare rocky mountains and entire absence of foliage is cheerless and depressing.

The lumbardai of Misgar had gone up to the Kilik to ascertain for me the feasibility of crossing by this pass on to the Pamirs, and I was informed would meet me the next day. As usual I declined the offer of a house to sleep in, preferring the outer world and my tent, where there was less chance of being invaded by hosts of live-stock, so prevalent in the native dwellings.

At Misgar the Mir's henchman left me to return to Hunza, and the faithful Piro, in conjunction with Giyani—who exercised

53

a careful supervision over my general well-being—now took up the reins of office, and right well he did it, serving me in a manner I shall ever look back upon with feelings of the liveliest satisfaction

The day we left Misgar there was a change in the weather, thick driving mists with occasional snow. The road lay through the same gloomy ravines, rendered the more so by the heavy clouds which rolled across the skies, dark and threatening.

Near Murkush I halted in a goatherd's hut for a scratch meal, and then pushed on to the point where the nullah bifurcates, one leading to the Kilik and the other to the Mintaka. Here I met the lumbardar of Misgar who reported the Kilik to be quite impassable owing to the deep snow.

There are two passes by which the Pamirs can be reached from the Kanjut valley—the Kilik and the Mintaka. The former is the easier of the two, the ascent to it being gradual and practicable for laden ponies. The Mintaka lies to the east and is therefore a longer route, the approach to it being steep and the going very bad over huge boulders. Both these passes cross the watershed of the Karakoram, and from the end of October until well on into May are closed to all but pedestrian traffic on account of the depth of snow, communication then being maintained by the Mintaka. This pass, though having a much steeper ascent, has less snow than the Kilik, hence it is preferred during the winter months. There is also another pass, the Gul Khwaja Uwin, which lies between the Kilik and the Mintaka, but has not been crossed for some years on account of the movements of glaciers and other obstacles which bar the approach to it.

The Mintaka is difficult near the summit, the gradient being severe, whilst there is also a large glacier to negotiate on the Kanjut side. The pass is practicable for yaks, which can usually tackle anything, but to take laden ponies over would be a matter of great difficulty. I decided to cross by this pass, and on the night of the 27th April, camped in the rocky nullah leading to it

It had been snowing throughout the day, and thick rolling clouds of mist blotted out the landscape on all sides. At times the threatening clouds would lift a little, revealing the heights on either side. The wind rising in fitful gusts drove the cold mist down the gorge, narrowing the field of view to a score of paces in any direction.

The outlook was not a cheerful one, and the prospects of successfully negotiating the formidable pass were far from encouraging. Moreover, two of my coolies were ill and unable to proceed further. Such medical skill as I possessed was now brought into play, their symptoms indicating a slight attack of fever, doubtless due to cold and exposure during the day, I doctored them with quinine, and made them as comfortable as possible in a goatherd's hut, a small stone structure built under the lee of a huge rock and occupied in the summer, when the Kanjutis move to higher ground with their flocks. Here I pitched camp, and the indefatigable Piroz Zaman served a more than passable meal after which, having taken a look at the sick coolies, I retired.

By dawn a complete change in the weather had taken place, the skies had cleared and the sun shone brilliantly, such a day as reveals the mountains in all their stately grandeur. Camp was struck and loads equalised and made as light as possible to facilitate the coolies' progress over the rock and boulder-strewn ground. The two sick men were left comfortably ensconced in the stone hut, whilst I pushed on with the remainder, who, after crossing the pass, would return the following day. Higher up, the ravine assumed a wilder and more rugged aspect, its sides bare and dreary, a striking contrast to the pine-clad heights of the Himalayas. Amidst this prospect of wild desolation and awe-inspiring immensity, the track skirts a frozen lake formed from a waterfall issuing from the mighty glacier that completely fills the upper end of the valley. I waited below the latter to allow the coolies to close up again. Thence the march was resumed the path leading along the side of the glacier and over

an ancient moraine littered with giant boulders amongst which
we had to pick our way.

A thousand feet below the summit a stiffish climb ensues,
and one that calls for determined efforts at this early season of
the year, but thanks to the pluck and grit of my Hunza coolies
we reached the top by noon.

A cairn of stones here marks the boundary line between the
British and Chinese Empires, and, standing there, one realises it

THE GLACIER BELOW THE MINTAKA PASS.

is the meeting place of great empires, the point where one leaves
the confines of civilisation and enters the weird and strange
dominions of the Flowery Kingdom.

Beyond lie the Pamirs, that vast and inhospitable region
truly termed, as already remarked, the " Roof of the World," and
a region which attracted much attention some years ago.

To the north-west lies the centre of the Asiatic continent, a
centre which, apart from its political significance, possesses much

interest by reason of its having been peopled in former times by great races whose deeds have left a mark in Central Asian history.

Standing on the crest line of the Hindu Kush, one is profoundly impressed with those stupendous barriers marking the northern confines of India and serving as natural frontiers between the Empires of Britain, Russia, and China.

From the summit of the Mintaka, or " Pass of a thousand ibex," I expected to see before me a great tableland, this, I

ON THE SUMMIT OF THE MINTAKA PASS (15,430 FT.).

think, being the popular idea of the Pamirs. Actually they comprise a series of wide open valleys with gently sloping sides, the average elevation being some 13,000 feet, many of the intervening peaks running up to 20,000 feet and over. They may also be compared to a succession of leads formed by the shale detritus which has accumulated through the ages, a mighty mass of lofty, high-pitched ridges and gables, with narrow valleys, hollows or leads between, desolate and treeless, and with a climate noted for its severity

Both from a political and sporting point of view, the Pamirs have attracted a considerable amount of attention, though their military value is a negligible quantity.

What are the origin of the Pamirs it may be asked ? The term signifies an upland plain and embraces the mountainous region of a remote corner of Central Asia Their origin rests somewhat in obscurity but authorities on the subject, such as Sir Francis Younghusband, explain them as ancient glacier beds and the detritus of shale brought down from the mountains the streams have been unable to carry away

The total area of the Pamirs is about 25,000 square miles, the greater portion being within Russian jurisdiction The Taghdumbash Pamir, situated within the boundaries of the Chinese Empire, is the only one now available to European travellers since the Russian Pamirs were closed to foreigners some years ago—a rule Russia rigorously enforces, keeping jealous watch and ward thereover

The chief object of interest attaching to this bleak and inhospitable land is the *Ovis poli*, whose horns form one of the finest trophies in the sportsman's collection This grand sheep, the largest of its class and the size of a donkey, carries long, curved horns, giving it a majestic appearance The existence of *Ovis poli* was first made known to the world by that famous traveller, Marco Polo, who traversed the Pamirs more than six hundred years ago, and from whom it derives its name

The people met with are the nomad Kirghiz, a tribe distributed over Central Asia, whose origin has been the subject of considerable speculation The dress of the Kirghiz consists of sheep-skin coats and trousers, with leather knee-boots. On the head is worn a fur cap, which can be pulled down over the ears The women dress in a similar manner, with the exception that coats lined with cotton wool are worn The headdress is peculiar in that it comprises a large turban of white cloth, those of the wealthier classes

58

being adorned with gold embroidery. The Kirghiz are of the Mahommedan persuasion, though they cannot be regarded as strict followers of the Prophet.

These hardy nomads gain a scanty subsistence by herding their flocks on the bleak uplands of the Pamirs. During the winter, when the snow and intense cold render life on the higher ground impossible, they retire to the valleys, some of them migrating to the Afghan Pamirs where the high wind sweeps the pasturage bare of snow, affording a meagre grazing.

A TYPICAL KIRGHIZ WOMAN.

The nomads of the Pamirs possess large herds of sheep, a species peculiar to the highlands of Asia. This is the " Dumba," or fat-tailed sheep, an animal, as the name implies, possessing a large tail in the shape of a pear hanging well down over its hind-quarters. The fat secreted therein is reputed to sustain life when the pasturages are snowed up in winter, or the sheep are otherwise unable to find sufficient nourishment for their needs. The presence of this fatty appendage imparts a curious aspect to the sheep, more especially when running, since it has a " wobbly " motion preventing rapid movement.

The habitations of the Kirghiz are the " yurts," or " khirgas," constructed of felt on a circular wooden framework, with an opening at the top to let out smoke from the fire lighted in the centre. The inside is carpeted with rugs and numdahs, and, in the case of the wealthier Kirghiz, is hung with embroidered cloths and coverings, imparting a pleasing and artistic effect.

A RIDING YAK.

The fuel in use on the Pamirs is yak or camel dung, which emits a pungent but not an offensive odour. There is another form of fuel known as " burtsa," a stunted scrub, the roots of which are inflammable and make quite a good substitute for wood. It is found in quantities along the valleys and collected by the Kirghiz for winter use.

The main articles of diet of the nomads comprise milk and mutton, while their chief beast of burden is the yak, an animal able to live at great elevations and endure intense cold but who

KIRGHIZ WITH YAKS WHO MET ME AT THE FOOT OF THE MINTAKA PASS.

dies in the slightest heat The yak is a member of the genus
ox, his peculiarities being long hair on the body and shoulders
and a big tuft of hair on the tail. He is indigenous to Tibet
and the Pamir region of Central Asia, where the high altitudes
are eminently suitable to his constitution He carries his head
downward, almost touching the ground, and this has given rise
to the belief amongst the Kirghiz that he is still searching for a
long-lost brother

The cold on the Pamirs is extreme, at times assuming a
rigour that renders life there the reverse of pleasant, whilst
there is usually a wind resembling such a hurricane as one
encounters off Cape Horn in December Here it is indeed a case
of the survival of the fittest, for only the strongest constitutions
can resist the Arctic severity of the long winter months But
centuries of wandering on these wind-swept uplands have inured
the hardy nomads to all the vagaries of the Pamir climate, though
their lives must be anything but cheerful amidst such rigorous
surroundings.

From the summit of the Mintaka I pushed on with Piroz
Zaman, as I had information from the Chinese side that the Beg, the
official in charge of the Taghdumbash Pamir, would meet me in the
valley below, with yaks for transport We slid and tobogganed
down for some two hours, and then three miles further along
the valley found the Beg, accompanied by sundry others,
waiting to greet me. They were a wild-looking set, all Kirghiz,
muffled up in huge sheep-skins matted with the dirt of ages
The head man hailed from Tashkurghan, the headquarters
of the Amban who rules over the Sarikol district and where
there is a small garrison of Chinese troops They had brought
with them several yaks and two camels, in relief of the Hunza
coolies who would now return to the Kanjut side

After I had taken a photograph of this motley crowd a
move was made down the valley where a yurt had been
pitched Here tea, served in a Chinese bowl, was passed round
and duly sampled, the ceremony being led off by myself,

though not repeated by me since I had no desire to taste
anew of a beverage touched by many grimy and unwashed
lips.

I left one of my men behind here with orders to load up the
kit and bring it to Mintaka, a distance of five miles lower down
The valley was fairly wide and open with sloping grassy sides,
rounded at the crest line and partaking more of the character
of the South Downs

Among the party meeting me at the foot of the Mintaka
Pass was a young Kirghiz shikari, Kurban by name, who
apparently knew all the best ground for poli, so I engaged him
I decided to proceed to the Wakhijiui and Kukturuk nullahs
to the west, these being considered the best on the Chinese
Pamirs

At Mintaka I found a yurt had been pitched for me, the
walls on the inside decorated with the embroidered cloths I have
before referred to   These yurts, when the felt is thick and
free from holes, are very warm and comfortable, with plenty of
room inside, the average diameter being some 18 feet   Here
more tea, dried raisins, cakes, cream, and milk were served in
quantities sufficient to feed a legion.   The Kirghiz are very
hospitable, and when one approaches their encampments, come
out and lead one's yak to the best yurt and produce tea   The
baggage arrived late in the evening, and, after making preliminary arrangements for a move to the poli ground on the
morrow, I retired to enjoy a much-needed rest after the fatigues
of the day.

From Mintaka I struck west to the Wakhijiui and Kukturuk
nullahs, following the left bank of the Karachukar River which
rises in the glaciers of the Mustagh Range near the Afghan
frontier and flows east towards Tashkurghan, through an upland valley of an average width of one and a half miles   The
gently sloping sides are covered with a scanty showing of grass,
whilst beyond lies the dark shale, so prominent a feature of the
higher ground   The day was brilliantly fine, the sun shining

64

through a cloudless sky, and the air so clear that the surrounding heights showed up sharp and well defined.

On the way I noticed several old horns of poli lying about, silent witnesses to the devastation caused by wolves and the hunting Kirghiz. Some of these I measured but could not find any exceeding 50 inches. One day when out shooting in the Kukturuk nullah I came on the scene of a former Kirghiz drive, counting over sixty heads, some of which—unlike those

THE TRACKS OF THE EXPEDITION ACROSS THE ROOF OF THE WORLD.

encountered on the way from Mintaka—would have constituted magnificent trophies.

The drives in which the Kirghiz indulge take place in winter when the snow being deep and soft, the poli are then more easily run down, and are conducted somewhat on the following lines : a point is selected, generally a narrow nek or ravine, where low stone sungars are constructed, from behind which the Kirghiz marksmen take up their position   The poli are then rounded up with the aid of dogs and manœuvred to make them converge on to the nek through which the majority pass in headlong flight   This is the Kirghiz opportunity for slaughter, an opportunity he takes full advantage of, usually bagging several poli. A good many of the natives possess Russian breech-loading rifles and, what is more, know how to use them   The object of these drives is to procure a supply of skins to make boots and clothes, whilst the meat is smoked and stored for consumption during the summer.

Wild dogs have also ever been a source of trouble, and to their ravages the diminution in the number of poli is doubtless to a large extent due   Lord Dunmore and other authorities on Pamir shikar speak of the havoc wrought by these beasts, and since it has been going on for generations, such a persistent onslaught must, coupled with the depredations of the wolves and the hunting Kirghiz, bring poli in time to the point of extinction and render a journey to the Pamirs for sport futile

Twenty miles up the valley from Mintaka I halted awhile at a yurt hard by the confluence of the Karachukar and Tagerman Su streams   The occupants were very hospitable and insisted on regaling me with tea and little cakes fried in fat, which I enjoyed, the keen air of the Pamirs giving one an ever-ready appetite   My shikari, Kurban, told me the poli ground was still some way up stream beyond the point where the Kilik nullah joins the main valley.   I therefore determined to make the most of the remaining hours of daylight and push on still further to a camp whence I could set forth on the morrow in quest of the coveted game   Leaving the yurt I trekked on for another two hours, camping in a depression of the ground where some shelter was afforded from the wind—always so disagreeable a feature of the Pamirs   Much snow was still here, the year being well advanced before it entirely disappears from the valley   At sundown a heavy snowstorm set in, and with such silent persistency did it fall that the tents were soon covered

66

with a thick layer, necessitating continual removal to prevent the poles breaking. Yak dung, the only fuel available, is difficult to ignite under such circumstances, but between us, with much blowing and coaxing, we managed to get a fire going, sufficient to prepare the evening meal.

A change in climatic conditions was now evident, for during the night it blew hard and snow continued to fall with unabated persistency. At dawn the outlook was a dismal one, but never-

TYPICAL POLI GROUND ON THE PAMIRS.

theless we started in search of " gulja," as the poli are locally known, the day being bitterly cold with a terrific wind blowing. We rode on yaks, keeping a sharp look-out and had not gone very far up the Kukturuk when we sighted a herd high up on the mountain side to our left. My shikari pulled up his grunting old yak and slipping quietly to the ground whispered " gulja." The herd was a small one some 600 yards off, feeding on the bare slope running down to the water's edge. I took out my powerful telescopic binoculars and scanned them carefully but could not make out any shootable heads   They kept well on the alert and constantly looked about as if fearing some danger, giving me ample opportunity to study their shape and curved horns which impart to them such a noble appearance.

Ovis poli is the blue ribbon of mountain shikar, a good pair of horns attaining a length of 60 inches and upwards, the record head being 75 inches, now in the possession of Earl Roberts

I then tried the ground towards the Wakhijrui but finding nothing, and the wind by this time assuming the proportions of a hurricane, retired on the camp about 3 o'clock, not too well satisfied with the first day after poli

I had had the camp pitched at the junction of the Kukturuk and Wakhijrui nullahs, reputed the best on the Pamirs, which is not, however, saying much   During the night it snowed hard, and though this ceased by 8 o'clock the next morning, the same terrific wind was still in full swing   I tried the Kukturuk again, and, coming across the tracks of a herd, followed them for some distance in the direction of the Balderling nullah   It was very heavy going through deep snow, but the yaks we rode tackled it as if to the manner born, though puffing and grunting vigorously   From the crest line above the left bank of the Kukturuk we tracked the poli by their footmarks in the snow, and kept to the trail till a blinding snow-storm put a stop to further operations, and forced us back to camp

The next day was notable only for the amount of snow that fell, and the increased strength of the wind which at times almost threatened to carry our "khirgas" away   During the afternoon the wind dropped considerably, but the cold was intense, and a heavy snowstorm was in progress   It was impossible to go out in such weather, so I remained within my tent, for the large yurt I had brought down from Tagerman Su was full of holes, and consequently so draughty that I deemed a canvas shelter preferable to living beneath an enlarged sieve.

A Pathetic Incident

I spent the greater part of the day reading, since nothing could be done outside. The view from the tent was dismal and foreboding, displaying a wide open valley wrapped in a snowy mantle, while to the north and south high ranges of mountains loomed out through the thickly falling snow, imparting a still stronger air of desolation to my camp on the Roof of the World, at an elevation of nigh 15,000 feet Around the tent were walls of driven snow, save in front of the doorway, where I had cleared it away. No sign of life was visible, all nature seemed hushed, and when towards dusk the wind died down a silence settled over the land, such a silence as one only knows on the Pamirs and the vast steppes of Central Asia

A strange incident happened that afternoon, one with a vein of sadness in it, and illustrative of the severity of the weather encountered on the World's Roof. Whilst deeply absorbed in reading, there appeared beneath the canvas walls of my tent a little bird, the size of the familiar wagtail He hopped in, and gazing up at me in wonder and amazement, seemed to demand shelter from the bitter cold without His appeal was not in vain, for with a tiny box which lay beneath my bed I made a comfortable nest of wool and installed him therein, partly covering up the box as some further protection against the rigours of the Arctic climate Whence he came, or how he had reached my tent, I knew not, but doubtless he had battled bravely against the icy blast, and on through the pitiless snow, until at last he found a haven of refuge from the fury of the elements Far into the night the snow fell with silent persistency, and the cold increased, until the land seemed locked in an icy grip, reducing everything to a state of frozen rigidity Several times I took a quiet look at the little inmate of the box There he sat, looking ill and weak, scarce able to move Before finally turning in for the night I again arranged the little creature's nest, and made him yet more comfortable Of food he would take none, the cold seemed to have struck too deep to render possible any movement on his part

69

The snow must have ceased before daylight, for when I awoke the sky was clear, and the general aspect more cheering than had been the case the previous day, when all was depressing and gloomy. I thought of the little stranger and how the rays of the sun would bring warmth and gladness to him I peeped beneath the covering There he lay in an attitude unmistakable. He was dead '

CHAPTER V

AFTER *Ovis poli* ON THE PAMIRS.

I HELD a council of war and decided to try the Wakhijrui nullah in the hope of coming across *Ovis poli*, should the weather continue favourable enough to go out with any reasonable chance of success

That morning, however, my Garhwali orderly, Giyani, complained of feeling ill with pains in the head and chest, so for the present all idea of shikar had to be abandoned, and means adopted to combat the sickness My medical knowledge was limited, to say the least of it, and when the day after the complaint had not apparently yielded to treatment I deemed the best course would be to endeavour to reach Tashkurghan, where a small military hospital in connection with a force of Cossacks was maintained by the Russians I had taken him into my own tent so that I could watch him through the night and render any assistance he might require. Two days were passed with no apparent change in his condition, days full of anxiety for the safety of my little comrade-in-arms. To reach Tashkurghan meant a trek of 60 miles through wind and snow, on the back of the sure, but withal very slow yak. Allowing him to remain where he was without proper medical attention was not to be thought of, so measures were taken to arrange the most comfortable form of conveyance and render the journey to Tashkurghan as easy as possible This I managed to do by fixing him on the broad back of one of the yaks. Leaving the camp standing, I took only a few necessary articles and set off with him down the valley for Tagerman Su, where I intended halting the night He bore the journey well, full of that pluck and grit so characteristic of

71

his clan, and which, when pervading the ranks of an army, contributes so largely to success

At Tagerman Su the hospitable Kirghiz placed their only yurt at my disposal, but as this would have meant turning them out had I accepted, I contented myself with billeting Giyani on them for the night, and slept myself outside, resuming the march at daybreak to Mintaka, where we arrived soon after mid-day. During the afternoon and evening the symptoms changed considerably for the better, with an absence of the rattling in the throat and difficulty in breathing that had caused me so much disquietude the first two days of his illness We occupied the same yurt I had passed the night in on the day of arrival from the Kanjut Valley, a large, roomy structure, warmed by the cheering glow of a "burtsa" fire The morning of May 5th saw a still further improvement, which was maintained, so this obviated the necessity of going to Tashkurghan.

The day after I decided to return to Kukturuk, leaving Giyani in charge of Mahomed, the head Kirghiz, who I knew would give him all necessary attention I waited another day to satisfy myself that the improvement was constant, and then, taking the shikari, marched back to Tagerman Su, the next morning reaching the shooting camp I had left some days before

It was wretched weather and bitterly cold, altogether a poor outlook for sport amongst the poli On May 8th I tried the famous Wakhijrui nullah, but not a sign of anything did I see, so, skirting the northern slopes of the nullah into the Kukturuk, reached camp once more, after a twelve-hour tramp through the interminable snows of the Roof of the World

I now decided to try the ground in the Balderling nullah, and left camp the following morning at 8 o'clock, intending to enter the valley from the south and work upwards in the hope of seeing some big heads Soon after leaving camp we sighted poli high up on the shale slopes at the entrance to the Kukturuk, a direct approach being barred by the openness of the terrain, so a long detour was necessary over some very broken ground covered with deep snow By keeping along the bed of the stream and thence under cover of a protecting spur running out from the main range, we worked beyond the poli and thus circumvented the wind, ever a source of trouble to the hunter During the night it blows down the nullah, changing soon after daybreak to an upward course, when stalking becomes a matter of increased difficulty, since the poli usually retire to higher ground during the day and any attempt then to approach them is futile, with the wind in their direction One must therefore get beyond and work downward against the wind On this occasion it was fortunately in the right direction

Once beyond the spur and out on to the slope on which the poli were feeding we became more or less exposed while in addition, the rattle of falling stones on the loose shale might easily cause the quarry to seek safety in precipitate flight By crawling along and taking advantage of slight folds in the terrain I finally reached a point beyond which any further advance was out of the question, for, by raising myself just above a lying posture, I could see the poli about 200 yards off

Evidently something had alarmed them, for they stood in a bunch gazing intently in my direction There were eight, all rams, so singling out the biggest I pushed my rifle quietly forward and, covering him behind the shoulder, let drive He toppled over, rolling some distance down the slope, whilst the rest of the herd betook themselves off in headlong flight We dashed down to the fallen monarch, blundering over sundry rocks in our eagerness The tape gave the horns at under 50 inches, a disappointment, as the head had appeared to be a good one

Poli heads are undoubtedly difficult to judge, but on my way from Mintaka, coming across many old horns, I, with an idea to gaining experience in the size, had set them up on rocks to view from a distance and then, judging the measurement, verified it afterwards by the tape I sent back for a yak on which to pack the poli I had shot, and when the former arrived loaded up and returned to camp

On May 10th, the day after bagging my first poli, I started out in the early morning to do the Baldeiling nullah to the northeast. It was terribly hard work in the soft snow, and the high altitude of over 15,000 feet, with consequent rarity of the atmosphere, made the going doubly severe. This day was destined to be another blank, one of unavailing toil, the close of it seeing the sportsman disconsolately wending his weary way back to camp, there to consult with his shikan as to what shall be done on the morrow. In this instance, as in most others, the said shikari looked wise, regretted that we had not been in some other nullah, or on some other ground, where poli would certainly have been found, and generally discussing the what-might-have-been.

The next day I sallied forth full of the hope that ever buoys up the true hunter, and searched the Wakhijrui from end to end, but fortune refused to smile on me, and, beyond experiencing a wind that would have put a Cape Horn nor'-easter to shame, sent me back empty to camp. I arrived about 2 o'clock in the afternoon, and sent Kurbán in the direction of Kukturuk to reconnoitre and report as to the whereabouts of the poli we had seen there some days previously. He returned having seen only one or two small heads, which for him must have been very small indeed, since anything with a head on it at all was usually reported to be a record one, and worthy of a mighty hunter.

Whilst in the Wakhijrui during the morning I had seen ibex on the slopes above the left bank, but a careful examination through my binoculars revealed only some indifferent heads. The ibex on the Taghdumbash Pamu are reputed to carry big horns, but though I saw a good many heads during my stay there I never came across any of a size sufficient to warrant serious consideration. One of the record heads of ibex was picked up on the Taghdumbash some years ago measuring 56 inches.

In the evening I again discussed the best means to adopt to further chances of bagging a record head of poli, and it was finally decided to move over into the Tageiman Su, whither local report said the poli had migrated, as the grass there was superior, while there was less snow on the ground. I set out next day in a blinding snowstorm and a hurricane blowing great guns, my shikari going ahead to survey the ground and note if any poli were about. The deep snow and terrific wind made progress slow, and one's temper short in proportion, whilst even the stolid yaks must have thought it a poor game struggling along in the teeth of a gale and half buried in snow.

WHERE THREE EMPIRES MEET.

There was nothing shootable in the Tagerman Su nullah, so I determined to trek on to the Payik, some 40 miles down the Karachukar Valley on the way to the Taghdumbash River. Three marches took us there, none of them very long but just too much to be done in two days. On the second day I camped at some Kirghiz tents, at the mouth of the Sárá Jilga nullah, the head man of which placed a "khirga" at my disposal, presenting me with sheep, cream, and other edibles, and doing his best to be obliging in return for which I gave him a substantial present on leaving the next morning He also provided a feast for my servants, to which they all did ample justice, especially Giyani, who was a famous trencherman and should have lived in the days of Falstaff

The weather had been wretched all day with the same high wind, so the shelter of the yurt was very welcome, and enabled me to write up my diary and notes in comfort The Beg had also prepared a large yurt for my staff and the culinary department, Piro serving up a dinner that would have done credit to the Ritz

My intentions were now to thoroughly explore the Payik nullah for poli, and if none should be found there to move on to the Khunjerab, some distance down the valley leading off from the right bank of the Taghdumbash River, thence on to Yarkand and Kashgar.

In the morning I bade farewell to the hospitable Beg and continued down the valley, camping that night some five miles up the Payik, a nullah leading off from the left bank of the Tashkurghan River. There is a karaul, or mud fort, at the entrance, which tower of strength is the outward and visible sign of Chinese occupancy The man in charge, with sundry other unwashed rascals, came out to meet me, but I did not stay, being anxious to get on to the higher ground in the nullah There were lots of hares in the vicinity of my camp that night and I shot a few for the pot, having become weary of a mutton diet

In the morning I went ahead with my shikari and another hunter I had engaged at the mouth of the nullah, Arzu by name, and a brother of Kurban s, and gave the others orders to come on later and pitch camp at the foot of the Payik Pass This pass is rather an important one, inasmuch as it lies on the road from Aktash, a post on the Russian Pamirs, to the valley of the Taghdumbash Its height is something over 15,000 feet, and, though steep and rocky near the summit, cannot be called difficult

It was, of course, covered with snow, even in May, and quite impassable to any but pedestrian traffic

The pass takes its name from the Payik River, which does not, however, rise in the neighbourhood, but a long way to the westward   The valley below the pass is broad and grassy, of an average width of about 250 yards, the sides sloping away gently and covered with gravel and rock as in the nullahs to the east   Behind camp was a nullah leading off from the left bank, the higher part opening out into a wide and grass-covered basin, but though we searched all this ground very thoroughly did not come across anything nor did we see signs of poli.   On the way back I noticed some good heads of ibex rotting in the bed of the stream, one or two of the horns running to 50 inches   My shikari informed me many large heads of ibex were once found in the Payik nullah, but that the wolves had committed sad havoc and very few were now to be encountered   I went out the following morning up the valley to the west, but did not sight any poli having heads of a shootable size

Higher up in a side ravine to the north two red bears were busy feeding on the short grass, but though I made great efforts to bag them they had other views and gave me no chance This bear (*Ursus isabellinus*) is also found in the mountains and valleys along the higher ground throughout the Himalayas and the ranges contiguous thereto. Its habits approximate to those of the black bear, with the exception that it is found at greater altitudes.   The fur is of a reddish colour and in the autumn, when the bears are in good condition, form fine trophies

All the bear tribe possess wonderful powers of scent and are able to detect the presence of danger at considerable distances   On the occasion in question the two I attempted to stalk were unusually wary, and the openness of the ground, coupled with the shifty nature of the wind, rendered all my efforts ineffectual

I then tried the ground towards the head of the nullah for poli, searching all the slopes thoroughly without seeing any, so late in the afternoon we rode back to camp—a three-hour journey on the yaks

On May 17th I started with Arzu after an early breakfast, and did the ground to the north-west, crossing an intervening range at a height of nearly 16 000 feet The country beyond was more open and the hills more sloping, resembling rolling downs It looked excellent ground for poli, and towards noon we sighted a herd high up on a long stony slope some distance along the valley We were on the northern side, so to get into touch with the herd crossed to the far side, jumping the river about a dozen times as it here flowed in several parallel streams Then commenced a climb through deep snow for some 1,500 feet, sinking to the knees and often to the waist I have been on a Pacific liner off the Aleutian Islands, where the wind breaks records, but that day it surpassed itself. Once on top we had to cross a long, undulating, snow-covered plateau, into which Arzu, being short, disappeared and reappeared like a Jack-in-the-box At last, towards 3 o'clock, after four hours' hard going in the teeth of the wind and being numbed with the bitter cold, I arrived within shot, but though from the other side the herd had appeared a good one, I could now see there was not a head exceeding 50 inches, and therefore nothing shootable, so steadily declined to open fire despite Arzu's persistent desire for blood

We had a strenuous time getting back to camp, for at 16,000 feet the air is so rarefied that one's heart thumps like an engine and the least exertion on a steep gradient is difficult and laborious. Ascending the summit of the range that night it took an hour to do 200 yards, for the snow only freezes on the surface, and by the evening, after the sun's rays have lessened its rigidity, one sinks in with an exasperating " flop " at every step.

Early on the morning of the 18th I was at it again, this time trying the entire ground lying between camp and the western end of the Payik nullah, but though I put in some terrific work there was no reward, and I did not even have the satisfaction of seeing any poli. That night I came to the conclusion that the

78

Taghdumbash Pamir now holds but few poli ; nevertheless, I determined to stay on until the end of the month, and then move across the Ili Su Pass and, if possible, down the Yarkand River to Yarkand.

On the 19th I spent the morning in camp, and sent out Arzu and Palang to look for poli, as I had a bad headache caused by being shut up in a stuffy, improvised darkroom the previous night developing a batch of plates. Arzu came in some three hours later and reported a herd on the stony slopes above

CAMPED ON THE ROOF OF THE WORLD.

the left bank of the stream towards the head of the nullah. He had left Palang to watch them, and when I arrived the poli, of whom there were only four, were still in evidence. I then commenced the stalk by making a detour to the east, and, when high up on their level, crept along under cover of some rough depressions in the rock and shale. Unfortunately the wind, which from the beginning had been bad, spoilt the stalk, and the last I saw of the tour they were going at a good speed up-hill, finally disappearing over the crest into the valley beyond

The next day I started before four o'clock The night had been clear and starry, but very cold and freezing hard We took the yaks and rode to the foot of the range crossed three days before, and there tethered the animals, proceeding ourselves on foot, over the summit and into the valley on the far side Again there was nothing to be seen, though we searched the slopes for some distance down, returning to camp in the afternoon

Having had enough of the Payik I decided to trek to the Oprang, a nullah at the upper end of the Taghdumbash Valley to the south, and try my luck there. Accordingly I had everything packed up, and we marched down the nullah, camping the night by the karaul at the mouth

I had rather an amusing experience that day when crossing the Karachukar River at the lower end of the nullah The yak I rode was meandering along in his usual confidential way, when on the far side of the stream having to get up on to a bank he took a sudden and tremendous leap which lifted me clean out of the saddle and deposited me in the water. I was rather angry with the yak, but it was so funny and must have seemed doubly so to my following, that I overlooked their suppressed hilarity at such a unique sight

On the 21st I did a long march to Tungtoos up the Taghdumbash Valley and camped that night by some Kirghiz yurts. I had paid off Arzu and Palang here, engaging another man in the person of Dai Khan who knew the Oprang and Khunjerab nullahs, ground with which the others were not acquainted The Kirghiz I met here were very hospitable and gave me a hearty welcome, placing one of their yurts at the disposal of my servants, though I preferred my tent

Throughout my stay on the Pamirs I invariably found the Kirghiz to be a congenial people, always cheerful, full of fun, and the soul of hospitality. None of the ladies are " purdah nishin," that is veiled, and are as jolly and coquettish as Swiss milkmaids.

We had great fun at this camp the following morning when starting for the mouth of the Oprang where I intended camping a few days in the hunt for big heads. The yaks, of which I required several, had all been brought in, except one very obstinate brute, who refused to be saddled, careering about wildly until at last secured. Again, however, he broke away with a mighty effort and dashed off, the saddle partly slipping

CAMP IN THE OPRANG (14,500 FT.).

over his tail and encircling his legs with the result that he indulged in some high kicks worthy of a ballet dancer.

The next day was wretchedly misty, but I nevertheless went out with the new shikari, trying the ground to the south of the Oprang, though the one herd we saw gave us the slip.

The 23rd was another bad day, with wind and driving snow, followed later by dense mists. After a climb in a wind that positively cut up our faces we sighted seven small heads. The stalk promised to be a most successful one, as I approached quite close, though the thick mists prevented my locating them exactly I waited for the mist and blinding snow to moderate a little, lying out on a shale slope for two hours and a half Then the mist lifted a trifle to reveal the poli moving off on the opposite side of the nullah. They had apparently moved of their own account since the wind was blowing up hill and not in their direction I attempted to follow but the mists and dense clouds rolling across the landscape effectually prevented my locating them again after they had once gone over the ridge on the far side of the nullah For several hours I had been on the track of this herd, but the adverse weather conditions prevented my reaping the reward of so much labour Sorrowfully we wended our way down the hill and back to camp in the teeth of a gale of wind and driven snow, arriving there at 5 o'clock, one mass of icicles and frozen snow, and almost perished with the piercing wind

In all the books I had read concerning the Pamirs I do not know one that chronicles such weather as I experienced The Roof of the World has a reputation for cold and winds, and it fully maintained that reputation whilst I was up there

I now decided to leave the Pamirs as I had had no luck, there being yet much ground to cover before my programme of sport would be completed and the far distant Trans-Siberian Railway reached Accordingly on the morning of the last day in the Oprang I sent off my camp to the foot of the Ili Su Pass, the nullah to which leads off from the right bank of the Taghdumbash River, where I joined it late that night I had had a blank day in the Khunjerab, not even having the melancholy satisfaction of seeing any poli, though, as usual, the Kirghiz encamped below the entrance to the nullah had assured me the place was full of them The return journey to camp in the Ili Su Pass proved a much harder task than I had anticipated, for it necessitated the crossing of two high intervening ranges, whence we had to coast along the far side down into the valley

In response to my request a Beg had arrived with an authority written in Turkish and Chinese to arrange transport on the road and assist me in any way I might require   The regular route to Yarkand lies through Tashkurghan, a fortified post in Chinese territory, thence east by a beaten track   I, however, determined to proceed by the Yarkand River and Kulan Urgu Valley to Yarkand, over a route never previously followed in its entirety. The Yarkand River and the country bordering on the Raskum Daria has been only partly explored, and not much information has yet been forthcoming as to its geography   I decided to move viâ the Ili Su Pass and down the gorge of the latter river to its junction with the Yarkand, thence to proceed as circumstances might dictate

I knew I should experience the utmost difficulty in forcing a way through the tremendous canyons of the Ili Su and the Yarkand River, and that the many passes to be crossed would present obstacles beside which those I had already encountered on the march from India would pale into insignificance

Although near the end of May it was yet too early to tackle high passes on the Pamirs, the snow not having melted in sufficient quantities to render them practicable without considerable danger

The Kirghiz on the Taghdumbash side declared I should never succeed in getting over the Ili Su Pass, and generally were very pessimistic on the subject of the venture   They knew nothing whatever about the country beyond, so I could gather no useful information as to the route and the amount of water in the ravine   Like all natives, however, though they had never been there they described the road in anything but rosy terms, one individual declaring by an admirable demonstration with his grimy paws that the track was that much wide, indicating a space of some 9 inches in width, adding much water was therein only waiting to claim us for its own

Prospects, therefore, of getting the large and grunting yaks through such narrow defiles did not seem very bright The Beg with me was, of course, quite unacquainted with the route, but expressed his willingness to do all he could and follow my fortunes into the unknown He proved to be a splendid fellow in every way and accompanied me as far as Kashgar, whence he returned to his home His name was Nadir and he was certainly about the best man I found throughout the whole period of my travels across Asia With him one's arrangements from place to place were a matter of ease, for the plucky, energetic Nadir was like Napoleon's General Vandamme, of whom it was said " He feared neither God nor devil "

I could only procure four yaks, just sufficient for the baggage, but the prospect of some hard walking did not perturb us, since a month on the Pamirs, with its attendant work and strenuous labour, had made every one very fit.

I struck camp on the 26th, sending off the baggage at 5 30 in charge of Giyani, with orders to keep moving and not allow the yakmen to loiter on the way, as is their wont An hour later, in company with Nadir, I started up the narrow rocky gorge now covered with ice and snow Some distance beyond camp the gorge narrowed to such an extent that sufficient room was not available for the yaks to proceed so they had to be off-loaded and the kit brought along by hand past these intricate defiles Precipitous ledges had to be scaled, weird snow bridges needed crossing, and some 150 feet below the summit a loose, shale-covered slide supervened, whose sides approached so nearly to the perpendicular that it seemed hopeless trying to negotiate it The yaks, however, tackled it as only yaks can, snorting and blowing, and halting every now and again to take breath, but reaching the top soon after nine

The summit of the Ili Su Pass lies at an altitude of 16,750 feet and is a small plateau, covered with many feet of snow, now frozen solid, and would probably remain in this condition until late in the summer, for the sun does not get an opportunity to exert full power until the year has well advanced   I halted a few minutes before continuing the march, taking a photograph of the caravan, and then began the descent.

The whole aspect of the country had now changed, for instead of wide open valleys and vast snow-covered uplands, we found ourselves lower down in a mighty gorge, shut in by high mountains falling away in perpendicular sides to the river banks   This narrow gully conducts one to the Yarkand River, a distance of nearly forty miles, in the track of a torrent racing down from the glaciers of the Mustagh Range   For the first five miles the passage of the gorge presents no great difficulties but beyond the water becomes more turbulent, being fed by an ever-increasing volume from the numerous tributaries that flow into it, afterwards expanding into a current which cannons and thunders through the deep and gloomy ravine to finally mingle its waters with those of the Yarkand River.

The fording of streams is done on the stolid and useful yak, and never did I admire this denizen of high altitudes more than in my march down the Ili Su. He can face the rushing cataract and cross it in safety where a man would be instantly swept away, working his way over huge boulders, and, breasting the foaming current, is quite undismayed by the roar and rush of the angry waters

From below the summit of the pass Nadir and I had gone ahead, leaving the transport to follow with Giyani in charge   The Ili Su was reputed to hold burhel, so I was in hopes of getting the chance of a shot at them   In places the ravine widens to a breadth of twenty-five and thirty yards, with a showing of grass that looked promising and indicative of a possible find for shikar of some sort   Three or four miles down I came on a herd of what at first sight appeared to be ibex, but on closer examination with the glasses proved to be burhel   I at once set about preparations for a stalk, Nadir being particularly keen and anxious to demonstrate to me his abilities as a shikari   The right bank of the stream was a tremendous precipice towering up thousands of

feet, whilst the left was broken and serrated, with pinnacles of
rock higher up, admirable ground for burhel but scarcely so
congenial for man, especially when encumbered with a rifle   The
herd was quietly grazing on the right bank some two hundred
yards further down stream and numbered about forty head, but
of these only ten or a dozen were rams

By keeping well over to the left bank I was enabled to take
full advantage of the configuration of the ground, which had a
tendency to rise slightly to a point lower down the stream whence
it dropped abruptly to the water's edge again   It was therefore
essential to coast along under cover of this, and by dint of much
crawling to gain the topmost point whence the burhel would afford
a fairly easy shot   Fortunately the wind was favourable, blowing
up the nullah as is usual in the early part of the morning   By
the time I was half way along the slope the caravan hove in sight,
a matter of four hundred yards up the ravine, but Giyani, noticing
my movements and divining from the manner I was hugging
the ground and pursuing a snake-like advance that something
was in the wind, halted the yaks and men under the lee of the
rocks   When I reached the crest and peeped over no burhel
were visible, so it was obvious they had taken alarm and made
off   I sent Nadir forward to reconnoitre and presently he looked
back, beckoning me to follow   Now, the ravine here was
of a winding nature, not permitting of a view in a direct line
for more than a hundred yards   Round the corner of the
next turn the burhel were spotted, making their way up
amongst the broken rocks on our side of the stream, and
evidently bent on migrating to less dangerous quarters   The
ground ran up from the river bank in a succession of ridges at
right angles to the ravine, with little hollows in between   There
was a chance that if I kept near the crest of one of these ridges
and worked gradually up I might get a shot   It was hard going
as the slopes were steep and rocky, affording scarcely any foothold, what there was being mostly loose rocks, which constantly
became displaced and clattered down with a noise that threatened

to render abortive any attempts at successful stalking   Patience, however, was rewarded, for when some way up the ridge I saw the entire herd on another which ran parallel to mine just under a hundred yards off

Not a single ram was visible, a most disappointing discovery, so it looked as though they must have gone one way and the females another   Nadir here interposed that burhel meat made good eating and suggested I should bag one of the "madeens," so singling out a plump one I dropped it with a shot behind the shoulder   At the report, probably the first they had ever heard in this distant and inaccessible corner of the universe, there was a tremendous stampede and a rattle and clatter of falling rocks as the herd bounded up the mountain side   A second later a couple of rams appeared on the crest line of the opposite ridge, looking about momentarily as if uncertain which way to turn   I rammed in another cartridge and, covering the best of the two, let drive, the shot told for he toppled off the ridge, bumping and rolling down until finally fetching up on an old moraine hard by the water's edge.

Nadir and I hastened down to the fallen beast and were soon joined by the yak men, greatly pleased at the prospect of much meat as also the skins wherewith they could repair their foot gear

On the way down the ravine I saw a great many more burhel and wished I could have remained a few days in their pursuit, but the increasing volume of water, brought about by the change in the weather and the brilliant sunshine now enjoyed, necessitated rapid marching in order to avoid our being shut in by the rising river

During the summer the ravine becomes quite impassable owing to the amount of water rushing through the resounding gorges, until in the month of July it reaches its maximum height, effectually barring all efforts at marching therein   Sometimes we crossed rocky parris, or passed round the edges of precipices, jumping from rock to rock in the river, the thunder of which reverberated throughout the narrow defile. The yaks negotiated these places with their customary skill, never getting in the least perturbed at the terrific current but quietly pursuing the even tenour of their way

Ten miles below the Ili Su Pass one gets into willow jungle, with occasional patches of grass where it is possible to find space for a tent. The change after the intense cold of the bleak and desolate Pamirs was most welcome, and I admired to the full the green grass and waving boughs of willow, a contrast as striking as it was pleasing. Through these patches of jungle it was necessary to cut a way for the animals, the denseness of the undergrowth preventing their getting along when carrying loads. Lower down the combined influence of vegetable life and the warm rays of the sun brought out the flies in considerable numbers, doing much to worry the yaks and causing us a certain amount of uneasiness, since they are very susceptible to the slightest heat and the worry of a large fly met with in the Yarkand country, a fly, as far as I could ascertain, similar to the tsetse fly of South Africa. The Kirghiz assured me this fly constituted a menace against which the animals would be powerless and to whose bite they would rapidly succumb

About four o'clock I decided to camp at the first favourable spot further down, as the ground I was then on was not sufficient to allow room for the whole of the caravan and animals. The amount of water in the stream was by now considerable, so this factor also contributed to a somewhat earlier camp than usual. Presently we reached a spot that seemed to afford the necessary accommodation, but as it lay on the opposite bank meant crossing the river again. At this particular point the ravine had widened to some fifty yards, the prospective camping ground being on the right bank and well above it, thus tending to lessen the fly nuisance. The river was a mass of rocks and boulders, amongst which the water tumbled and roared like the cataract of Niagara above Prospect Point, whilst on the far side were some willow trees whose branches projected over the stream and would afford some hold should one be lucky enough to reach them The width was about thirty feet and occupied only a comparatively short time to negotiate, but in that space of time how much exciting incident is crowded when struggling in the grip of a mountain torrent the force and speed of which must be experienced to be adequately realised

Standing on our side of the ravine it seemed impossible to gain the opposite bank, but I determined to try, so Nadir and myself went forward and with the aid of the yaks, without whose assistance little could be done, did battle with the raging cataract, edging across as opportunity offered and getting deluged with water The others followed our example and, arrived on the other side, Giyani soon had the camp pitched, whilst Piro, indefatigable as ever, busied himself with preparations for a well-earned supper It was not an ideal spot for a camp but the best under the circumstances

On both sides the ravine rose in a solid wall exceeding a height of 1,500 feet, whilst both up and down stream the same prospect of rugged grandeur met the gaze. The noise of the river as it thundered through these sombre canyons was deafening, and to make oneself heard at all needed a stentorian voice

The best time for trekking is the early part of the day before the sun is up, as later, when the warm rays have acted on the snow, the rise of water is much greater and fording consequently out of the question During the night the snow on the higher ground freezes hard, the volume of water being thereby restricted, but by noon the upper surface commences to thaw, every side nullah and gully becoming a feeder to the main stream and assisting to turn it into a flood tide against which all the efforts of man are vain We therefore rose at dawn the next day to the music of the waters as they raced onwards to the Yarkand Valley, and, having breakfasted, loaded up the yaks and proceeded on our way.

It was another brilliantly fine day with the sun shining through a cloudless sky, just such a day as would bring the water down from the snows above in record quantities   For the first five miles it was exceedingly narrow and difficult, indeed to such an extent that it was only with the utmost exertion we could get along at all   I had hoped to reach the junction of the Ili Su with the Yarkand River that evening, but it turned out to be impossible, the numerous fordings with their attendant difficulties and dangers hindering us so much that I gave up the idea   Five hours of struggling through these turbulent waters and along the face of precipices brought us to Issok Bulak (hot spring), where I halted for a scratch meal, appreciating a brief respite from perils and dangers by land and water   Lower down we reached a point where a mighty avalanche of rock had descended in bygone days, completely blocking the way, so the only alternative offered was a climb over the rocks and boulders above at the imminent risk of being cast into the river below

There was no track of any sort, simply a vast conglomeration of rocks amongst which the yaks would have to pick their way and get across as best they could   Yaks are about as steady on their feet as any animal in the world, and can get over ground that would be the despair of most human beings   On this rock slide we passed an hour, working against great odds, whilst the ever-present possibility of starting the entire slope in motion was not pleasant to contemplate   Further on the ravine again widened to a breadth of some twenty yards or less, the sides being covered with dense undergrowth through which a way was hacked with axes   Past this uncanny spot I camped in a small grassy clearing by the water's edge and distant less than a quarter of a mile from the Yarkand River, the valley of which I could distinguish ahead   Above the steep slopes on the right bank of the latter the ground was worn by paths leading up to the summit of the Tupa Dawan, a track made by the Kirghiz with their herds of goats.

It was this last ford across the Ili Su which prevented my camping the night in the main valley, since the volume of water and terrific strength of the current necessitated the abandonment of such a course. I made great efforts to negotiate this final ford, the one remaining obstacle between me and the Yarkand River, but no creature, animal or otherwise, could have lived in that boiling torrent, roaring and rushing through the gloomy canyons, and striking terror into the hearts of my Kirghiz, whose dismay was intense when I expressed an intention to try it.

THE GORGES OF THE YARKAND RIVER.

As mentioned before, if anything on this earth can get through a mountain stream it is a yak, so I deemed it advisable to put *Bos grunniens* to the test before risking our own lives in such a watery inferno. We secured a halter round the yak's neck with a good run of line on the end, enabling us to haul him back should he be carried away by the current. We were not long in doubt about this, for no sooner had he taken to the waters than he was instantly swept away, but assisted by the line attached to his halter managed to struggle ashore lower down, where he calmly proceeded to nibble the long grass as though nothing had happened.

This little test of the water's power was sufficient to convince me that a crossing was out of the question, so I decided to camp and effect one the following morning Daylight, however, brought no appreciable diminution in the volume, and after several vain attempts to get over I had a path cut through the dense jungle on our side along which the yaks were passed, and thence over another rock slide as steep and formidable as the one we had crossed the day before We succeeded in getting over the Ili Su lower down, an undertaking that involved much agility amongst giant boulders, the least slip from which might easily have cost us our lives

However, luck was again with me, and I stood at last on the banks of the Yarkand River, down which I hoped to travel on to the plains of Chinese Turkistan

The Yarkand is the chief river of this corner of the Celestial Empire, and takes its rise in the glaciers of the Karakoram Range hard by the well-known Karakoram Pass, the latter rising to a height of over 18,000 feet, and notable from the fact that it is the highest pass in the world used as a trade route The upper waters of the Yarkand flow through the Raskum Valley, famed, as I have already indicated, for the Kanjuti raids, of which it was formerly the scene It is a rushing torrent shut in by high mountains, until reaching a point just beyond its junction with the Ili Su whence it flows through tremendous gorges whose sides fall away in sheer precipices It is these gorges that prevent the traveller following the course of the river, especially during the spring and early summer, when the water therein constitutes an impassable obstacle Beyond the point where it issues from the mountains it flows through Kashgaria, doing much to assist in the cultivation of tracts of land in this district.

CHAPTER VI

By an Unknown Route to the Kulan Urgu Valley

The date of my arrival in the Yarkand Valley synchronised with the maximum rise in the river, usually reached about the end of May or beginning of June. It was hopeless trying to proceed down the river by the left bank, so the only course open was to ford to the opposite side and work my way down the right bank. I therefore went up the river for some considerable distance, over some very nasty slopes, bare of rock or stone, but none the less dangerous since the bottom ended in a precipice beneath which the Yarkand River rolled and splashed in all its might and majesty.

The valley was here about half a mile in breadth, both sides shut in by high ranges of mountains, the ground along the river banks being covered in places with a reed undergrowth known in this part of the country as " khamish " Here and there clumps of trees afford a certain amount of firewood to those who pass this way, which I should say is very seldom, for the valley in addition to being extraordinarily hard to penetrate, is much harder to find a way out of.

The width of the river where I forded it is about two hundred and fifty yards, the current swift, and the water a deep mud colour. To gain the opposite bank was now a problem to be solved and one that bid fair to offer more than the usual run of excitement. The guide I had brought with me from the Ili Su chose a point some way up the Raskum Valley where the river ran in three channels and the dangers of crossing would be to some extent minimised, in consequence of the water being distributed over a great area with a proportionate decrease in the depth. So, confiding myself to the tender mercies of this individual, I took to the swirling waters, leaving the baggage to follow as soon as we ourselves should be over in safety.

One great advantage in fording the Yarkand is the fact that the bed is smooth and firm wherever one can touch it, so there is no distressing blundering and struggling amongst huge boulders and rocks, every one seemingly put in its particular position as a pitfall for the unfortunate traveller.

VIEW OF THE RASKUM VALLEY.

Now, to attempt the crossing of a big and rushing river a good acquaintance with the fords conducting from one side to the other is essential, though even this knowledge is sometimes stultified by the seething current which catches the forder in its folds, throwing him about like a cork, and lucky he be if not washed away and drowned. The guide professing to be well up in river lore of this nature was deputed to take the lead, and pilot us through the billows, a post not appealing to him, but

one which force of circumstances compelled him to fill   The yak
tackles most fords with comparative ease, on this occasion further
justifying his reputation as a wader of rivers of a high order
More than once mine was carried off his feet, but with an admirable coolness he breasted the current, battling against it until
bottom was touched

On the far side I rested the yaks before despatching one
back with the guide who brought over the baggage animals,
an operation pleasanter to look back upon than watch, since
the chances of all one's worldly goods being swept irretrievably
away are very strong

In the jungle amongst the reeds and willow trees I halted
awhile, before commencing the ascent of the Tupa Dawan, the
path leading high up above the right bank of the river.   I partook
of a frugal lunch inside an old ruined log hut there, a rough
structure, doubtless built many years ago judging from its dilapidated condition

It was a long and stiff pull to the summit of the Tupa Pass,
over a bare and otherwise desolate stretch of ground sloping
down at an extremely steep angle to the river bed far below
The summit is likewise bare and in addition covered with
fragments of rock

A descent of about 1,500 feet takes one into the nullah,
the head of which leads over into the Kulan Urgu Valley by a
high and exceedingly difficult pass   The path winds down in a
succession of zigzags to the nullah in question, these running
directly under one another, a fact we were summarily apprised
of by miniature avalanches of stones caused by the yaks
above us, for Nadir and I had, as usual, gone on ahead

I camped that night some four miles up the nullah leading
to the Qoqoi Qotchkor with the intention of pushing on at
dawn and getting over the pass, the guide saying it was high
and very difficult   This man, like all natives high and low,
assured me the pass was " not far," and that we should reach a
Kirghiz encampment in the valley on the other side by evening

His ideas on the subject of distance were limited, as I was destined to discover by practical experience. Just how much "not far" represented in his computation was at the moment a problem I could not solve but I certainly was sanguine enough to hope the close of the day might see us in the valley on the far side.

It was a quiet, restful spot where I camped, a grassy patch by the brook, whose rippling waters flowed almost noiselessly down the narrow valley, a pleasing contrast to the rush and roar of the Ili Su. I spent the evening in re-packing and arranging the loads in readiness for the ordeal of the morrow, since I was sure it would be a formidable one. Whilst thus occupied some fresh yaks arrived in accordance with arrangements made the previous day, when I had despatched one of the Kirghiz drivers with orders to that effect. This worthy had disappeared into the hills with the object of rounding up fresh transport, though from where I knew not but he had assured me scattered groups of Tajiks and Kirghiz lived in even these inaccessible parts, and that from them he would be able to secure other yaks capable of tackling the ground ahead leading down to Yarkand. He omitted to mention the main reason of his anxiety to secure fresh animals was that it would permit him to return to the Pamirs with his own yaks, and thus avoid the probable loss of his life on the perilous Qotchkoi Pass.

The yaks with me were suffering from exhaustion and the hardships of the march down the Ili Su, and were consequently quite unfit to tackle the still more difficult portion of the route ahead. The arrival of the fresh animals gladdened the hearts of the yak men from the Pamirs, and mighty pleased they were to turn back and avoid treacherous and unknown routes with their manifold dangers. When I paid them off the next morning in solid coin of the realm their faces beamed with delight, and we parted the best of friends, they to return to the snows and wind-swept uplands of the Pamirs, I to cross into the Kulan Uigu and Asgar Sai Valleys on my way to Yarkand.

I started that morning soon after half past five, the road lying through a narrow valley some seventy yards broad, with grass patches and wood jungle here and there. The ground on both sides ran up in a series of grassy slopes, intersected by many side ravines and gullies, whilst beyond the grass it was rocky, approximating more to the nature of cliffs.

Shortly after leaving camp we sighted burhel on the grass slopes of the right bank. They did not seem to be in the least surprised at our sudden appearance, merely contenting themselves with moving slowly off up-hill, halting every now and then to gaze back, probably wondering what strange creatures we could be, for I doubt if they had ever seen much of man before Higher up we sighted another herd coming down the hill from the right slopes of the valley and which, crossing some distance in front of us, went off up-hill on the opposite side Both here and in the Ili Su I saw a number of burhel, but high water in the rivers and the possibility of being shut in for the summer did not permit of my tarrying ; indeed as it was we had to trek fast in order to avoid being held prisoners by the rapidly rising water

As regards the Ili Su it might repay sportsmen trying this spot for burhel, since it is only a day's march from the Taghdumbash Valley, and as no one ever shoots there some good trophies would doubtless be obtained

The Ili Su is also reputed to hold ibex, but whether they would repay pursuit is another question. Certain it is I saw no' large heads either there or on the Taghdumbash Pamir, though as to whether any frequent those uplands or not I can express no definite opinion.

At 8 o'clock I halted for a light breakfast, the while giving the yaks time to forge ahead, for the ground we were then entering upon was more stony and arduous, and a yak, though very sure, is at the best of times a slow moving creature At 10 o'clock I left the last patch of grass and wood jungle behind and entered

a narrow, stony ravine, whose sides reminded me of the Ili Su
The way was littered with huge boulders over which we had to
scramble, there being no visible track and a prolonged climb it
was over this rocky débris at an ever-increasing gradient. The
ravine from now onwards became wilder and more rugged, its dark
sloping sides covered with moraine and the detritus of avalanche-
swept shale, whilst beyond the ground stretched away up into the
region of eternal snow. Amidst such a scene of rugged grandeur
and sombre immensity we toiled upward, at noon reaching a
point where the nullah bifurcated, one branch leading to the north,
the other being the road I was to follow, and the one the guide
had informed me was " not far." There was grass on the only
open patch at this parting of the ways, so we rested there, gathering
energy for the wilderness of rocks and boulders ahead   It was
a long, unbroken ascent over masses of slate and shale, where to
gain a footing at all was a work of art, the labour intensified by
its sliding propensities, causing much blundering and struggling
on the treacherous surface.

Such a road, leading as it did, at a steep angle, over heaps of
detritus and ground that is one vast moraine, is most distressing for
the baggage animals, and their struggles over the terribly rough
going were pitiable to behold   As mentioned before the rarity of
the atmosphere at these high altitudes puts a great strain on
men and animals alike, and the hard work entailed by such
precipitous ascents causes the heart to beat like a sledge
hammer, and one gasps for breath in the attenuated air   It
had always been my practice never to hustle the animals
over such ground, but allow them to go their own pace, a
slow, but withal a sure policy, working out better than any
attempt to rush them through   At the same time it obviates
a heavy mortality consequent on continued exertion combined
with great height and its attendant evils

The secret of success in crossing high passes lies in ascending
them slowly, with due regard to the respiratory organs, which at
high altitudes. and the resulting lack of sufficient oxygen, can

only perform their functions under difficulties still further accentuated by any attempt to force the pace.

At two o'clock we were a long way below the summit, apparently further off than ever, but the guide still stuck manfully to his guns and declared we were now quite close The ascent, now over a long and exceedingly steep moraine, momentarily became more laborious and exhausting A pony I had brought from the Ili Su had to be left behind at the last patch far below, as, though marching unladen, he was quite unfit to proceed even over the ground further down, which in comparison to that we were now on was a mere bagatelle The inconceivably rough going was too much for him, but the yaks on the other hand bore the ordeal well, accustomed as they are to live at considerable heights, although it was only at the cost of much puffing and grunting, and frequent halts to gather breath for renewed attempts

At half past three we crossed patches of frozen snow, just beginning to melt under the warming influences of the sun, and reached a basin shut in by the surrounding heights. Some 400 feet above we could discern the razor-back crest denoting the summit of this appalling pass It was a last supreme effort up a slope approaching so nearly to the perpendicular that it seemed a hopeless task trying to gain the top. But patience and perseverance have their reward, and at a quarter past four I stood on the summit, calculating the height with my instruments to be 17,400 feet, and the highest pass I had yet crossed Having reached that altitude one is quite content to go no higher, unless there be something tangible at the end of it in the shape of a good trophy of ibex, burhel, or other horned denizen of the mountains.

From the top a grand view unfolded itself, a panorama of peaks and glaciers stretching away north and south over the mighty Mustagh and Kuen Lun Ranges. It was a fine display of snow-capped heights, with great spurs running out parallel to the main ranges, the valleys and ravines in between being lined along their lowest levels with a thin silvery thread denoting a rushing torrent flowing from its glacier bed above. There in the distance stood out bold and exceptionally well defined the Ili Su Pass I had crossed some days previously, and the peaks on either side of it, whilst farther south one could distinguish the giant summits of that grand chain of mountains, the Mustagh Range, rising above the Raskum Valley, the highest peaks attaining an altitude of more than 26,000 feet.

Turning to the east and looking over that portion embracing the Kulan Urgu Valley, down which I was now to travel, almost the same scene of savage grandeur met the eye, with the exception that the peaks were not so high, nor the line of snowy summits so complete as that spreading itself out to the gaze in the Karakoram and the Mustagh from the western aspect of the Qotchkoi Pass

Soon after reaching the summit one of those remarkable changes of weather common at high regions came on, and in the place of a cloudless sky and brilliant sunshine, a dark and driving mist supervened, boding ill for the descent and causing us to hasten preparations for the downward journey The summit of the pass was a narrow razor-backed ridge, with a huge snow-cornice overhanging the eastern side. The descent looked exceedingly steep and dangerous, and the snow-cornice, frozen solid, offered no means of getting down to the slope beneath The yak men went along the top endeavouring to find a way for the animals, whilst I assisted Piro and Giyani at tightening ropes and generally readjusting the loads in order to facilitate the downward passage of the laden yaks.

Presently the drivers returned and reported the only practicable path through the snow-cornice was a difficult one, and asked me to inspect it before allowing the yaks to proceed This I did and it certainly seemed very hazardous as there was merely a 12-inch ledge leading down at a most acute angle for twenty feet, thence a long, stony slope supervened for a distance of quite 2,000 feet to the bed of the ravine, the surface being covered with shale and frozen as hard as steel. I gave orders that the path through the snow-cornice should be enlarged as much as possible, and that the yaks should be assisted down by all the men, of whom I had eight. This was done with the aid of the tools we possessed, and the path widened slightly to the commencement of the slope, which was frozen so firm that it seemed impossible for any animal to maintain a footing. The wind, now rising ominously, drove the mist across the summit, confining the view to a matter of some fifty yards at the most, and filling my party with the direst forebodings. The path having been prepared I marshalled all hands, and with the object of testing it sent an unladen yak ahead to prepare the way for the others, and make as secure a hold in the treacherous surface as could reasonably be expected.

The laden animals were then passed down in succession, assisted by everyone, some holding on to their tails, whilst others at the lower side steadied their progress and prevented any sudden precipitation down the slope. By the time this dangerous part was successfully negotiated, it was 5 o'clock, and a dark misty afternoon. Already the feeble light was rapidly waning, night coming on apace as it ever does in the East, and I began to realise nothing could get us to the foot of this incline without disaster. We were now on the eastern slope, where it became necessary to proceed with the utmost caution, to save yaks and men from an untimely descent to eternity.

At times the mist would lift somewhat, revealing only that sweeping slope going down it seemed to us to the bottom of the earth. The surface was as slippery as glass, and I did not like the outlook at all, as the ground was certainly the worst we had been on, while the gathering gloom, foretelling the approach of darkness, rendered the task of getting the laden animals down a well-nigh superhuman one.

On reaching the summit I had scanned the whole valley to the east but saw no sign of habitation, nor indeed any traces of the Kirghiz encampment the guide had assured me existed just below. It was then too late to visit any of the trouble on he who had committed us to this desperate country, doubtless out of ignorance, so I merely contented myself with bringing down my invective on the author of our impending misfortunes All that remained to be done was to find a way out of the difficulty and endeavour to reach the foot of the pass in safety if possible

To add to our embarrassments the cold wind increased, turning everything into a state of frozen rigidity, so that the fleeting moments became of vital importance. It was impossible for the laden yaks to maintain a hold, some slipping thirty feet or more on the glassy surface, only recovering themselves when a friendly rock intervened to break the force of their descent and afford them a chance to regain a footing Yaks are fine mountaineers but it seemed as though one were asking too much of them in the descent of the Qotchkor.

We had brought the animals down about fifty feet when one of them slipped again. and although desperate efforts were made to save him, it was useless on a slope continuing for full 2,000 feet. I was a little distance below endeavouring to hack a path in the icy surface so as to alleviate in some measure the difficulties of getting the transport down As the yak slid backwards I hoped against hope he would be able to pull himself up, since he carried my most important kit, negatives, uniform, and presents destined for Chinese officials in Turkistan. One of the yak men was holding on to the halter rope and it looked as though he too would be dragged to certain death, but having gone about seventy feet at a tremendous speed, he let go and saved himself by cannoning into a rock, somewhat bruised but otherwise safe The yak, however, continued his headlong flight, and by the time he had slid the first 150 feet was gathering a terrific impetus that nothing could check. I realised there was no chance of his saving himself on that glacial surface, so resigned myself to the inevitable. It was indeed a bitter moment to stand there and listen to the crash of my boxes being literally smashed to matchwood, coupled

with feelings of regret at the untimely death of the poor beast.
The Kirghiz above were in an agitated state of mind, weeping
and wailing, calling on Allah to save them, and generally behaving
as though their last hour had come. I at once gave orders for
the remaining yaks to be off-loaded, and the kit stacked on the
spot, intending to come up the next day and man-haul everything
down. I left Piro in charge, directing him to bring the unladen
yaks on as rapidly as possible to the Kirghiz encampment, still
a long way down the valley, in search of which I now set out
with Nadir and Giyani. On the way we endeavoured to get an
idea of the direction the fallen yak had taken, but the gathering
gloom and mist overhanging the slopes beneath the summit
prevented our seeing anything of him. We went down several
hundred feet following parallel to the course of his descent, but
beyond the same terrific slope, of seemingly illimitable depth,
could see nothing, so concluded he must have fallen a tremendous
distance, in which conjecture we were right as was proved by our
investigations the next day.

Some 2,000 feet below the summit we passed a solid wall of
frozen snow and ice, now rapidly developing into a glacier that
would probably in future years come down the valley and block
up entirely the path through the ravine, though at the time
there was no immediate indication of this. From here we passed
through the bed of the ravine, a mass of rocks and shale, and
then over a gravel and mud-strewn moraine rendered heavy and
sodden by the fast-melting snow. A further descent brought us
to open grassy slopes with a narrow ravine on either side through
which flowed streams fed from the snows above, finally uniting
at a point further down the valley

I searched the entire ground here hoping to sight the Kirghiz
encampment I had heard so much about from the guide, but
nothing could be seen except the rocky bed of the streams and
the walls of dark moraine above them. Continuing for some
distance we reached the confluence of the streams, thence went
along the valley on the right bank, where the grassy slopes were

covered with numerous well-defined tracks hollowed out by the Kirghiz flocks

Further down, and a good nine miles from the summit, we heard the barking of dogs, denoting the camp we were in search of. Descending into the valley and rounding the corner of a spur jutting out from the main ridge, we came on it, a solitary yurt with a small stone hut, the only sign of human habitation in this dark and gloomy wilderness. It was 9 o'clock when we reached the yurt tired and weary, but the Kirghiz, with characteristic hospitality, placed it at my disposal, the occupants disappearing through a low door into the stone hut close by, like rabbits into a warren

We were glad to rest awhile after sixteen hours hard work over what may be termed one of the most difficult passes in the world. I, together with Nadir and Giyani, enjoyed a meal of barley boiled in milk, which a pretty Kirghiz girl prepared for our delectation. I then sent off for reinforcements from a Kirghiz camp, some miles away, in an adjacent nullah, and later in the night despatched a second man to hasten their arrival, since I wished to return to the dreaded pass the next day and go over the ground where the yak had fallen, in the hope of recovering some of my property, particularly the negatives and photographic plates, articles I could ill afford to lose After supper Nadir proceeded to appropriate sundry numdahs and felt rugs to provide me a couch for the night, while he also brought in firewood from a stack near the yurt, and which had been cut from the willow jungles found in the valley down stream.

We gathered round the blazing fire and, warmed by its cheery glow, discussed the day's events and the outlook for the morrow The dancing light lit up the interior of the yurt, the primitive though warm and comfortable dwelling of the Kirghiz nomad The walls were decorated with the usual embroidered cloths, whilst from the staves of the wickerwork constituting the frame on which the yurt is built depended a native guitar, not indeed of the type met with in Europe, but yet one that could give forth melodious music when manipulated by a master hand. Along the sides of the yurt were bowls hollowed out of wood, forming the eating and drinking utensils of the owners, while part was curtained off, serving the double purpose of a place of repose for the lady of the yurt, and pantry, which contained bowls of milk and cream covered with dirt and dust, always a strong feature in the nomad's dwelling I enquired as to the country I had now to traverse, and the information gathered indicated it as being of a formidable nature, but I was not perturbed, having already covered much ground beset with many difficulties

The Kirghiz here were greatly interested in my adventures down the Ili Su and on the Qotchkoi Pass, parts of the universe they had never visited, and I doubt if they ever will, especially after my description. The loss of the yak seemed to be a serious calamity in their eyes, for the docile creature represents much worldly wealth to them, the mere fact of my having lost an important kit not appearing to be anything like so disastrous as the loss of its hairy carrier

At dawn the next morning the Kirghiz reinforcements had not arrived, but at 6 o'clock Piro and the yakmen came in. They had spent the night at the foot of the pass amongst the rocks and boulders, having found it impossible to make any headway in the darkness, while in addition men and animals were tired out from the hardest day's work they had ever experienced. Soon after their arrival, as the Kirghiz had still not put in an appearance, I collected all available hands and, leaving only Piro and his party in camp, set out for the pass It took us five hours to get there over a road which would have made the patient Job weep tears of grief and sorrow. Arrived at the foot of the glacier we had encountered on our way down the previous night, I marshalled the party into line with the object of working up hill and thoroughly searching the slope Fortunately it was a fine day with another of those cloudless skies, prominent in the East when clear weather is the order of the day, so there was still a chance something might be recovered.

Judging from the mist and clouds enveloping the pass and the ravine below it the evening before, I had looked upon a fall of snow as highly probable This would have rendered the search doubly severe, since most of the articles might have been buried and all traces of the yak's descent obliterated But luckily for me nothing untoward happened, and with fine weather to carry out operations I confidently expected to see again some of my missing goods and chattels

The first thing we found after commencing the upward march in line was a copy of Napoleon's Memoirs with the cover torn off, and after this articles came to hand fairly fast, including, amongst others, a History of the Russo-Japanese War with the maps out and scattered about over the icy slope Shortly after our own arrival we sighted the Kirghiz reinforcements coming rapidly up the narrow ravine. They had reached the yurt soon after my departure, pushing on at once to my assistance, mounted on fresh yaks, who tackled the rocks and boulders in a way that did one good to see These men were in charge of a most excellent Beg, or head man, and getting them into line we worked gradually up the slope There were fourteen all told, the new arrivals, armed with ropes and ice axes, wearing a business-like air It was impossible to do anything on the frozen slope without the aid of ropes and ice axes

We found the yak fully 2,500 feet below the summit, wedged in between blocks of ice, with his head jammed in a tiny crevasse through which raced an icy cataract He was naturally in a mutilated condition, pieces of skin having been torn off from contact with jagged rocks. and several teeth missing, some of which the Kirghiz actually found during the subsequent search The tremendous distance he fell must have broken every bone in his body Not a vestige of the two boxes attached to him remained, only the loading ropes still trailing by his side

The Kirghiz behaved splendidly, working up the precipitous slope, hauling each other up with ropes, and cutting footsteps in the ice with their axes. A number of articles were recovered, although they strewed the slope for hundreds of feet. How it happened I shall never know, but three bottles of Liqueurs carried in one of the yak dans were found unbroken, so the prospects for some Amban to indulge were still bright The discovery of these unbroken bottles greatly impressed my followers, and Nadir, holding them up, declared my luck in this connection was good, and that the gods could hardly be considered angry with me. Above this another useful find was made in the shape of a bag of money, ever a welcome commodity

Higher up, the slope approaching more than ever to the perpendicular, I scratched out a hollow in the surface and sat down to direct operations, having no desire to qualify for an early grave.

Some of the Kirghiz climbed to where the loads had been stacked the previous night and man-hauled everything down, a task only a hardy mountaineer could accomplish, and one they disposed of in a commendable manner.

The Beg told me the pass was considered exceedingly difficult and rarely used, even by the Kirghiz, to whom few passes come amiss, adding that they would think twice before going over the Qotchkor It had never previously been crossed by a white man so I have the doubtful honour of being the first.

Unfortunately I did not recover my photographic plates, bar the tin holding them, and even that was damaged almost beyond recognition Some of the negatives were certainly discovered far down near the foot of the pass, but, of course, exposure to the light had rendered them useless.

On the way back to camp that night we sighted a herd of burhel the chief telling me numbers were to be found in the Kulan Urgu, and that amongst his people were shikaris who occasionally hunted them for the skins and meat The ground certainly seemed favourable, so I much regretted time would not permit of a few days in their pursuit Doubtless some fine heads could be secured there since no Europeans ever pass that way, and the country being almost undisturbed, must surely be a happy hunting ground for the particular game it contains Whilst in camp the following day a Kirghiz shikari came in with a 25¾-inch burhel head, offering to show me a part of the valley containing others of a similar nature Unfortunately I could not avail myself of the opportunity, for the rapidly rising water in the ravines meant our being shut in if we did not trek fast.

It took a further three hours to reach the yurt. where Piro greeted me with a good supper, a pleasing close to another hard day in the mountains.

The next morning I despatched a few Kirghiz back to the pass with the object of endeavouring, if possible, to retrieve further articles, but they returned in the evening having found nothing beyond a few cartridges and some odds and ends. I spent the day in camp drying everything, overhauling the kit, and generally preparing for the march down the Kulan Urgu Valley. The Kirghiz said the latter would prove hazardous in the extreme owing to the rise in the river and the terrific current resulting therefrom.

Before leaving I paraded the Kirghiz and others who had assisted me on the pass, paying them handsomely, and also discharged the men who had accompanied me from the Ili Su. The owner of the ill-fated yak, who did not apparently expect to receive any compensation for the loss of his defunct steed, was most agreeably surprised when I presented him with the price of a new one, as well as his hire for the time he had been with me.

The Beg came some distance down the valley and piloted us through the first of the fords As I have already indicated, at this season of the year the volume of water in the streams is very great owing to the melting snow, and fording them is attended by the gravest danger, so much so that at this period it is often attended with fatal results, men and horses being swept away and drowned. The river was now a roaring channel, the sun had reached the zenith of his power, and the effect on ice and snow resulted in every ravine being turned into glacial rivulets, each contributing its quota to the main stream.

The width of the Kulan Urgu Valley varies at different points, in some places being as much as two hundred and fifty yards and in others narrowing to forty paces. At intervals along the valley are signs of cultivation, mostly in the shape of barley, whilst here and there groves of apricot trees surround the tiny mud-built houses of the inhabitants in this out-of-the-way corner of the world. The valley is shut in on both sides by stupendous mountains rising abruptly from the water's edge, and recalling the mighty canyons of the Fraser River in British Columbia, through which I travelled some years ago.

CHAPTER VII

OVER THE MOUNTAINS TO YARKAND

THE Kulan Urgu River rises in the glaciers of the Kuen Lun Mountains, and, flowing northward, gathers volume from numerous tributaries racing down from the snows above, until its waters join those of the Yarkand River. It is of deep and abiding interest to note a river throughout its different phases, to observe its source, to watch it gathering strength from the currents which pour down the mountain side, until finally becoming a mighty cataract it sweeps on with irresistible force, its deafening waters resounding throughout the narrow gorges

Such a river was the one I was about to travel along, where, the snows having become melted by the summer sun, progress is a matter involving much risk.

The first ford lay some way down the valley, beyond which I should have to cross and recross the river frequently, following the devious windings of the path as it meandered from side to side. Mamanur, the Kirghiz Beg, said the river must be forded in the early morning as the night's frost would restrict the amount of water, and that after noon I should find it impossible. I therefore hoped to negotiate several the first day out as a continuance of the prevailing warm weather would bring the water down in a deluge.

Arrived at the river bank, Mamanur took the lead, I following with the rest of the cavalcade, all mounted on strong yaks the best to be procured for the task. The current was well above the saddle flaps and rushing like a millrace Crossing at right angles was impossible owing to its depth and force, so we

"THE GORGES OF THE KULAN URGU RIVER."

were carried some way down stream before finally securing a foothold on the opposite side, the wonder being it did not sweep us away entirely. Just why it did not do so is a mystery I shall never be able to solve. The yaks behaved well, displaying that admirable coolness so characteristic of them. At such a critical moment they remained undismayed, breasting the current splendidly with their heads always in the right direction. When lifted completely off their feet by the rush of water there would only be a quiet struggle and a gradual edging towards the bank.

Twenty-six of such fords did we do in one day, so that we had more than our fair share of adventure will scarcely be denied. Sometimes in place of having to ford the river we were able to keep along under the lee of the rock-bound gorge where the water flows in diminished violence. Journeying on we occasionally passed oases of waving poplars with a sprinkling of apricot trees and a little cultivation, sights that gladdened the eye after the bleak and sterile wastes previously traversed. The air too was becoming perceptibly warmer, while the atmosphere no longer had about it that rarefied character, which makes breathing such a labour. We had left the icy blasts behind, and a feeling of joy took possession of us. To fully appreciate the significance of such a change one must travel for a lengthened period over rocks and snow where nothing relieves the eye beyond the same vista of dreary desolation.

There were a number of chikor, or hill partridge, amongst the open patches in the ravine, and I shot some for the pot, as well as a few pigeons I came across.

At Yaghzi I encountered the first hamlet of stone huts inhabited by a few Tajiks from the Yarkand Valley. These dwellings were of the ordinary mud-built type with flat roofs, the light illuminating the interior being let in from a hole in the roof that also served as an outlet for the smoke.

Beyond the village was another ford to cross, and it was touch and go whether we should manage it or not, for the day

was already well advanced and the increase of water pro-
hibited any further risks being run   However, we gained
the opposite bank, moving on down to Baldir another village
of stone huts similar in every respect to that just passed
through   I camped near the river bank in a delightful little
orchard of apricot trees, whose spreading branches afforded
grateful shade from the noonday sun   The inhabitants totalled
some fifty souls, the majority coming down to view the new arrival
from the outer world. I had no difficulty in procuring supplies,
the people showing considerable readiness in producing eggs,
milk and fruit, arrangements having been made by the energetic
Nadir. The local headman had prepared a house for me, spreading it with carpets and numdahs, but I preferred the apricot
grove and my tent

Judging by the force of the current in the river, now
at its maximum fury, I foresaw an obstacle to my forward
movement on the morrow, as unless a considerable diminution
occurred before morning there would be no hope of crossing,
since nothing could live in that raging cataract, swirling onward,
a seething mass of waters   The villagers said that during
summer they were often imprisoned for weeks at a stretch, cut
off from all communication with villages either up or down
stream, and that if any bold spirit desired to cross he generally
accomplished it on a raft made of inflated goat skins.   This is
the usual method adopted by the natives here in crossing rivers
and transporting their worldly goods from one side to the other
They also transport their women by the same means, though
the ladies must have a rough experience at flood time.

The water had risen considerably the following morning,
and the truculent manner in which it confronted me dispelled all
chance of getting over   One of the villagers, knowing the ford
well, brought his horse, and waded hither and thither searching
for a passage, but his efforts were futile, so I was compelled
to wait   Hopes were held out of some decrease in volume
occurring between 8 and 9 o'clock, but when noon came and

with it no change in the situation I began to think we should never succeed in crossing at all.

The only alternative route was a track leading up the mountain side and along a perpendicular wall of bare rock, five hundred feet above the river. It was an exceedingly difficult path, a matter of hanging on and playing the part of a chamois. I mustered every available man in the place, and divided all the kit into small portions for the coolies, who then started, picking their way along the cliff, hauling each other up with ropes, and passing things along, a hazardous work lasting till 2 o'clock. The look of this uncanny place did not favourably impress me, so preferring to run the risk of a watery grave rather than a five hundred foot drop, I mounted a fiery mustang and, accompanied by one volunteer, plunged into the foaming current, and was instantly swept down stream.

It was a great struggle, but my Bucephalus exerted all the energy he possessed, and though we constantly cannoned into rocks and boulders, and the water rushed like an express train, we attained the opposite side amidst the shouts of the villagers, who confidently expected us to be completely carried away. There were still three fords to do, which we managed alright. Fortunately I found fresh yaks on this side and at once engaged them to accompany me as far as the valley of the Asgar Sai.

Leaving the main stream of the Kulan Urgu, I moved up a narrow stony ravine leading off from the right bank to the foot of the Kara Dawan, or Black Pass. My plan of campaign was to work over into the Asgar Sai and down to Yarkand, and in order to do this it would be necessary to cross two more passes, the Kara Dawan and the Sundal. From the Kulan Urgu to the foot of the first-named pass we moved through precipitous defiles and over ground strewn with detritus and particles of rock cast down from the frowning heights above. The gorge through which the track passed was strikingly impressive. A mile or so up the nullah we turned north again into a side ravine, whose

I 2

walls were so narrow that at their tops one could almost have
jumped across the intervening space Clearing this defile we
passed into a grassy depression shut in by high mountains

In front of us stretched patches of grass with here and there
picturesque clumps of fir and pine From these slopes the
mountains rose on either hand, their lower reaches dotted with
bush and flower, the green sward beneath giving the scene
a pleasing aspect High up in this mountain retreat and at
the foot of the slope leading to the Kara Dawan, I found two
mud-built huts, the temporary home of shepherds who retire to
the uplands with their flocks during the summer. On the grassy
heights around, herds of yaks and goats were grazing, taking full
advantage of the ample pasturage stretching away in every
direction Whilst waiting for the kit to arrive I conversed with
the hardy shepherds who told me they had never before seen a
white man in their valley, and wondered what could have induced
me to undergo so much in the attempt to penetrate these
mountain fastnesses Game, they said, was to be found here
in the shape of burhel, or blue mountain sheep, as also the Ram
Chikor. Of the latter there were indeed any number but far
too wary to admit of approach.

These people provided me with milk and firewood, and cleared
a space for the tent They considered I should experience no
difficulty on the morrow in crossing the Kara Dawan, some
1,500 feet above us As it was then clear weather I did not
myself anticipate any difficulty, though in the mountains
changes in the weather occur with remarkable rapidity, a
brilliantly fine day often developing quickly into a sky black
with clouds bringing snow and wind in their wake, the latter
always the danger most to be dreaded

The last of the yaks came in at 8 15 p m. and Piro turned an
old disused stone hut, that was half underground, into a kitchen,
where he proceeded to light a fire, a desperately smoky affair,
but Piro and Giyani were used to smoke and breathed it with as
much joy as a *prima donna* taking lavender

I intended moving the next morning at 4 o'clock but all were very sleepy when the time came, though Nadir rose like a giant refreshed and went round rousing the camp, putting the fear of the Lord into the shepherds, who must have thought the end of the world had come to judge from the stentorian shouts he let in upon them.

From here it was a steep climb to the summit, up over a long grass-covered slope. Near the top we encountered fresh snow, fallen during the night, but there was not enough to impede progress. Here I stalked a herd of about twenty-five burhel,

MY CARAVAN ON THE SUMMIT OF THE KARA DAWAN (14,000 FT.).

of which only eight or nine were rams, but none having good heads I did not trouble further.

The summit of the Kara Dawan is covered with rocks, and although the ascent from the Kulan Urgu side presents no difficulties in itself, the descent is hard for laden animals, leading as it does over huge rocks and boulders for a thousand feet. Beyond this we reached more down-like country, where I again came on burhel, this time quite a big herd, but, alarmed at the sight of my caravan, they made off up the mountain side.

disappearing over the crest   There were, too, numbers of Ram Chikor about to an extent I had not previously met with

The height of the Kara Dawan is 14,000 feet, and only used by the natives when moving with their flocks from valley to valley. Below the pass are numerous undulations over spurs jutting out from the main range, until descending into a ravine whence a nullah leads to the Sandal Pass   The latter is the final pass to negotiate before reaching the valley of the Asgar Sai. Being weary of tramping through mountains and canyons I determined to get across that day and camp on the far side. It, however, involved a hard day's work over two small intervening ranges to the bed of a nullah, thence up the rocky ravine leading to the pass

Again there were numbers of Ram Chikor about and I went after them, but it was only vexation of spirit for I never managed to get a shot. The Sandal Ravine was hard going though only the lower portion was really difficult, being over rocks and boulders, and taxing the yak's powers to the utmost   Higher up the track wended over a vast moraine, a conglomeration of rocks and slabs of shale to the summit, the latter at the time quite free of snow   The snowfall is probably not great, as the top of the pass faces north and south so that there is always a certain amount of sunshine bearing on it The height of the Sandal Pass is nearly 16,000 feet, the crest line being sharp and serrated, though the actual summit is free from rocks. I gained the top at 4 30 in the afternoon, whence a long and stony descent ensued to the valley of the Asgar Sai. Here and there patches of snow, now fast melting from the sun, covered the hillsides, while numerous rivulets trickled downward, rendering the ground sodden and heavy, mud exuding from the shale-strewn slopes

On the way I saw a herd of some thirty ibex feeding on the grassy ridges above the left bank of the river, but a careful examination through the glasses revealing no good heads I left them in peace.

Far below in the valley I came upon a solitary yurt occupied by a Kirghiz shepherd and his wife, who were about to move to the higher ground for the summer with their flocks   Here I camped the night after a record march, the yaks coming in at half-past eight

From other Kirghiz inhabiting a side valley I secured fresh animals for the journey down the Asgai Sai, and, having paid off the men from the Kulan Urgu, started the next morning at 5 o'clock, crossing and recrossing the stream at frequent intervals   It held little water so the operation was accomplished without any of the danger and excitement we had encountered elsewhere   I was now entering an inhabited and more or less cultivated country, the hills becoming lower, grassy and more rounded, whilst native villages, nestled amongst orchards of apricot trees, were in constant evidence

I halted at Zumchi about mid-day to exchange the yaks for ponies, as the former were unable to proceed further in the low altitudes, since they are out of their element in even a moderately warm climate   I was able to raise sufficient pony transport and again pushed on to Thayis, arriving there after another 14-hour march   The valley was here about a mile and a-half wide, with numerous trees and cultivation, though the hills off the line of the oasis preserved a desert aspect, in striking contrast to the cultivated areas between

At Tar Aghzi, a few miles above Thayis, I passed under the lee of some remarkable stratified loess formations that from afar have the appearance of rocks   At Thayis I camped in a large orchard belonging to one of the head men

Apparently the passing of a white man is an uncommon event for the natives came in crowds to pay their respects and present cakes, fruit, milk, and similar articles   Giyani played the part of a showman and exhibited my X-pattern bed and collapsible table, which quite mystified them.   They live their lives far away in the heart of Asia, unmoved by the turmoil of the outer world, and oblivious of the mighty march of civilisation and the marvels it brings in its wake The meanest thing is to them a nine days' wonder, and the passing of the " Feringhi " from regions beyond their ken is the event of a lifetime No parliaments occupy their attention, no Press sway their opinions, no suffragettes exhibit their importunities They till the soil, guard their flocks and return at night free from care and worry With them the struggle for existence is reduced to a minimum, and content in their humble surroundings they heed not the passing of empires and the onward march of progress

I had now descended to an elevation of 6,000 feet, encountering a land of trees and cultivation and the warmth of an English summer day. How restful it all seemed and what an air of serenity it bore after the vast Pamirs and the regions of eternal snow, where it is but a white expanse, dark moraines, and the whistle of an Arctic blast I was weary of those uplands and the intense cold, weary of the numerous high passes, of the bleak camps in that inhospitable region, North Polar in its severity, so determined to march hard for Yarkand and Kashgar, more congenial climes Though I did not camp till 7 o'clock I left the next morning at five, and with a change of good ponies, continued to break records Ten miles beyond camp a twenty-mile strip of desert had to be crossed to reach Khan Langur, on the Yarkand River

Unfortunately a hurricane was blowing and by 9 o'clock a tremendous dust storm was in full swing, the force of it at times making travel an impossibility, so there was nothing to do but turn the horses round and sit down covered with coats and rugs to avoid the stinging of driving sand Never had I encountered anything resembling it, the strong wind whirling up the sand and grit and blinding us, forming on all sides a darkness which was often profound These dust storms are of frequent occurrence in Turkistan, due to the desert and level nature of the country

At Khan Langur I rested in the house of the local Beg, where Nadu picked stones and lumps of dirt out of my eyes The baggage animals came in at 6 o'clock, having had a very poor time, but I pushed on another four miles to Aktum, camping in a garden the property of a wealthy Beg   I think we were all satiated with the incessant marching, for we had been doing something like 14 and 15 hours daily, on one day crossing two high passes, fording rushing torrents and travelling unusually fast   In the last two days I had traversed the whole length of the Asgar Sai, having covered 70 miles and was now within 30 miles of Yarkand   Through the energy of Nadir I again obtained fresh ponies here, so moved at half-past five the next morning for Yarkand   The road runs mostly through avenues of tall trees, with a considerable amount of cultivation flanking it

Speaking generally Chinese Turkistan is a land of deserts and sand dunes, the rivers rendering cultivation to some extent possible by means of irrigation channels constructed to this end   Only in the neighbourhood of streams is cultivated land met with, since, the rainfall being practically nil, all watering has to be done by irrigation   The result is these portions consist of strips of land along the streams, the ground beyond giving place to the desert   Throughout my ride from Aktum to Yarkand I was passing through these leafy avenues and over tiny irrigation channels that continually crossed the road   Running parallel to these avenues were deeper canals, all part of a system of irrigation which time has evolved for the reclamation of land threatened by the hungry wastes of sand on every side   The larger water-ways, where they cross the road, are spanned by wooden bridges of an ancient make and usually comprise layers of logs and brushwood sprinkled over with earth, a structure that creaks and groans ominously as one's horse passes over

Here and there are seen groups of houses, built of mud, with flat roofs, low pitched places of sombre mien, in keeping with the sandy wastes around   All are single storied with usually only an opening in the roof to admit of light   The better class of house has its orchard with picturesque groves of fruit trees and running rivulets, giving life to the ground beneath and imparting a sense of peace and comfort to the mind after weeks of wandering through inhospitable and arid lands.

At the village of Posgam I struck the main trade route from Ladakh to Yarkand, not, as the name might imply, a brilliant example of the road maker's art, but as good as one can reasonably expect in Chinese Turkistan. Lines of trees give grateful shade, and compensate to some extent for any unevenness in the road.

Beyond Posgam I reached the Yarkand River, here crossed in huge flat-bottomed boats, and unfordable at this time of the

CROSSING THE YARKAND RIVER.

year. The current was swift and the width at the ferry about one hundred yards. Whilst waiting for the kit to arrive I sat down on the bank and watched the operation of transporting some Turkomans with their horses.

First of all the barges were moored as close in to the bank as possible, the horses being then led up and, in default of gangways to facilitate embarkation, were made to jump into the barge, a feat some of them accomplished though others came to grief in the water, causing energetic action on the part of the natives to save their plunging steeds. The real fun, however, came when the ropes were cast off and the barge floated out into midstream The current was rapid, and once away from the shore the barge was caught like a cork and swirled down stream. This galvanised everyone into an activity that showed itself in frantic shouts and yells, all at the acme of excitement, whilst the sturdy boatmen pulled with giant oars from the stern, bringing the unwieldy barque with a bump into the opposite bank that nearly capsized all hands More shouting and gesticulation ensued as the disembarkation took place, until finally all were ashore, when the boat was towed up stream and brought across to transport more voyagers By this time my caravan had put in an appearance, so we loaded up and took them over, the exciting incidents I had previously witnessed being repeated

From Aktum I had been accompanied by the Beg's son and a Yuzbashi, a minor official, whose title signifies " Head of a hundred " They are responsible for districts under Chinese Government comprising one hundred houses With these two worthies and Nadir I left the caravan after crossing the Yarkand River, and pushed ahead through shady lanes, doing the greater part of the distance at a good canter Some four miles outside Yarkand I was met by the British Aksakal, a native Consular subordinate appointed to watch the interests of British subjects and assist them generally Thus escorted I rode on through the outskirts to the gate of the city, whence we entered streets flanked by shops and low mud houses, until reaching a house prepared for me by the Aksakal It was two-roomed, the larger of which I turned into a living room, the other being relegated to the needs of the kitchen and my staff. There was a verandah running round three sides of the courtyard, the fourth looking out over the garden, where I was able to enjoy some delicious fruit. Inside my pavilion the floor had been spread with carpets and what furniture there was to be found in this outlandish part of the world Windows of coloured glass and lattice work let in the light and sunshine, throwing brilliant rays across the interior. The Aksakal and his many compatriots brought loads of fruit, in the shape of apricots, melons, plums and a whole host of sweetmeats, to say nothing of Russian biscuits and cigarettes.

My first duty was to order a supply of Chinese visiting cards for the purpose of official calls on the Governor and others. These cards are long strips of red paper, about 8 by 4 inches, and one's name is written thereon in Chinese characters, or as near as the Celestial writer can get to it I discovered the result in my own case fell short of the original, but as it had at any rate the merit of a name of some sort I did not worry These cards arrived in the course of the afternoon, and I sent one with my passport to the Yamen, or official residence of the Chinese Governor, intimating my desire to call on him the following day. I also sent another to the Commander-in-Chief of the Chinese forces at Yarkand with a similar message Return cards came from both these good people soon after, with a communication to the effect that they would be pleased to see me. Giyani therefore unpacked my full dress uniform and furbished up buttons and brass work in readiness for the audience of the morrow

In the afternoon I walked through the bazaars with the Aksakal and sundry others who had attached themselves to me, to get an idea of this, the largest, city in Chinese Turkistan, and once an important centre in the days of old Tartary.

Yarkand has a population of some 60,000 inhabitants, the great majority of Mahommedan persuasion, with a sprinkling of Chinese It is one of the chief trading centres of Kashgaria, and from it roads radiate to Kashgar and Maralbashi on the north and north-east, whilst to the south lies the main trade route to British India, the latter giving to Yarkand its present-day importance

It is a 30-day march from Leh in Ladakh (Kashmir) over a road crossing some of the highest passes in the world, which as a trade route between two countries is the loftiest in the universe.

The World's Loftiest Trade Route.

Owing to the great physical obstacles trade is carried on at a considerable disadvantage, and every summer during the period when the passes are open a heavy mortality in baggage animals results   This is consequent on the high altitudes, the desolate nature of the country traversed, devoid of grass or any kind of pasturage, and the enormous glaciers to be negotiated   Of late years the Government of India has done much to mitigate the difficulties and dangers of this important trade route by the construction of supply depôts for grain, the erection of caravanserais for the use of men and animals, and in generally assisting traders to overcome the immense natural difficulties confronting them   At points along the road improvements have been instituted and carried through with a view to rendering it much easier than in former days, so that the entire route is now very different to what it was a few years ago

CHAPTER VIII

Across the Plains to Kashgar

THE people of Yarkand do not impress the traveller, their air and bearing being that of a race showing them to have suffered many vicissitudes They display an entire lack of energy and enterprise, or indeed of any interest in life, doubtless due to the many wars that have from time to time raged in Kashgaria between the Chinese, Mahommedans and others for supremacy, leaving traces deep rooted in the character of the Turkoman

The dress of the men consists of a loose flowing robe of black or coloured material, exchanged in winter for one lined with cotton wool. Beneath this are worn pyjamas tucked into leather boots reaching to the knee, of peculiar make in that they boast neither heel nor sole When the wearer goes abroad he dons a high-heeled shoe that is kicked off on entering a house On the head is worn a cloth or silk cap, but in winter one lined with fur is preferred

The dress of the women is similar to that of the men, with perhaps a greater abundance of nether garments peculiar to the feminine world, on which I do not feel qualified to express an opinion Very few of the ladies are veiled, the rules regarding the seclusion of women not being so strict as in other Musulman countries. A veil is, however, worn, a network affair attached to the cap and thrown forward over the face, or carried on the top of the head at will The usual practice is to wear it in the latter position, the majority of the ladies, as far as one could see, not being overburdened with modesty

There are a large number of shops in Yarkand built of mud, or sun-dried bricks, with nothing of architectural beauty about them. All are open in front as is customary in the East, the shopkeeper sitting cross-legged in the midst of his wares, extolling their virtues but discreetly saying nothing about their vices. The bazaars have covered-in roofs of matting, making the thoroughfare cool and shady, though it tends to keep the many odours arising from shops and people in constant evidence.

Notable at many of the gateways of Chinese towns are prisoners condemned for various offences. A common sight is the "cangue," a heavy square board fastened round the neck and

A PRISONER SUFFERING THE PUNISHMENT OF THE "CANGUE."

varying in weight from 25 to 40 pounds. The unfortunate individual undergoing this punishment must perforce carry this formidable instrument during the whole period of his sentence, making sleep a difficulty and life for the time being a torture. Often when thus exposed they are the butt for the jeers and missiles of passers-by.

During my stroll through the bazaars of Yarkand I met several Indian traders, some having served with well-known English travellers and being intimately acquainted with the country

towards Ladakh and Kashmir   The Indian element in the population of Turkistan is small, mainly consisting of those engaged in
the trade between Yarkand and Kashmir and others permanently
settled in the country   There are a number of persons of mixed
blood, known as Argoons, the result of marriages contracted
between Yarkandis and Ladakhis   They are mostly employed
in shopkeeping in the larger towns and villages, or gain a liveli-
hood on the trade route as servants and caravan men   There
are also some Hindus in Yarkand posing as money lenders, who
seem to do well out of the simple Turki   In pursuit of their
calling they apparently stick at nothing, and their behaviour
in the general conduct of their business has called for stern
repression on the part of the British Consul at Kashgar
They are an enterprising set, and had even extended operations into Russian Turkistan, making themselves so obnoxious
that the Russians had them expelled from the country, to
the encouragement of thrift and the enhancement of Russian
reputation

Many Russian-made goods are displayed for sale in the native
shops, those of a flimsy nature, such as handkerchiefs and table
cloths largely predominating, while there are also looking glasses
in little boxes, and a mixture of trunks of gaudy hue covered with
much brass and tinsel work

The Russians are, from their geographical position, better
able to introduce trade into Chinese Turkistan than we are, since
the road from Osh, the nearest point on the Russian Central
Asian Railway, to Kasghar and Yarkand, can bear no comparison
to that from Yarkand to Kashmir in point of physical difficulty.
and the length of time taken to traverse it

One sees very little of the Chinese in Yarkand, who although
the ruling race, do not represent more than 5 per cent of the
total population   They, in common with other towns in Turkistan,
reside in a walled city of their own, distinct from the Musulman
quarter

In a country where sanitary measures are non-existent plague and pestilence might reasonably be expected to account for a large proportion of the people, but such is not the case The type of complaint most prevalent in the Yarkand country is goitre, a disease generally supposed to result from bad or hard water, though its exact origin still lacks scientific determination. Its characteristics are a swelling in the glands of the neck, giving the sufferer the appearance of having a large ball located in the throat. The disease is painless, and so far has not shown itself amenable to treatment. It is much in evidence in Yarkand, but at Kashgar there is almost a total absence of the complaint, perhaps due to the difference in the water A certain amount of malaria also obtains in the city, possibly accounted for by the number of stagnant pools existing. Each of these must be a hot bed of microbes, since they are never cleaned out, and consequently full of the dirt and filth of ages

The Aksakal brought a large supply of vegetables, fruit, and fresh meat from the bazaar, so that night Piro provided an unusually good dinner, or at any rate I thought so after the weeks of Spartan living I had experienced. Judging from the feast Giyani and the rest of the staff prepared for themselves they evidently intended to celebrate their return to the flesh pots and the mountains of rice, meat, and fruit must have gladdened Giyani's soul

I slept till late the next morning, as the visit to the Amban and Commander-in-Chief was not timed to take place until 4 o'clock I had had my camp bed moved on to the verandah where the cooling breeze the scent of flowers and twittering of birds was a delightful contrast to the snows of the Roof of the World The only occupant of the courtyard beside myself was a Turkoman soldier sent from the Yamen to be in attendance during the period of my sojourn in Yarkand, and whom I had posted at the inner gate as doorkeeper to restrain the curious minded anxious to gaze upon the new arrival from distant lands At 3 o'clock the Aksakal with a crowd of satellites appeared on the scene in readiness to escort me to the Yamen Donning my uniform, and accompanied by Giyani, and a host of others riding two abreast in rear, I set forth in procession through the bazaars on my way thither, a distance of more than a mile

The sight of a British officer in full regimentals is not a common one in Central Asia, for the natives flocked in crowds to see us as we rode through the streets   One man went ahead with a long and formidable stick and belaboured every unfortunate individual who failed to make himself scarce   We occupied all available space on the road, and when any other horsemen were encountered they were unceremoniously hustled into side alleys, or sent cannoning into shops, to the delight of Giyani and the energetic protestations of the shopkeepers, who resented the intrusion by vociferous shouts, adding to the general commotion raised by my prancing cavalcade.

A mounted man preceded me to the Yamen, intimating I was on my way, and on reaching the entrance I found a large crowd assembled   I rode on into the courtyard through numerous gates, and then dismounted   There was a raised dais in front with a big door in the centre, which was thrown open as I approached it   The retainers followed by a side door, and then, preceded by a minion of the Amban holding my card before him, I marched through the inner courtyard, being greeted at the end by the Amban   After cordially shaking hands we passed through more doorways into the reception room, the walls decorated with Chinese scrolls, while a small table was placed at one side of the room spread with sweetmeats, fruit and Russian cigarettes.   We then carried on a conversation through interpreters.   I spoke Hindustani to the Aksakal, who translated it into Turki for the Amban's interpreter, he in turn rendering it into Chinese and thus delivering the substance of my conversation to the Amban.   It is difficult to converse on these lines, though we succeeded better than might have been expected   As the Chinese officials either do not know Turki or profess ignorance of it they employ interpreters, a wearisome mode of procedure and one hardly conducive to the brilliant exchange of ideas.

The Amban enquired after my health, and as to my journey from India. At the same time he expressed his extreme regret at not receiving earlier notice of my approach to Yarkand since it would have enabled him to meet and welcome me in person to his capital. This was, of course, only exaggerated politeness on the part of the Celestial, and would be colloquially designated in this country "swank."

In the meantime tea was served, the Amban himself handing me mine with a graceful bow, and sugaring it, a compliment I returned with interest

There are some curious customs to observe when amongst the Chinese, one being that the ceremonial tea is not taken until one is ready to depart, so having done mutual honours we resumed the conversation. He asked me if I had experienced any hardships on the road and I replied I had, but that the pleasure of coming to Yarkand and meeting him had entirely obliterated the thought of them from my memory He said London must indeed be a gorgeous city, to which I replied it could not be compared to Pekin. He thought England was a mighty country, with which remark I mentally agreed, though my reply was to the effect that China was a Paradise on earth. He was very anxious for me to dine with him, an invitation I cordially accepted. When I had perjured my soul sufficient to warrant eternal damnation I drank the ceremonial tea and departed for the residence of the Hsei Tai, or Officer Commanding the troops The Amban accompanied me to the outer courtyard, where, having again shaken hands, I mounted my charger, and followed by the same prancing bodyguard rode out and into the Brigadier's Yamen a short distance away

I found the officer a charming personage, no longer in his youth, but well on to the allotted span of three score years and ten. He had seen much fighting in China and related some of his exploits, which conveyed through the channel of three languages must have lost some of their piquancy by the time they reached me He was greatly interested in my wanderings, but could not fathom why I should want to visit the Pamirs and undergo much personal discomfort exposed to the vagaries of a rigorous climate, for the sake of shooting a few animals, whose horns were valueless from a monetary point of view Having visited China during the Boxer rebellion of 1900 I was able to discourse on this theme and the country in general to the old man's visible delight.

After leaving him I rode back through the bazaars now even more crowded than on the outward journey It seemed as though the entire population had taken a holiday to see the procession, and when we reached my quarters it required more than the usual display of stick to force a passage

The following morning the Amban and Commander-in-Chief returned my call, sending a retainer to announce their approach They arrived together, being met by me at the gateway, and ushered into the reception room. Both remained over an hour, discussing a variety of subjects. The venerable officer was much taken with a bottle of saccharine I produced, and to prove that it really did possess sweetening properties I dropped four tablets into his tea This must have been too much even for a Chinaman, since he failed to muster sufficient courage to drink it

The Amban appeared to be up-to-date and appreciated things European, in this respect being unlike the usual type of Chinese They were much taken with my battery, examining the rifles with evident interest. At the conclusion of the visit both took their departure in little two-wheeled carts, each drawn by a large black mule richly caparisoned. Accompanying them was a goodly following of retainers, spearmen, umbrella carriers and others, who always surround a Chinese official when he moves out of his Yamen.

During the afternoon a contingent of Indian traders called and extended an invitation to an entertainment they desired to give in my honour in a garden outside the city. All were rich men and had met most of the famous travellers who had passed that way In religion they were Mohammedan, the majority hailing from Bajaur, a district to the north-west of India under British suzerainty. We remained in conversation for some considerable time, discussing the trade outlook and the country in general The elder ones related stories of the early days and the times of Yakub Beg, when the country was in the throes of a long and bitter struggle.

The Amban had arranged a programme for the following day to commence at 9 a.m with an inspection of the Chinese school and the scholars therein

Giyani and Nadir looked forward to it with much gratification, for the Oriental love of " tamasha " was strong within them, so when after an early breakfast I prepared to sally forth they both appeared on the scene looking very chic, Nadir in flowing robes like a Sultan, Giyani in the smartest of his regimental mufti. The dinner was to be given in a garden the Amban had engaged for the occasion outside the city. The inspection of the school being the first item on the programme we rode there through the bazaars. The Amban gave me a very cordial greeting and together we took our seats in the courtyard to watch the boys at drill. Their ages varied from 8 to 17 or 18, and they were drawn up in two lines under a Chinese master armed with a sword, the Liliputian dimensions of which reminded me of nursery days

The children then went through their drill, a form of exercise on the Swedish model, acquitting themselves creditably. The close of the parade was signalised by a march round the ground singing a song that the Amban informed me had been specially composed with a view to instilling into the children a love of country, and is, I understand, now in vogue in all the schools throughout China We then proceeded to the schoolroom to watch the children at lessons, and their struggles with the brush, for the Chinaman is no wielder of the pen in its literal

sense   Rather he excels as a painter, his prowess in this respect
being responsible for many gorgeously decorated documents,
of which my passport was an interesting example. As to just
how long it takes to turn out a finished scribe in China I am not
competent to express an opinion, but judging from the laborious
exertions of some of the pupils, I imagine it must be many moons
before one can be said to be a wielder of the brush of a high order.

The Amban continually asked me what I thought and seemed
much pleased at the praise I had to bestow   Here indeed one
had a Chinese official who really wished to move on modern
lines, and foster any scheme tending to further those ideas
After the inspection we moved on to the garden, a well-shaded
spot graced by many trees   In the centre was a raised pavilion
open round the sides with a flight of steps leading up to it   The
whole of the Chinese aristocracy had been invited and kept
arriving up to noon   All were arrayed in full dress, being most
punctilious and polite, and bowing profoundly. There were
Treasury Officers, Secretaries, the Governor of Maralbashi,
whom I was to meet later on on my way through his district,
and many others   The old Colonel also arrived looking very
pleased with himself and beaming all over like a schoolgirl
out for a picnic

There was, too, the Amban in charge of the Customs a clean-
shaven individual with the build of a bruiser, and the air of a
" chucker-out " Whilst the reception of the guests was in
progress we were enlivened by the strains of a Turkistan band,
a rude assortment of native instruments, and dancing by men
and boys, who squirmed heavily, but whose knowledge of the
terpsichorean art was limited, at any rate from the European
standpoint   The ladies of whose dancing so much is heard were
not forthcoming, so we had not the pleasure of gazing upon these
females reputed to be so prepossessing.

At intervals, tea, cakes, melon seeds, and other delicacies in
Chinese eyes, were served, of which everyone partook with great
gusto   The Chinese when giving a dinner certainly do it well as

far as quantity goes ; and on this occasion a repast was provided
for the servants of the guests, the preparations for which were
viewed with undisguised satisfaction by my retainers.

The dinner started at 1 o'clock with two courses, but it
was only a preliminary canter. An interval of two hours supervened the while we watched the dancing, and I took photographs
of the assembled guests. Then we resumed the repast, this time
in earnest, the feast lasting till 6 o'clock. It was a trying ordeal,

GUESTS AT THE GOVERNOR'S DINNER IN YARKAND.

course succeeding course, until I lost all count after twenty-five.
There were shark's fins, bamboo shoots, and bamboo roots,
pigeon's eggs preserved in chalk, lotus seeds, stag's tendons,
liver of all kinds, and a host of weird and strange comestibles,
that might well have appalled a stomach of iron. I suffered the
whole programme even to tackling a sea slug with as many legs
as a centipede. Each dish was served in small bowls, the guests

being provided with chop sticks, but out of consideration for my barbaric up-bringing the Amban had furnished me with knife and fork   The acme of politeness at a Chinese feast is for the host and others to single out any choice morsels on their own plates, or from the table, and deposit it on the plate of the chief guest As I had the doubtful honour of fulfilling that *rôle,* everyone proceeded to bombard me with questionable tit-bits in a manner highly gratifying to them but not conducive to the well-being of my stomach

Whatever the various ingredients may be there is no doubt the actual cooking is excellent, the preparation of the dishes calling for considerable skill on the part of the chef   The wine list was limited, consisting of Chinese brandy served hot—evil stuff—the very smell of which is sufficient to make one seasick. By 5 o'clock the guests were in hilarious mood, an orgy beside which the rowdiest night at Mess would pale into insignificance.

Some strange tricks were played at this Chinese banquet, one of them being to hand round a lighted match stuck in the end of a match box, and the unfortunate guest in whose hand it goes out has to quaff more brandy, the result in some cases being highly exciting   Then one of the guests will extend three or four fingers to another, and yell something in Chinese, he responding by thrusting his hand across the table with a similar yell that sounds like the crack of doom, the loser in this fast and furious game then lowering more brandy   The old Colonel, who sat on my right excelled at this pastime, and I imagine his experience in this connection obviated easy defeat

At 6 o'clock the Amban announced that, as so far we had not enjoyed anything substantial, he proposed giving us a spread, upon which bowls of meat and rice were brought in, the Chinese guests, whose capacity seemed unlimited doing ample justice to them   At the close of this Gargantuan repast all present took their departure, one of the customs at a Chinese dinner being for the guests to leave immediately after the function   Having bade adieu to everyone I also retired, and mounting my charger, iode away, after an outing, the memories of which will long remain.

The following morning the Custom's Amban sent his Secretary and caid with a message intimating his desire to call, but I put him off as I was feeling unwell from the effects of the queer dishes at the previous day's banquet.

The Indian traders were to be "At Home" that afternoon at 4 o'clock, but unfortunately shortly after noon a tremendous dust storm sprang up, locally known as a "buran," and upset the arrangements, so I did not go out. These dust storms are of common occurrence in Turkistan, the high winds frequently prevailing there catching up the sand, and darkening the atmosphere until the whole sky becomes black and threatening, shutting out all objects so that at a distance of even fifteen paces it is impossible to distinguish houses and trees, whilst the fine dust penetrates everywhere despite the closing and barring of doors and windows. Owing to these frequent storms the atmosphere in Turkistan is invariably hazy, and for months at a stretch distant ranges of mountains, which elsewhere would be apparent to the eye, here remain invisible.

In the evening I went to tea with some Swedish missionaries located in Yarkand and who carry on a religious work. They have recently opened a dispensary in connection with the mission, which should prove a great boon to the natives if only they take advantage of it.

I also visited a house outside Yarkand in a large and well-stocked fruit garden, where several European travellers have stayed. There is a bridge in the garden with a number of famous travellers' names carved on its balustrades, but the house itself has fallen into disrepair, and is at present unoccupied.

There is little of interest in Yarkand though I went all over it accompanied by a Beg, one of the minor officials from the Yamen, who had been detailed to show me round.

At the close of the rebellion under Yakub Beg against the Chinese the latter built forts in close proximity to the larger

towns with the object of securing a fortified retreat in case of
local revolt. These forts are surrounded by solidly built mud
walls of considerable height. loopholed along the top, though
they would be incapable of withstanding a siege on modern
lines, but against a local enemy might serve their purpose. The
tops of the walls are sufficiently wide to admit of a carriage and
pair being driven along them with space to spare on either side.
At intervals, heaps of stones are collected intended for use

THE WALL OF THE CHINESE CITY OF YARKAND.

against an enemy, going far to show the primitive state in
which military science languishes in Chinese Turkistan.

The construction of these forts show a total disregard to
tactical requirements, in many cases the walls being commanded
by hills in the vicinity from which hostile fire could be brought
to bear. They seem to have been built merely to meet purely
local needs, and without any thought of aggression on the part
of European-trained troops.

Rapacious Shopkeepers

One gets a good idea of the size of Yarkand from the walls of the Chinese city, but the view is in every respect a disappointing one, with little to relieve the monotony of plain mud roofs Even the temples or " musjids " of the Musulmans possess nothing that strike the eye, architectural features in them, as in all other buildings in this country, being conspicuous by their absence

By the great gate of the city I passed the police station where half-a-dozen men acted as guardians of the peace. Their ideas on the subject of discipline were distinctly original, for all, including the officer in charge, were busy gambling. The policeman on duty had dropped a formidable battle-axe, the mere sight of which ought to strike terror into the heart of the evildoer, and joined his comrades inside, leaving the law and its keeping to take care of itself

A variety of Chinese and native shops exist here, the latter displaying handsome brass jugs, known as chaguns   Through the energy of the Aksakal I was enabled to purchase a beautifully embroidered Chinese robe, only met with to any extent in this part of Turkistan   I also acquired some ancient brass work, and other interesting articles, but generally it was difficult work bargaining, as the shopkeepers demanded exorbitant prices, especially the Chinese, who must have thought I had journeyed to the country for their especial benefit, judging from the value at which they assessed their goods.

The Amban's dinner had been such a success that the Hsei Tai also determined to give one, an intimation causing me not a little uneasiness   He was anxious to make it an all-day sitting but I pleaded press of work, and did not put in an appearance until 4 o'clock   The dinner was to be preceded by a review of the garrison, and as I had not seen much of the soldiery of Chinese Turkistan before, I anticipated an enjoyable afternoon My departure for Kashgar was timed for the same evening, so I engaged carts for the baggage and servants to go ahead, I intending to follow later

During the day several of the Indian traders came to tea on my invitation, I having been unable to meet them at the entertainment given in my honour the previous day Afterwards I sent off Piio and Nadir with the baggage and arranged another conveyance for myself and Giyam to await me outside the city walls, where I proposed joining it after the Hsei Tai's dinner

At the entrance to the military Yamen the gallant officer received me, the garrison being drawn up on either side of the approach to the main doorway The troops were of all ages from 16 to 60, while their armament was decidedly antiquated, some being provided with old Tower muskets, whilst others had nothing more formidable than blunderbusses and spears. But if there was a paucity of arms of serious worth enough banners were in evidence to fit out a Drury Lane pantomime, so if victory could be gained by the display of a plethora of flags and "jhandis," then the Chinese certainly ought to achieve it As might be expected, all the weapons were in a state of dirt, brought about by generations of neglect, so that to fire one would doubtless require a few days' notice The garrison is, I believe, returned at some five hundred men, but the total strength on parade did not exceed one hundred and ten

At the close of the inspection we adjourned to the banqueting hall, where the repast was served. As I was to leave for Kashgar afterwards I partook in moderation, steadily parrying all attempts levelled at me by enthusiastic guests The Hsei Tai had arranged for an escort of cavalry to accompany me, whilst the Amban detailed a member of his staff to attend me to the limits of his jurisdiction

After dinner, which comprised the same assortment of delicacies I had encountered when dining with the Amban, I bade farewell to my genial hosts, riding out to the conveyance awaiting me under the great walls of the city. The vehicle in question is known as a "mapa," an instrument of torture resembling an oblong box on springless wheels, its tyres studded with huge hob nails. As the roads are full of ruts and pitfalls, and the bridges spanning the numerous streams are constructed of rough logs, the bumping experienced is sufficient to last a lifetime A " mapa " being short, it is impossible to lie in it at full length, hence the traveller has to be content with a cramped position, which, coupled with the jolting and its general unsteadiness, gives him an idea of the days of the Inquisition Its average rate of progress is about five miles an hour, any increase on this speed would simply mean shaking the very soul out of one

I reached Kok Robat, twenty-five miles from Yarkand, at two o'clock in the morning, where I discharged my cavalry escort, much to their delight, for riding along in the wake of a " mapa " at midnight was not at all to their liking. Here I found Piro and Nadir with the baggage, they having arrived the previous evening : Piro with his usual energy providing me a substantial supper on the verandah of a house. Later I received a visit from the local representative of Chinese might and power, who enquired my pleasure, and was highly gratified when I dismissed him to return to his pipe and couch

I found the arrangements made by the Chinese authorities excellent, and had no trouble in securing fresh carts, so loading up sent them off at 4 o'clock, starting myself at six, *en route* for Ak Robat, fifteen miles ahead, where I arrived shortly before noon

From Kok Robat the route lies over a desert of sand and gravel, dreary looking country, and a good sample of what Chinese Turkistan really is. Throughout the journey from Yarkand to Kashgar there is very little oasis, the country being a stony waste except where villages are situated, and even here there is little beyond a few trees and sparse cultivation.

At Ak Robat is a posthouse, and a small serai for the use of travellers, but I remained only long enough to give the ponies a rest and have some tiffin in the courtyard of the former A further fifteen miles brought me to Kizil, where I halted till seven in the evening It was still a desperately uninteresting land, nothing but a sandy waste as flat as a billiard table. Fifty-five miles of bumping had well-nigh shaken us inside out, though my sturdy little orderly, being short and about as broad as he is long, had more on which to take the concussion, so did not undergo such distress as his less stout master

I halted three hours in Kizil and having engaged another horse for my " mapa " pushed on to Yangi Hissar, a distance of thirty miles I arrived there at 4 30 the next morning in a battered condition, feeling as though I had spent a lifetime on the rack I established myself temporarily in the Chinese rest-house, sending my card and passport to the Yamen in accordance with custom

I had brought Nadu with me from Kizil, and he presently returned accompanied by the Aksakal, bringing a large quantity of fruit, as well as biscuits and tea, so I indulged in an impromptu meal beneath the verandah In the meantime cards arrived from the Amban and the Officer Commanding the garrison, who expressed a desire to pay me a visit, but as I was anxious to reach Kashgar without undue delay, I sent a message that I should be grieved if any deleterious effects resulted from their being disturbed at such an early hour, a subterfuge having the desired result, since they did not appear

I arranged horses for myself and Nadir, and the Amban ordered an escort of four cavalry soldiers, so at 8 30 I rode out of Yangi Hissar It is fifty-six miles to Kashgar through a fairly well-cultivated country, and we travelled so fast that only one of my escort was able to keep up. After twenty miles my horse naturally began to tire, so I hired another from a villager near by, and then pushed on to Yapchan, where I obtained a fresh mount for Nadir Leaving one of the escort to bring on the owner of my horse into Kashgar, I again forged ahead and passed through Yangi Hissar, the new city situated six miles outside Kashgar, arriving at the British Consulate there just after 3 o'clock

Captain A R B Shuttleworth (Indian Army), having been advised of my approach by a mounted orderly, very kindly met me outside the city, and together we rode to the Consulate,

where I was to stay as his guest during my sojourn in Kashgar
It was a pleasure to see Europeans again and to be once more
in an atmosphere of refinement. Captain Shuttleworth had been
stationed here a year, officiating as His Britannic Majesty's
Consul in the place of Mr. G Macartney, C I E , then on leave

In 1908 the Government of India determined to establish a
Consulate in Kashgar, a step duly recognised by the Chinese
and Russian Governments   The result has been beneficial in
every way   Chini Bagh, the site of the Consulate, is situated
on the right bank of the Kizil Su, and from it extensive views
are obtainable across the river. There is a large and well-stocked
fruit garden, and along the terraced walk above the river bed a
row of towering poplars imparts added charm to the scene,
giving grateful shade for the early morning constitutional

On arrival I found some of the Swedish missionaries in the
garden, so we had tea together, discussing current topics, which
possessed a deep interest for me, I having been so long without
news of the outside world   One or two of the missionaries
remained to dinner, the table displaying snowy linen, glass and
silver that was a revelation to me.

I spent the following day quietly, my kit not arriving until
the evening.   Captain Shuttleworth, despite the pressure of
State business, good-naturedly devoted the morning to me, he
imparting much information concerning Turkistan, a subject
with which he was well acquainted   Attached to the Consulate
is an English-speaking Munshi, and a staff of clerks and orderlies,
as also a dispensary with a qualified native hospital assistant
from India in charge.

CHAPTER IX

A DESERT MARCH TO KUCHAR

KASHGAR is the chief city of Southern Chinese Turkistan, and from a political standpoint enjoys considerable importance, while since the Russians have accorded increased trade facilities to merchants from Russian Turkistan it has assumed greater prominence   The roads leading from the city to points on the Russian Central Asian Railway present no serious obstacles so that trade prospers under the circumstances

Kashgar is similar to Yarkand, though its population is less, amounting to 35,000 or 40,000 in all   The province of Kashgaria has passed through troublous times, and been the scene of war and tumult which, as I remarked in the case of Yarkand, has left its mark upon the people

Prior to the revolt under Yakub Beg in the sixties of last century, the country had been devastated by constant rebellion against the Chinese first one side and then the other gaining control   In 1877 the province again came under Chinese domination, and has since remained so   The Kashgarians possess no martial qualities, and as they have neither the power nor inclination to rule themselves, or leaders amongst them capable of conducting a revolution, are content to remain under Chinese government as being the lesser of two evils, since they are not unduly harassed and allowed to go their own way. The people rest happy in their present condition showing no desire to improve it, and even were a change to ensue it would probably not concern them

China appears desirous of consolidating her power, and since the Russo-Japanese War is awakening to a sense of her

WASHING HORSES IN THE KASHGAR RIVER.

responsibilities and the latent strength she possesses, apparently realising that to get at the root of the evil she must first purify her system of administration, corrupt and rotten to the core This in a small way she is endeavouring to do, though time is needed to cleanse and remodel a system in vogue for centuries

With the formation of the New Model troops, the management of schools on modern lines, and reforms in the administration, signs are not wanting that China aspires to a place amongst the Powers During my travels in Chinese Turkistan and other parts of the Celestial Empire, I met many Chinese officials who showed a desire to raise their country above its present low level, some even holding advanced European ideas.

Two days after my arrival in Kashgar Captain Shuttleworth kindly accompanied me in a call on the Chinese officials, for which purpose we donned our full-dress uniforms, Giyani accompanying and looking as usual very smart.

To differentiate between the various grades in the Chinese official classes is a difficult matter to the uninitiated, but I would here remark that Chinese Turkistan forms the New Dominion of the Celestial Empire and is administered by a Viceroy resident at Lanchufu, in Western China The actual Governor of Turkistan resides at Urumchi, the headquarters of the provincial government The province is further divided into four districts, Kashgar, Aksu, Kulja and Urumchi, each presided over by a Taotai Subordinate to the Taotais are other officials in charge of towns, sub-districts and the various departments of the governmental machine We visited all those resident in Kashgar at the time including the Hsei Tai (Colonel Commanding the Kashgar garrison), the Hsein Kuan (City Magistrate), Tung Shan (Official for Foreign Affairs), and the Governor of the city The Taotai of the Kashgar district, who administers the adjacent districts of Yangi Hissar, Yarkand and Maralbashi resides in the Yangi Shahr, or New City, six miles outside Kashgar itself All these officials returned my call, and much impressed me with their charm of manner and evident desire to cultivate friendly relations with the British.

I also called on the Russian Consul, whom I found to be very affable, he showing me much kindness and hospitality during my stay in Kashgar.

In the afternoon we drove to the New City in the Russian Consul's " tarantass," a low four-wheeled vehicle common

CHINESE OFFICIALS IN KASHGAR.

enough in Russian Central Asia, but the only specimen of its kind in Kashgar. It is a pretty drive there through villages and cultivation fostered by an extensive system of irrigation. Yangi Shahr is the Chinese quarter and the seat of the Taotai, and is surrounded by a high wall loopholed and provided with towers, the object of these fortifications being to furnish a place of retirement in case of necessity.

From shops in the city I bought several articles under the

guidance of M. Bohlein, a Swedish missionary speaking Chinese fluently and acquainted with the wiles of the Celestial, an experience of much value in dealing with John Chinaman.

Time passed pleasantly enough during my stay in Kashgar, the Russians doing much to make it congenial. We entertained them to dinner one evening, the company including the Consul, the Manager of the Russo-Chinese Bank, of which there is a branch here, the two Cossack officers of the Consular escort, and

THE MARKET PLACE IN KASHGAR.

the Postmaster, the latter rather an important individual in Russian eyes, dressed in a white uniform and carrying a sword. The dinner was a cheery affair and passed off remarkably well, the guests enjoying themselves immensely, especially the Postmaster, who was very entertaining.

A detachment of sixty Cossacks forms the escort of the Russian Consul, so I had an opportunity of seeing these much-vaunted troops. The annual reliefs had just taken place, a fresh troop from the Orenbourg Cossack Regiment arriving They gave one the appearance of being workmanlike, and handled their rough ponies with considerable skill.

In the afternoon, when Captain Shuttleworth had finished the duties in connection with his onerous office we usually strolled through the bazaars and the surrounding country, one day paying a visit to a tomb, outside the city, known as Hazrat Apak, the only building of any architectural pretensions I had seen in Turkistan

There are a number of ancient tombs of Musulmans here, and a great many horns of burhel, poli and ibex are piled on the walls and round the tomb of Hazrat Apak A poli horn we measured taped 72 inches almost a world's record, so some unknown shikari had evidently encountered great luck

Market day in Kashgar is an animated sight, and is quite a gala day, the crowds being augmented by hosts coming in from neighbouring villages

As a rule the women are decidedly handsome, and some of them would have no difficulty in securing prizes at a beauty show, possessing as they do fine complexions, long dark tresses, good teeth, and a graceful carriage for which all Eastern women are noted

There is also a Swedish mission in Kashgar; the missionaries often called and we occasionally enjoyed their hospitality They were genial people, not affecting a missionary garb or an Their object in life is to convert the heathen Turki and Chinese, but I fear they do not experience much success As at Yarkand, there is a dispensary attached to the mission and it must be a boon to the natives, nine-tenths of whom are afflicted with unsavoury diseases The missionaries do much good in a quiet way, though the lack of any desire in the infidel to become a Christian must indeed be disheartening

I was anxious to bag a specimen of the Yarkand gazelle (*Gazella subgutturosa*), found to the west of Kashgar and throughout the Yarkand and Maralbashi country Its habitat is the open desert tracts, and an exceedingly difficult animal it is to approach, being in fact the wariest creature I have ever seen. Captain Shuttleworth kindly made arrangements for me to go to a village called Opal, some thirty-five miles west of Kashgar, reputed to be good gazelle ground, and despatched men to report on the probability of my encountering the coveted game. I sent off the kit on June 20th, riding out myself the following day and found my tent pitched in a garden belonging to the local " Qazi " or Judge

Two shikaris appeared in the evening and reported many " jeran," as the gazelle are locally known, on the stony plains to the west, but as the natives' " many " usually resolves itself into an infinitesimal quantity, I was not hopeful of sighting any quantity by the time I reached the ground on the morrow

I started at half-past three in the morning for the plains to the west and north-west of Opal The country was quite open, merely a sand-covered waste, so that stalking was no easy task I saw three gazelle during the day, but could not work sufficiently close for a shot. They kept out of range in the most tantalising manner, always too far away to chance an attempt at them with any hope of scoring a hit Though much akin to the Indian chinkara, or gazelle of the plains, they could easily give them points in the art of evading the shikari Despite my most persistent efforts to stalk them I was not successful, so abandoned operations late in the day and returned to camp I could only spare two more days in their pursuit, with unfortunately the same barren result, so returned to Kashgar, as much yet remained to be done ere the Thian Shan, many hundreds of miles to the north-west across the illimitable plains of Chinese Turkistan, could be reached.

I stayed a few more days in Kashgar, and then on July 2nd sent off my kit, in charge of Giyani and two new servants engaged in place of Piroz Zaman and Nadu, who now returned to their homes at Tashkurghan and Hunza respectively. The parting with these two men I never ceased to regret, for they had served me well, and had been moreover thoroughly honest, certainly rare qualities in Eastern servants

It was my intention to proceed via Maralbashi Aksu and thence east to Kuchar and northwards over the eastern Thian Shan into the Great Yulduz Valley, the principal, though little known, valley of this range of mountains This route, I gathered, would embrace many difficulties, but having heard a variety of wild sheep existed on the Yulduz Plains I wished to spend a few days there in the hope of bagging some.

On July 3rd, therefore, I took leave of Captain Shuttleworth, after three pleasant weeks in Kashgar, and accompanied by one of the Consular orderlies, rode forty-eight miles to Faizabad, reaching there shortly before six in the evening   I changed mounts half-way, which gave rise to an amusing incident   Horses in this part of the world are not flyers, the Turkoman being content to meander along the road in a style unsuited to the European temperament   The consequence was when my steed showed signs of weariness we cast about for fresh means of locomotion. At that moment the Consular orderly espied a mounted villager some distance away and promptly chased him before I could intervene. The wretched man took to precipitate flight pursued by the orderly who, overtaking him, administered a clout over the back which brought him somewhat ungracefully to earth, more frightened than hurt, though he soon recovered at the sight of a *douceur* I gave him

Being desirous of pushing on the same night, in order to avoid the heat and flies during daylight, I at once donned my uniform on arrival in Faizabad and called on the Amban, whom I had met in Kashgar   I arranged for fresh carts, and after he had returned my call, packed up and trekked on

It is practically impossible to travel through the Maralbashi country during the day owing to the heat and flies, so one is glad to rest in the shade rather than journey in a moving purgatory   I therefore travelled during the night, halting each day until five in the evening.

A Barren Land

I was now passing through a flat and uninteresting country, and going on through the succeeding night, stopped just before noon at Urdiklik, or the place of the duck, a great breeding ground for the latter, though at this time of year they were well out in the swamps of the Tarim River

After breakfast I gave Giyani some lessons in swimming in a small lake near by, and at sundown commenced an all-night trek through the villages of Kara Kulchun and Churga to Maralbashi, where I arrived at seven on the evening of July 6th   This town, one hundred and fifty miles east of Kashgar, is presided over by an Amban whom I had previously met at the Governor's orgy in Yarkand   I camped in a large garden outside the town and stayed the following day there to call on the Amban and have a look round, perhaps a waste of valuable time, since there is nothing of interest to see, it being an exact replica of Yarkand, but on a smaller scale   The Amban returned my call and pressed me to stay another day to dine with him, but of Chinese dinners I had had enough, so like the guests at the wedding of Biblical renown began to make excuses and escaped, though not altogether gracefully

Whilst strolling through the bazaars I met an Indian trader who informed me he had been in the country twenty years and was very anxious for me to honour him by taking tea at his house, so, as it was asking very little, I cheerfully agreed. He was a Pathan from the Swat Valley and spoke Pushtu and Persian, hence we were enabled to converse without the tiring aid of interpreters. He had some fine old brasswork in the house I was keen to purchase, but as he declined to accept money no business resulted

I started again at 5 30 and travelling through the night reached Ak Tumchuk, thirty-three miles distant, at 10 o'clock next morning. I passed through Charbagh at midnight, halting only long enough to give the horses a feed and rest.

Over this part of the trek to Aksu there is scarcely any cultivation, it being simply a scrub-covered waste with occasional

153

patches of trees. At Ak Tumchuk, after engaging fresh carts to go to Yakka Kudak, thirty miles east, I trekked to Chadir Kul and stopped for dinner outside the village. The water was brackish and almost undrinkable. but as there was nothing else we had to accept it.

A HALT FOR BREAKFAST ON THE DESOLATE PLAINS OF CHINESE TURKISTAN.

This being the main road to Peking the villages *en route* boast Chinese serais, or inns, which were opened for me, though as they mostly suffered from an undesirable accumulation of dirt I preferred my tent. The serais in question comprise a low single-storied building surrounded by an outer and inner courtyard, the former for the use of men and animals with the carts, the latter for the high and

154

mighty traveller The main and only door opens on to a central hall, with a raised mud dais at the further end and two rooms on either hand, the windows of which are latticed and the holes therein pasted over with paper At one side of the room is a high dais, the portion beneath being hollow to admit of a fire in winter, so that the guests have a species of heated bed upon which to repose The walls are usually decorated with ancient scrolls illuminated with hieroglyphics, probably containing injunctions to the wicked and solace to the wise

I arrived at Yaka Kudak at three in the morning and halted till evening The jungles in the vicinity are said to hold the Yarkand stag (*Cervus yarcandensis*), a near relative of the Kashmir stag, or "barasingh " Its numbers have dwindled considerably of recent years, due to the belief prevailing amongst the Chinese that its horns possess medicinal properties and they command a long price when in the unformed state, consequently he is hunted relentlessly

Two shikaris appeared here and volunteered to show me game in the jungle, also informing me gazelle were to be met with in the neighbourhood I decided to sally forth in the afternoon, gun in hand, so sent these worthies ahead with orders to bring in any information they might acquire I started with Giyani about 2 o'clock, keeping along an irregular watercourse running through the jungle On the way I was much amused to come on the two Nimrods peacefully snoozing under a tree, totally indifferent to the interests of the chase One had a gun, an ancient weapon with a long forked attachment for resting on the ground when shooting This gun I quietly abstracted from its place by the hunter s side and hid it behind an adjacent bush When I returned to camp these two sportsmen came in stating the devil had dropped from the clouds and annexed their rifle, a source of much grief not unmixed with astonishment to them After enjoying their discomfiture for some time I advised them to search the surrounding jungle as possibly his satanic majesty might have left the gun there, so away they went. Later they returned to camp much elated at recovering the gun, I hoping the lesson might have a salutary effect

I obtained fresh horses in Yakka Kudak, and, leaving there in the evening, moved on to Chilan through Yaidu, a grim-looking spot with nothing to recommend it but tamarisk, mosquitoes, dirt and heat

At Chilan I halted beyond the village on the Aksu road, and again hired fresh horses The entire population was out for the day at a place called Kalpin, some distance to the north, so I was unable to procure any supplies beyond an egg or two, which my apology for a cook could do nothing with I had engaged this blot on humanity in Kashgar, with another equally as bad, to replace Piroz and Nadir, as there would have been considerable difficulty in returning the latter to their homes from the distant Thian Shan. I daily regretted the loss of their services, as I afterwards thought satisfactory arrangements could have been made for their return to Hunza

I trekked again on July 11th the road leading over a level sandy country, hard going for the horses. I halted three hours at Chol Utak, a march of eighteen miles, where the water was horribly brackish Another seventeen miles took me into Sai Arik, a wearisome trek over the same sand and scrub-covered plain, the going being exceptionally heavy, with occasional stretches of muddy and swampy ground

From Sai Arik one reaches a cultivated country again, and this continues with intervals up to Aksu, twenty-one miles beyond I had changed horses and carts at Sai Arik, so was able to resume with renewed zeal

I crossed the Aksu River in huge flat-bottomed boats and camped in a large garden beyond the Chinese city, which, as usual, is distinct from the Turkoman one.

On arrival I sent my card and passport to the Yamen, and the Governor, despatching his in return, invited me to dine with him that evening I accepted, and met there two Americans who had travelled across China from Pekin on their way to Kashgar and India. Their expedition was a scientific one under the auspices of the United States Government. I waded through the dinner without the dire consequences usually associated with these functions, though I felt a deal of perturbation as to the probable after-results, not being possessed of an armour-plated stomach.

The following morning the Indian traders in Aksu called on me, and I regaled them with a light collation and cigarettes, during which we carried on an interesting conversation.

The weather was hot in Aksu and the mosquitoes in

"I CROSSED THE AKSU RIVER IN HUGE FLAT-
BOTTOMED BOATS."

my garden were a great pest. In common with other cities in Chinese Turkistan, Aksu is a filthy place, the streets being positive quagmires of mud and water.

Every one in this land of sin and sorrow is intent on making the most of his opportunities and enriching himself at the expense of the central government, so it is a matter of complete indifference to the Chinese officials whether the streets are in a sanitary condition or otherwise.

From the walls of the city I obtained a first view of the mighty Thian Shan Range, which, as already indicated, run east and west, dividing Kashgaria from the Ili Valley and Northern Turkistan, the western portion extending far into Russian Central Asia, and the eastern abutting on to the Mongolian plains. After the long trek of many hundreds of miles it was a glad sight, this view of the Celestial Mountains, as the Chinese style them, with their snow-clad peaks, truly a scene of sublime grandeur comparable only to the panorama disclosed by the Rocky Mountains from the prairies of Alberta.

AT THE GATEWAY OF AKSU.

One afternoon the Americans took tea with me, and we spent a pleasant hour, having much in common.

There was little to see in Aksu, and my only recreation was in walking along the walls, whence a view of the city, such as it is, can be had. I was accompanied on these excursions by a very stout Beg, sent from the Yamen to be in attendance on me during my stay. Once, when exploring one of the curious

158

corner towers gracing the walls of Chinese cities, we nearly disappeared through the floor, the building being rickety and dilapidated After that I made the Beg precede me, a task not at all to his liking, but the best course for me to adopt under the circumstances

Aksu was certainly the dirtiest town I had seen in Turkistan, sufficient criterion that the local officials were busy looking after number one I gathered there were a number of soldiers here, those I saw being a mixed lot, some old and decrepit, and all utterly useless I never passed a police station without seeing the guardians of the peace busy gambling, more intent on raking in the shekels than worrying their pig-tailed heads about mundane things They were armed with sticks, three-pronged forks and scythes, murderous looking weapons, the very sight of which should be sufficient to overawe the most unruly

Whilst in Aksu I called on the Taotai, whose authority extends over the whole of the Aksu district and surrounding country, and who is responsible to the Governor-General at Urumchi

I left Aksu on July 15th, going out to the Khona Shahr, or old city, some five miles further on, to attend a feast given in my honour by the few Indian traders there They had prepared a courtyard with some fine carpets, rugs, and a shamiana in the centre, and were kind and hospitable

I met a delightful and entertaining old man there, Mahomed Amin, hailing from Peshawar, but who had lived forty-five years in Turkistan and had served with several noted explorers The old man was well the far side of eighty but nevertheless hale and hearty He desired to see again the land of his birth in far-away India, and I strongly advised him not to delay but undertake the journey, arduous though it be, at once He had long deferred his departure, being appalled by the difficulties of the route, and now, realising that advancing years were weighing heavily upon him, determined to set forth He showed me many letters received from famous travellers, such as Shaw in

1868, and others, and he much prized a special letter of thanks from the Viceroy of India for services rendered to British travellers He was deeply affected when I told him the fate of various explorers he had met in years gone by and now long since passed to their last account, whilst much interested in others risen to fame and fortune and still in the land of the living

I left the Khona Shahr at six in the evening, halting five miles out, at a place called Mazar, merely a caravanserai, but as it was pitch dark when we arrived I saw nothing of it   The road was now partly through scrub and cultivated land, and over numerous watercourses, muddy and heavy going for the carts   We were bogged in one of these channels, and a Beg I had with me distinguished himself by beating a wretched wayfarer for not coming to our assistance

I reached Jom, a little village twenty-five miles from Aksu, at eight in the morning, and camped the far side of the bazaar under some trees   The local Amban sent me a present of sheep, but as he was only a minor official I did not think it necessary to call on him   I went on in the afternoon over the same vast plains, desolate and seemingly limitless, stretching away into the unknown. where man has never yet set foot, and presumably does not wish to.

Outside Kara Yulghun I forded the Muzart River , it was not difficult, the water being low and the current moderate.

It is a desperate country to travel in, this land of Chinese Turkistan, immense sandy plains, occasionally scrub-covered, and truly a veritable Sahara.   The water found is so brackish as to render it almost undrinkable, and even in the form of tea the disagreeable taste is strongly apparent

At 4 o'clock on the morning of the 17th I left for Yakka Arik, an oasis in the desert, where I changed horses   We forded three rivers between here and Bai, arriving in the latter place, a small town with a petty Amban, late in the afternoon   Though these rivers were successfully forded, it proved an operation productive of much shouting and a deal of Turki Billingsgate. I sent my card and passports to the Amban and made arrangements to hire fresh horses, though they were a long time appearing, but then one needs much patience in China.

I still continued to miss Piro and Nadir, both of whom had been most useful, and, energetic and hardworking, were a great contrast to the two I had engaged in Kashgar. I fired one of these out at Aksu, he being a useless waster, not knowing his heel

IN "MAPAS" ON THE ROAD TO KUCHAR.

from his elbow, and exciting Giyani's most withering contempt. which afforded me a considerable amount of quiet amusement.

From Bai I pushed on at midnight, halting next morning for a rest and breakfast at a tiny village called Sairam. Seven miles out from Bai I crossed the Kara Su, the water flowing in several streams and everywhere fordable. I left Sairam at noon and trekked on to Kizil, over plains with intermittent cultivation,

crossing the Kizil Su just outside the village   North and south
of the road were low ranges of hills, of an average height of about
2,000 feet, bare red sandstone, in keeping with the aspect of
desolation around.   I camped beyond Kizil, till one o'clock in
the morning, on an open stony plain, where the road assumes
an upward gradient to Shildar, a small post and customs house
in charge of an old Chinese munshi, who insisted on regaling me
with tea and cakes in his dwelling

I reached Kuchar on the afternoon of July 20th, and camped
in a pleasant orchard   I had been met by the seven or eight
traders who live here, and they were very kind and attentive.
The following day I called on the Amban, an old man long past
active work, being accompanied to the Yamen by a brilliant
escort of traders and others dressed in the height of fashion.
We made a gallant show riding through the bazaars and the
whole place was *en fête*, for the spectacle of a Sahib in full war
paint was even more unusual than in Yarkand

At the interview we discussed my intention to strike north
from Kuchar and cross the Thian Shan by some doubtless difficult
passes I knew must exist there   After shooting in the Great
Yulduz Valley I wished to trek west to the Tekkes Valley, in the
neighbourhood of which the best ibex and wapiti shooting is
obtainable   The Amban, however, advised me to go *viâ* the
main road to Kulja, running through Karashahr and Urumchi,
saying he knew nothing of the northward route and that it was
impassable, no one ever going that way, and insisting I should
perish in attempting it.

On his returning my call he reiterated these remarks and
urged my following the main road, but I pointed out the object
of my journey was sport, and that it could not be found in the
bazaars or gazing at the shops, arguments which were unanswer-
able.   There were no horses here for sale, nor could I at first
find any on hire, though I offered much more than the usual
rates   Later, however, I concluded arrangements for hiring.

The Amban declared there was no road by the route I wished

to follow, to which I replied it would be a good opportunity to try and find one. He further informed me the country beyond was full of rogues and rascals and that we should inevitably meet with violent deaths amongst the freebooters of the north. He was an aged specimen of the Mandarin, capable of little more than a pull at the opium pipe, and probably a distinct failure as Governor of a large district such as Kuchar.

"A DWARF FROM KHOTAN DANCED."

It may be of interest to tell of Chinese procedure in so far as supplying transport is concerned. The Amban issues orders to the Begs (minor officials) to produce so many ponies or carts, or whatever may be wanted. These worthies go forth into the highways and by-ways, and annex the required number, without troubling to consult the wishes of the owners. This is the Beg's chance for an illicit commission. The former buy this individual off for a small sum, when he retires, repeating the performance until he has made a good haul, and at last

163   M 2

Across the Roof of the World.

obtaining the animals from some unfortunate not so well able to satisfy his demands. Knowing this to be so, I interviewed the Beg detailed to bring the ponies required, promising him a *douceur* for each animal produced by the following afternoon if effected without recourse to unfair means Needless to say they all arrived punctual to time So much for Chinese methods! The owners of the ponies wore long faces when they appeared in the garden, but an immediate change ensued when I informed them they would receive high pay and rations as long as they remained in my service

I halted three days in Kuchar, and one evening attended a feast the Pathan traders had prepared in my honour. Music was rendered by a Turki band, while a dwarf from Khotan danced, and a good exponent he was of the art No ladies appeared on the scene, so I cannot express an opinion as to their capabilities in this direction.

The bazaars were of the same nature as those in Yarkand and Kashgar, with the exception that a greater display of Russian goods was noticeable A river runs through the town and in the evening crowds congregate on its banks, listening to the stories of wandering dervishes and travellers from afar I photographed one of these gatherings collected round a professional raconteur, the crowd listening open-mouthed to the wondrous tales he told, but whether they doubted his veracity was not apparent, although his remarks as a whole may have been taken *cum grano salis* The untutored Oriental, having no experience of the Western world and its marvels, is undoubtedly sceptical concerning all he hears thereon. Whilst on the Pamirs some Kirghiz one day enquired if England was as big as the Taghdumbash Valley. I assured them it was, and moreover added that for its defence we maintained a great many warships, the cannons thereon being capable of firing over ranges I endeavoured to indicate Never having seen a ship, nor able to divine its purpose, it was not hard to account for their looks of utter incredulity

CHAPTER X.

In the Great Yulduz Valley

FROM Kuchaɪ I was accompanied by a dragoman-cum-soldier, one no longer in his first youth, and were it not for his latter-day military costume might reasonably be supposed to have come out of the ark   His martial qualities were of a poor order, though his ideas on the subject of personal comfort left nothing to be desired, for, in addition to a roll of blankets carried on the pommel, two leathern bags depended from either side of the saddle, bulging with Turkistan bread   To mount without assistance was an operation quite beyond the powers of the aged warrior, so he was assisted over the mountains of bread and blankets into the saddle

I struck camp on the morning of the 25th and moved at 5 o'clock across an undulating plain to the foot of the first range of hills, thence due east down a stony and dried-up river bed, flanked by low hills   Further on the track turned north-east up a narrow valley, in places broadening to grassy pine-clad stretches, with here and there a profusion of wild flowers giving added charm to the view

I saw nothing in the way of shikar that day beyond a few partridges which Giyani pursued, stalking them as is the native wont, but not lucky enough to get within shot

I halted early in the afternoon on a wide stretch of grass at the mouth of a narrow ravine coming down from the west. Here was a solitary log hut, inhabited by some shepherds in the summer when tending their flocks of sheep and goats, and guarded by a number of savage dogs who ferociously attacked us, but after a time we beat them off, though the assault was lively work while it lasted   These people knew little about the north-ward route into the Great Yulduz Valley, and when they learnt I wanted guides stealthily disappeared into the mountains, aghast no doubt at the mere thought of a journey to unknown lands   This was rather disconcerting, but, knowing the general direction to take, I comforted the Turkis with me as well as possible, making light of their fear and trembling, and forged ahead the next day.   The route lay up the valley, beautiful pine-clad slopes, with rich green grass

Three miles out of camp I reached a small pass leading down into the valley on the far side.   This, according to my calculations, I thought should conduct me to the passes leading into the Yulduz Valley   We had little difficulty in getting over the small pass in question, as it presented no serious obstacles   Paths to the summit, though steep, ran in a succession of zigzags formed by generations of the nomads' sheep wandering in search of pasturage   At the foot of the descent was another hut constructed of rough logs thrown together, forming a shelter from wind and weather   It was uninhabited, and its ruined appearance gave the idea it had not been occupied for many years.   Past this tumble-down dwelling the track turned north-west through the main valley, the slopes of which were lined with fir and pine, and occasional expanses of grass, the latter capable of affording excellent pasturage to herds of cattle and horses

Far down amid the sylvan reaches of this vale I halted for tiffin, sending on the baggage and intending to overtake it later   The site of my frugal luncheon was a grassy sward in a clearing of pines   Behind, the hills rose in a gradual sweep, whilst in front an icy torrent, fed from the innermost depths of the Celestial Mountains, raced onward through this picturesque valley

Some distance beyond I reached a point where the nullah divided, the main stream continuing north-west, and a branch striking due west   From an elevated knoll I observed its general trend higher up to be in a northerly direction, and this I judged must be the correct route to pursue   I therefore went up this ravine for about two miles, over some difficult ground above the left bank of the river, through clumps of forest, anon descending into the valley, where the going above did not admit of a direct course being followed

Again I turned north for two and a-half miles, over some very swampy ground, thence commencing the ascent of the intervening range over rocky débris and through dense bush to the summit, 8,200 feet, on the northern side of which was a lake   The shores sloped away precipitously, giving the idea of great depth   From above, the water looked beautifully clear, but whether it held fish no evidence was forthcoming From the lake the path still continued in a northerly direction through a broad valley with low hills on either side   There was grass in abundance, in places reaching to our knees, the quality and quantity of which would constitute it a fine cattle country.

A mile or more along this grazing ground I reached the ruins of an ancient fort, which the old cavalier from Kuchar told me was a relic of bygone times when wars and rumours of wars were the order of the day   It was sixty paces square, with corner towers and one entrance, and constructed of mud and wooden beams with a mixture of stones to stiffen the walls and impart solidity   Judging from the condition, generations must have elapsed since its occupation as a battlemented stronghold, probably in the days when Kalmuk, Kirghiz and Chinaman fought for mastery   The country to the south was commanded from its walls, whilst to the north a still more extensive view was obtainable   A stone's throw beyond the fort the ground dropped away to another lake which filled the southern limits of a broad grassy valley , while at the far end clusters of trees were visible.   The valley sides sloped up in ridges to a height of several hundred feet, the lower reaches being dotted with pine and fir, imparting an air of majestic solemnity to the scene

Hard by the fort walls I came on a covey of chikor and shot one, but he spoilt the chances of the pot by rolling into a deep marmot hole, so visions of a good supper were rudely dispelled. I had perforce to follow a circuitous route into the valley and round the shores of the lake. Several duck were about, but as they

A TURKI WOMAN AND CHILD.

were well out on the water I could not get a shot. It was admirable duck ground, the banks being covered with weeds, where they love to paddle and feed.

I moved two miles up the valley, the central part being very boggy, and as no one with me was acquainted with the country the greatest caution had to be exercised in crossing to avoid being engulfed   At the upper end of the valley I camped by the edge of a tiny mountain stream tumbling down from the icy regions above   There was an abundance of wood, a welcome sight, for, the evening being cold and a dismal rain setting in, a fire imparted an air of cheerfulness to our surroundings

Just before reaching camp I passed some Kalmuks from the Yulduz going down to Kuchar with a large herd of horses, some being fine animals, and all showing traces of the abundant feed for which the Yulduz plains are famous   These men assured me the pass into the Yulduz, now a few miles higher up, was stony and difficult, and the descent on the northern side impracticable for laden ponies.   I would rather not have met these people, for the information they imparted only tended to still further alarm my followers, to which the unkempt appearance of the Kalmuks added   I felt they were only awaiting an opportunity to decamp, so, to frustrate their attempt in this direction, had the horses picketed near my tent.   I informed them that any one deserting would run the risk of being robbed and beaten, perhaps killed, by the Kalmuks, between whom and Musulmans there is no love lost   The real ground of their fears lay in the land to the north of the pass, which, the Amban in Kuchar had said, was infested with freebooters, and a bad corner of the Celestial Empire, where measures of reprisal were difficult to carry out by reason of the inaccessible nature of the country

The British Consul in Kashgar had informed me the nomads of the Thian Shan cared little for the Chinese, and would pay but scant attention to any remonstrances the latter might make   Personally, however, I felt able to deal with any trouble these Central Asian brigands might cause, but the caravan men viewed the situation in quite a different light, and it required all my energy and wakefulness to prevent them absconding during the night

It would be hard to exaggerate the many difficulties and obstacles met with in the march through this wild country to the plains of the Yulduz, difficulties which were accentuated by timorous caravan men, and predatory bands of robbers who were a constant source of danger.

The next morning I struck camp to cross the pass, it requiring considerable efforts to instil a little life into the wretched specimens of humanity with me, who moved about their tasks as though condemned to death I started at 7 o'clock, marching up the valley towards the pass, through pine woods, and over intermittent grass slopes Despite all my precautions one man had absconded during the night

The path I was following I hoped might be the right one, since the Kalmuks had said though there was more than one pass, the one by which they had crossed from the Yulduz was the best As the nullah branched off further up I was not certain which road to take, so chancing it followed the one to the north-west. A mile or two higher up the ravine became narrower with long sloping ridges, covered with grass on the right bank, the left clothed occasionally with clumps of fir and pine Here I reached the bivouac of some nomad shepherds encamped with their flocks Their temporary home was located beneath a spreading pine tree, consisting of merely a few branches supported on cross poles and forming a rough protection from the elements, the ground being strewn with leaves and brushwood.

I halted an hour here to adjust loads for the ascent of the pass, now facing me at the upper end of the ravine, a dark mass of rocks and shale, precipitous, but almost devoid of snow, except for patches on the summit I commandeered one of the shepherds to pilot us over into the valley beyond his attempt at flight having been anticipated and measures taken accordingly. The top of the pass was only a mile and a-half away, the ground leading to it being along the hillside over steep grassy ridges, to the point where the moraine and shale intervened, whence ensued an upward sweep over rocks and débris to the crest line Once beyond I should be in the Yulduz, or rather on its southern confines. Could I but succeed in getting my depressed and trembling caravan men down into the valley I did not mind if they incontinently fled, since I felt sure of getting transport from the Kalmuks there who during the summer months frequent the Yulduz plains for the pasturage

Arrived at the further limit of the grassy ridges I could see the actual approach to the summit would indeed be a tough proposition ; two hundred feet higher up was loose sliding shale at an angle of 60 degrees   This surmounted, I should be on the top and substantial progress made   Giyani headed the little column and Rahim, the cook, followed in the centre, I bringing up the rear to urge on caravan men and horses, and incidentally prevent the guide from suddenly absenting himself

Beyond the rocks and boulders, which we negotiated alright, was the loose shale mentioned, and which proved to be the undoing of the animals   Two slipped on the treacherous surface and rolled down the mountain side   One of them was badly hurt and the other, saving himself by contact with a rock, was able to regain his feet, serious injury being averted by my Wolseley valise he carried having broken the concussion   With ropes, and the combined efforts of all hands, the other ponies were hauled up. The fallen animals were off-loaded and I then had everything man-hauled to the summit, now a distance of two hundred feet, work in which Giyani greatly distinguished himself, labouring like a Trojan, and as befitted his noble calling

The height of the pass is only 11,400 feet, but that is no criterion as to its difficulty   The crest line marks the division between Kashgaria and the Great Yulduz, the entire range in this section consisting of rocky serrated ridges.

The scanty information possessed on this portion of the Thian Shan would appear to be incorrect in several details. Notably it has been stated that the southern slopes are steeper than the northern ones, and much broken by narrow ravines, and that their higher reaches are prolific in glaciers   As far as my observations go I encountered no glaciers, nor did I see signs of any to east or west when on the summit of the dividing range.

Moreover, I found the northern slopes of the Thian Shan more precipitous than the southern   The passes from the Yulduz to Kashgaria are said to be extremely difficult owing to the steepness of their gradients, and the masses of rock and boulders with which they are covered.   This is undoubtedly true, the Kara Dawan especially being unlikely ever to prove a popular route.

This region of the Thian Shan is wild and little known, and would appear to offer a favourable field for further exploration and geographical research   The average height, where I crossed the range, would not exceed 11,700 feet

The actual summit of the Kara Dawan was only sixteen feet broad, with one or two patches of snow thereon, now rapidly melting under the rays of a warm sun.   Thence we descended a distance of four hundred feet, and along a rock-strewn slope above the right bank of the ravine to a small intervening range jutting out from the main chain

A further descent ensued, with another climb of six hundred feet, bringing us on to a range overlooking a dark ravine running parallel to that leading directly down from the summit of the Kara Dawan   The far side of this range was exceedingly steep, and much time was occupied getting the ponies down, and then only by dint of securing them with ropes and steadying their progress by every means in our power.   In the ravine it was just a scramble for three miles through water and over rocks and detritus cast down from above, the track being too narrow to admit of our marching high and dry, the water taking up all available space

At 6 o'clock we reached a small grassy clearing at the confluence of two ravines, and camped there the night, the nullah being here fifty paces broad, and very stony.   On the open patch, where I had camp pitched, was a cairn of stones, the top graced by the skulls and horns of some fine ibex, one taping over

50 inches. Both sides of the ravine were treeless though grass-covered, the upper reaches giving every indication of first rate ibex ground, which no doubt it is, though to ascertain this by actual experience would have entailed a prolonged halt. I could not afford the time for this especially in view of all the circumstances, and the questionable crowd of followers I had with me.

I struck camp at seven the next morning, and with one of the Turkis decided to move down through the rocky ravine, which,

"WE REACHED A SMALL GRASSY CLEARING AT THE CONFLUENCE
OF TWO RAVINES."

at a point opposite camp, narrowed to ten feet. The baggage was to cross by a low pass to the north-east, as the guide I had pressed into my service the day before informed me the road through the ravine was impracticable, which was a lie, as I afterwards found out, the track, though mostly through water and over a vast amount of rocks and stones, being quite passable for the transport. Certainly at one particular spot where the way led down a chute between two perpendicular ledges of rock it was a little difficult but the caravan could have negotiated it with assistance   I scarcely liked leaving them to the care of Giyani and Rahim   but the former said he could manage alright so I did not worry

I went on till noon, and then halted to await the arrival of the ponies, but as they did not put in an appearance by 5 o'clock, I turned back a couple of miles, and met them coming down the valley, they having had a very hard time up hill and down dale over a rough path.

Apparently the guide knew nothing of the country, and had advised the upward road through mortal fear of the one through the ravine   I moved on and camped in a dip in the undulating ground on the right bank   The valley here widened to half a mile, the left bank rising in grass-grown ridges, the right having low rolling hills bordering the undulating ground.

It was very swampy and sodden, and infested with large numbers of horse flies whose bite caused the ponies much misery   The altitude of this camp was 8,500 feet, the air being cool and pleasant, and after sundown and the disappearance of the flies, was really quite enjoyable.   I was away again the next morning at 7 o'clock down the valley which gradually broadened to three-quarters of a mile, the rich grass giving it the aspect of meadow land

Seven miles took me to the end of this valley which debouched on to a wide grassy plain some twenty miles wide, with snow-covered mountains to north and south   This was the Great Yulduz Valley, famed for the grass and the pasturage it affords to countless herds of horses and cattle of the Kalmuks, who migrate here during the summer   Its length is about thirty miles, and the average breadth twenty, but towards the west it increases to some twenty-five miles   To the south, on the slopes bordering the valley below the Thian Shan the ground is damp and marshy, the central part of the plain towards the east being the same, but in the portion where I later on camped that day, it was firm and dry. It is rich in grass of an average height of nearly a foot. A river traverses the length of the valley, fed by numerous small streams coming down from the mountains to north and south.

I had heard there were a number of Kalmuk auls throughout the valley, but as the population is a floating one no precise estimate of the actual numbers could be ascertained. At the time of my visit there were some 360 auls distributed over the

MY CAMP IN THE GREAT YULDUZ VALLEY.

Yulduz, the number of cattle and horses running into many thousands, judging from the immense herds I saw during my stay there.

Far away across the plain in a north-westerly direction I noted some faint specks which, on examination through the glasses, proved to be Kalmuk auls, or felt tents, surrounded by herds of horses and cattle. I accordingly moved in their direction over

175

undulating hills sloping down in gradual sweeps to the central part of the valley The distance was most deceiving, for on leaving the hills it did not appear to be more than two or three miles to the auls It, nevertheless, took us three hours of steady marching, thus giving some idea of the deception peculiar to travelling across great plains

I pitched camp beyond the group of auls, and then interviewed an intelligent Kalmuk I found there From him I learnt that their Chief lived a considerable way off, in the Little Yulduz Valley to the east Their ideas as to his exact whereabouts were rather vague the distance apparently being anything from five to fifty miles. They could do nothing without the orders of their Chief as regards the supply of horses, although the whole plain was covered with them for leagues

The Chief, or Khan of the Kalmuks as he is called, is an important personage in this part of the world and the liege lord of all his nomad tribesmen I therefore decided to go over the following day and see him in person The Kalmuks near my camp, contrary to expectations, displayed no curiosity, none coming to stare at us, as is customary in other parts of Central Asia for which act of grace I was exceedingly thankful

Here I paid off the Turkis, also giving them sufficient supplies for the return journey, and heartily glad I was to see the last of them and to have finished with such a cowardly set of creatures.

The Kalmuk who had been spokesman when I first arrived at the auls, now volunteered to accompany me to the residence of the Khan, so I decided to start at dawn the next morning, leaving Giyani in charge of the camp. I took Rahim as interpreter as, of course, no one in this out-of-the-way corner of the universe spoke Hindustani or Persian, only Turki, with which language my acquaintance was limited.

The horse flies in this portion of the valley were a great nuisance, my tent being full of them, and the space between the inner and outer walls swarming with the buzzing insects They reminded me of some lines a miner wrote on a tree outside Coolgardie in Western Australia—

D—— the track both there and back,
D—— the flies and d—— the weather,
D—— Coolgardie altogether.

Substitute the Yulduz in place of Coolgardie and we have it.

I started about ten the next morning, accompanied by the Kalmuk guide, riding some eight miles across the plain to another collection of auls. Here the Kalmuk appeared in his true light He said the Khan lived 50 "putai" away, a small matter of 125 miles, and that it would take many days to get there, his horse would die on the way, and he himself would starve

We argued for an hour and I at last induced him to proceed, by which time it was past noon I little knew what was in store for me We rode on and on, trotting and cantering, and at six in the evening reached a Kazak yurt by the banks of the river, where I commandeered fresh horses and then pushed on harder than ever By 8 o'clock it was pitch dark, and soon after we had to ford a deep and wide river three times, which at night on tired horses and in black darkness is naturally hazardous. Luckily the Kalmuk knew the way and we managed the first ford without difficulty The second was not so easy and my steed could only by the greatest exertions keep his feet in the swirling waters which sped on with alarming velocity. The third ford was a mile further up, and when half-way across I heard the tinkle of bells and on the opposite bank encountered a long file of camels They were laden with tea and other articles going into the Great Yulduz to barter amongst the Kalmuks for skins and felt These people told me the Khan's camp was still a long way off, and that there were at least 500 auls there

Towards 10 o'clock we reached some more yurts, and here the Kalmuk wished to stay the night, saying the home of the Khan was still miles and miles away I, however, insisted on proceeding, so we rode on through the same low valley, bordered with hills, the main feature being their rounded aspect looming

through the darkness as we cantered on   I mentally wished the
Khan somewhere, being tired and weary of the long ride and the
search for his apparently phantom dwelling-place, seemingly
further off than ever.

It was nearly midnight when I did at last reach the camp,
where, of course, everyone was sound asleep, the only person
1 discovered not in a somnolent condition being a drunken
Kalmuk, who hiccoughed in the orthodox fashion and was of
as much avail to me as the proverbial sick headache.   But if
no people were about, dogs were numerous, and the noise they
made simply beggars description   We were surrounded by a
yelling pack, the din of which was terrific

I rode all round the camp with Rahim, but it was hopeless
trying to find anyone , and though the dogs made sufficient
noise to drown a brass band of the most strident proportions
it did not worry the slumbering Kalmuks   The ride had wearied
me so entering one of the auls I rolled myself up in my long
choga, or cloak, and lay down to sleep thinking what an
arduous undertaking it is to carve one's way through the wilds
of Central Asia.   It was very cold and the wind blew under the
ragged sides of the aul until I was nearly perished.

When I awoke at daylight, after an uncomfortable night,
there were two big 12-pointer wapiti heads hanging up in the
aul, having been brought in, I was later informed, from the
Jirgalan Valley some distance to the westward   These horns,
like those of the Yarkand stag, have a medicinal value when
in the unformed state, and hence are much sought after

I then sallied forth and beheld the camp of the Khan to
interview whom I had come so far.   This was his home surrounded by the auls of his Kalmuk subjects, a people with whom
one comes largely in contact when travelling in the Thian Shan

The Kalmuks are a race of nomads of Mongolian origin,
and though they have come under Chinese influence have
preserved their own language as also their national customs
and traditions, some of which are peculiarly interesting   During

the eighteenth century they were settled on the Volga under Russian jurisdiction, but in 1771 took place the migration of all the Kalmuks there established (to the number of nearly half a million) to Dzungaria and the Thian Shan districts of Chinese Turkistan, a trek immortalised by De Quincey in his "Flight of a Tartar Tribe." This celebrated journey, surpassing that of the great Boer trek from Cape Colony in 1836 to the country north of the Orange and Vaal Rivers, occupied a period of eight months, during which the Kalmuks suffered many vicissitudes through the hostility of Kirghiz and Russians whose territories they were traversing Towards the close of the year in question they reached the province of Dzungaria, then recently conquered and depopulated by the Chinese Here they were in hopes of finding a permanent place of settlement and of forming an independent kingdom. In this they were disappointed, for the Chinese had taken over the country ; so but two alternatives presented themselves, either they must become subject to China or turn back on to the Kirghiz and Russians, hard upon their trail They preferred to remain under Chinese domination and were accordingly permitted to settle in the Kunges and Tekkes Valleys, where ample pasturage was obtainable for their immense herds of cattle and horses

Those Kalmuks within the boundaries of the Chinese Empire pay an annual tribute in kine to the authorities, and also furnish the mounted levies established along the border and in the western part of the Tekkes Valley For purposes of administration they are divided into sections, presided over by officials, who are responsible for judicial and military affairs in connection therewith, the higher grades of those in the Ili Valley being nominated from New Kulja, the headquarters of the Viceroy

The supreme head of both the Kalmuk and Kazak tribesmen of this portion of the Celestial dominions is the Governor-General, or Chang Jung, who resides at Suidun twenty-four miles west of Kulja. This official is a Manchu of high rank, and his authority is absolute in all matters connected with the government of the nomad tribes.

In religion the Kalmuks are Buddhists, and their hair is worn in pigtails similar to the Tibetans. The type of feature is distinctly Mongolian, with almond-shaped eyes and prominent cheek-bones. In stature they are above the middle height and a fine-looking race, always cheery, excellent hunters and good on the hillside.

Whenever possible they prefer to be mounted, but are none the less able and willing to walk when out shooting, as their foot-

A KALMUK RIDING AN OX.

gear is suitable for the purpose and their attributes as hillmen of a high order. When not hunting the Kalmuk always rides, and should a horse not be available he is equally at home astride the lumbering ox.

As in the case of the Tibetans, they evidently pay scant attention to the old adage that cleanliness is next to godliness. Nevertheless, they are a fascinating race of people, appealing strongly to an Englishman for their love of shikar and their sporting instincts.

Strange Burial Customs.

The manners and customs of the Kalmuks are in many respects remarkable, more particularly in regard to the disposal of their dead   The corpse is put out on a hill or point in proximity to the camp and there left to be disposed of by dogs and vultures   Should the body not be demolished within the space of a few days, the departed is deemed to have led a wicked and wayward life, a presumption that is visited upon his relatives in the shape of severe chastisement all round

Marriage plays an important part in the life of the Kalmuk, betrothals being arranged early in life, and scant regard paid to the wishes of the lady   A wedding is a great event, the bride being usually carried off by force by the suitor, to which arbitrary proceeding the parents make no objection   When interrogated on the subject, one of my Kalmuks afterwards told me should there be several aspirants for the lady's hand she generally manages to fall into the grasp of the swain she regards with the greatest favour   Ordinarily marriages are arranged and the girl handed over after the ceremonies connected therewith have been concluded.

The Kalmuk dwelling is the aul, the same warm and comfortable habitation so often met with in Central Asia. When moving to fresh pastures, if the distance to be compassed is short, the aul is carried bodily by men and women, but for a longer journey it is dismantled.

Having sent notice of my arrival in the camp I went in search of the Wazir, or Minister of the Khan who received me hospitably, and apologised for the unofficial reception, due to his being unaware of my visit. I conversed through Rahim, and the Wazir arranged transport, also placing a spacious aul at my disposal where a substantial Kalmuk breakfast was provided for me

Unfortunately the Khan himself was away, he having apparently gone on a visit to the Chinese Governor at Urumchi His mother sent a message to say she was unwell and regretted her inability to receive me

The village of auls here was by far the largest 1 encountered
in the Thian Shan, there being nearly 300. Those belonging to
the Khan and his suite were situated within a large square formed
by other auls, several of the royal dwellings being as large as
marquees. The material used in their construction was of the
best quality, and profusely adorned with strips of red felt,
imparting a regal air to their otherwise sombre mien   A
large number of watchdogs were about, each wearing a
scarlet collar, and specially kept to guard the Khan's tents;
the same noisy fiends who had greeted my arrival the night
before.

After settling details regarding transport I proceeded to
breakfast in the aul prepared for me   Its usual rôle was that of
a durbar hall, where the Khan administered justice and settled
any cases arising amongst the community   Just above the
doorway was a formidable whip with an abnormally thick and
heavy lash, which, the Wazir informed me, was employed when
sentences of castigation were awarded   Judging from its appearance it must need a hide of leather to withstand the shock of
such an instrument

After breakfast I held a *levée* at which most of the Kalmuks
in the camp were present, and they took great interest in me on
learning I had come from India, asking many questions concerning
Tibet, towards which, as Buddhists, they turn a reverential eye.
They were especially enamoured of my rifles and shot-gun,
examining the barrels and expressing considerable admiration
at the polished surface   Some of the more wealthy were keen
to become the possessors of such weapons, one man offering two
of his best horses for either of the three, whilst another made
equally tempting offers on somewhat different lines, but to no
purpose. Whilst my reception was in full swing two Kirghiz headmen arrived from the Jirgalan Valley some distance to the west,
with a report that a large number of horses had been stolen from
the Kazak herds by predatory Kalmuk horse thieves   The
Wazir and the principal men retired to discuss the matter,

returning shortly after to renew their acquaintance with modern weapons and the wonders of expanding bullets

The Khan's mother sent his visiting card, a gorgeous sheet of red paper, handed to me by a varlet in blue and red robes and a plumed Chinese hat

In connection with the Khan I afterwards heard a curious story On attaining the age of 25 years he vanishes from this world and a new Khan reigns in his stead. The mode of his disappearance from mortal ken rests somewhat in obscurity, but from what I could ascertain the end is brought about by means of poison The present Khan, whose views on the subject differed considerably from those of the high priests and elders, being undesirous of qualifying for an early grave, had fled from the cares of state and gone ostensibly on the visit above mentioned In this he showed a commendable amount of wisdom and circumspection, for not even the prospect of perpetual bliss in the society of other defunct Khans could tempt him to give up the ghost Of a truth uneasy lies the head that wears a crown in the Yulduz Valley !

CHAPTER XI

To the Happy Hunting Grounds of the Thian Shan

I COULD gain no information in the Great Yulduz Valley on the subject of shikar, as none of the Kalmuks were aware of the existence of wild sheep on the plains or the hills bordering thereon. There were said to be some in the ranges by the Naret Pass and near the headwaters of the Kok Su, but at this season of the year, owing to high water in the streams, it was impossible to get there—at any rate from the eastern side

I had hoped to find sheep of the *Ovis karelini* variety amongst the hills to the north of the Great Yulduz, but despite exhaustive enquiries failed to glean any information nor did I notice signs of sheep during the few days spent there   All agreed that the Tekkes was the noted hunting ground, so as no prospect of sport presented itself in the immediate neighbourhood of the Yulduz I determined to reach the Tekkes as soon as possible

I therefore arranged for the ponies to follow, and leaving Rahim to take charge. bade farewell to the Khan's camp   It was a quarter past eleven when I rode off, accompanied by the Kalmuk guide, down the valley, here about two miles wide, and shut in by low rounded hills, treeless and grass-covered, and fine grazing grounds for the nomads herds   I had to ford the same river on the way back, a task in broad daylight shorn of part of its dangers

I reached the Kazak aul in the afternoon, the one from where I had commandeered fresh horses the day before, and halting to change mounts took over those left here on the outward journey.   The only occupants of the aul were the

184

Kazak and his young wife, who pressed me to partake of
some boiled horse-flesh, a delicacy I declined with many
thanks, but which my Kalmuk tackled with great avidity. This,
however, was not the only item on the bill of fare, for the owner
had recently bagged some marmots—a little animal found at high
altitudes and more particularly on the uplands of the Pamirs—
and served them up as an *entrée*. I gave the Kazak some silver,
at which he beamed all over his dirty face, and then mounting
our steeds we rode off to camp, still more than 30 miles distant.

KALMUKS MOVING AN AUL.

I arrived there at 6.30 in the evening, tired with the long journey
and the exertions required to reach the Khan's home, to say
nothing of a ride of nearly 100 miles over rough country in the
previous 34 hours. Giyani had shifted everything up to a spot
nearer the northern edge of the valley, and hard by another
group of auls, the occupants of which provided us with milk,
and fuel for the fire.

As there is an entire absence of wood in the Yulduz plains,
camel and horse dung is used, and hard material it is to ignite,
especially when a strong wind is blowing.

Across the Roof of the World

The following morning the ponies arrived, and I spent the remainder of the day preparing loads and overhauling my outfit. On the morning of Tuesday, August 3rd, I started across the plains to the north-east. It was an easy march, over undulating ground thickly carpeted with luxuriant grass.

The famous Russian explorer Prejevalski states that the name Yulduz, signifying "star," was perhaps bestowed on the country on account of its altitude, or from the fact of its being the promised land of cattle. According to this authority it may have been at some distant period in the earth's history the bed of an inland sea, and its alluvial clay soil goes far to support this theory.

Twelve miles out of camp I reached the opening in the northern range leading to the Khanpui Pass. The crest of this range marks the dividing line between the valley of the Yulduz and that of the Tzanma, the latter a broad valley through which the Tzanma River flows.

Leaving the plains of the Yulduz, I entered the nullah over grass-grown ridges, whence the track winds along the slopes on the right bank, the going everywhere being easy and presenting no difficulties to the baggage animals.

A mile up the narrow valley I turned east, passing round the southern end of a lake of clear blue water, which the Kalmuks informed me was of illimitable depth. Its extent was about 800 yards long by 300 broad, the banks sloping away precipitously from the water's edge, and giving every appearance of great depth as the Kalmuks had intimated. There are no outlets to the lake, but at its northern end it was fed by a stream flowing down from the snows above, not, however, in any great quantity. The water is slightly brackish, but not more so than that of the Sairam and Ebi Nor Lakes I afterwards visited to the north of Kulja.

I skirted the eastern shore and then turned north across grassy slopes to within a quarter of a mile of the summit, where the going is over rocks and stones to the crest line, then free from snow. The view therefrom is a pleasing one, the aspect of the country being diametrically opposed to that on the Yulduz side. Beneath was a descent of 500 feet, past rocks and shale, while beyond stretched a narrow valley, its sides clothed with fir and pine and carpeted with rich herbage, so prominent a feature of the northern slopes of the Thian Shan.

KALMUKS AND KAZAKS WATCH US STRIKE CAMP.

At the far end of this valley I could discern a broader one, the Tzanma, its breadth being some two to three miles, dotted here and there with clumps of fir and spruce, imparting an air of restful comfort after the monotonous plains of the southern ranges.

I had been informed by the Kalmuks of the Yulduz I should

meet with another tribe the Kazaks, in the Tzanma Valley, and on debouching from the ravine below the pass I encountered several auls occupied by Kazaks The ground was here covered with long grass and fairly well wooded, whilst through the centre of the valley flowed a river whose waters joined those of the Jirgalan and Tekkes further west

I camped near the Kazak auls in an open grassy clearing, and sent for the headmen with a view to securing fresh ponies, as the Kalmuks from the Yulduz now informed me they knew nothing of the country beyond and that it belonged to the Kazaks, who were a lawless people and would inevitably steal their horses on the return journey

Judging from the appearance of the Kazaks there certainly seemed to be a good deal in what the Kalmuks said so I agreed to let them return to the Yulduz, provided I could secure a change of ponies The head-man in charge of the Kazak auls here arrived shortly after, and on producing my Chinese passports and other documents said he could arrange transport and guides to the Tekkes Valley, adding it was only three days' march to the west This petty chieftain or Zung as he is called in the vernacular, was quite a young man, wearing a large white flowing robe fastened at the waist with an embroidered girdle, and carrying on his shaven pate a fox-skin cap. High-heeled boots reaching to the knees completed the dress of this Central Asian cavalier, and imparted to him a decidedly swash-buckler air

As already indicated the Thian Shan is inhabited by three races of nomads—Kalmuk, Kazak and Kirghiz. Of these the first is the dominant race and the one with which travellers to these mountains come mostly in contact

The origin of the Kazaks rests to a considerable extent in obscurity Many theories have been advanced as to their rise, the leading ethnographical authorities inclining to the opinion that they are descended from Turkish tribes who in days gone by marched through Asia conquering the territory they traversed and forming

The Nomad Kazaks.

settlements thereon, and extending their boundaries towards the east into the Chinese Empire. In course of time they became involved with the Sungarians in a struggle for supremacy, and being unsuccessful dispersed through Central Asia, the greater portion of them remaining in Russian territory, whilst others

A KAZAK.

settled in the valleys along the northern side of the Thian Shan, where their descendants roam at the present day.

In appearance the Kazaks are about the middle height, and of sturdy build. The cheek bones are high and prominent and the general cast of features is decidedly Mongolian, the complexion being clear and bronzed and the hair dark.

Their dress consists of a long robe reaching below the knees and fastened at the waist with a girdle. Pyjamas of skin or cloth are worn tucked into high-heeled boots, and a cloth cap turned up at the sides, or in winter a fur one coming down over the ears and nape of the neck.

The women dress in much the same way as the men, with the exception that the robe is worn loose without a girdle.

On the head is worn a large white square-shaped turban, the hair being plaited down the back at the end of which ornaments of silver and copper depend

In religion the Kazaks are Mohammedan, and they shave the head as is the custom amongst the followers of the Prophet The language spoken is Turki, but varying somewhat from the dialect of Kashgaria in the mode of pronunciation and other details, so that usually some difficulty is experienced in first conversations with them

The Kazak mode of salutation differs from that of other Musulman races—who raise the hand to the forehead in token of respect on meeting a stranger—in that they doff their caps and make a low curtsy by bending the right knee rather a graceful way of greeting

In horsemanship the Kazaks excel, women as well as men and they manage their rough ponies with admirable skill. All the ladies wear high-heeled boots, and acquit themselves on horseback with remarkable ability They often exhibited their prowess, and on one occasion a restive steed, the despair of Giyani was captured and readily subdued by a fair equestrienne. This particular girl was one of the best riders I saw, and she laughed with great glee when the horse had been caught by her and mastered.

Pedestrianism is not popular amongst them and they prefer being mounted where they are more at home than on foot, while their high-heeled boots are eminently unsuitable for walking Moreover the Kazak can lay no claim to any of the attributes constituting the ideal shikari, and from my experience of them in this respect their room is preferable to their company

They devote much time to cattle breeding, the wealthier possessing large herds of horses, sheep, goats and camels Oxen are also met with but not to the same extent The pasturage found in the valleys of the Thian Shan is of the best, and as there is an unlimited quantity of it sustenance is afforded to vast herds.

A Queer Beverage

In the winter many of the nomads move to the higher valleys where the pasturage is more open, due to the high winds which sweep it bare of snow.

The home of the Kazak is the familiar "aul," or felt tent, of the same shape as those met with on the Pamirs and in Mongolia. There are few good points about these people, but there is one way in which they appear to be superior to their Kalmuk neighbours and that is in the matter of cleanliness, although their other drawbacks outweigh this desirable attribute

The food of the Kazaks comprises milk, cream, mutton and horse-flesh, the latter looked upon as a great delicacy. The most popular article of diet amongst them is, however, "kumis," fermented mare's milk, the taste of which must certainly be an acquired one I have sampled a number of beverages during wanderings on five continents, but have yet to meet anything rivalling "kumis." The drink in question is made in a leathern receptacle and frequently stirred until fermentation, when it is considered fit to drink It has the reputation of being invigorating and constitutes a staple article of diet Whenever a halt is made at an aul, or a visitor arrives, he is proffered the flowing bowl and does full justice to it There is no accounting for taste even in Central Asia !

The Kazaks are distributed over the land lying to the north of the Thian Shan, but are more in evidence in some valleys than in others, notably along the Jirgalan and eastern and central portions of the Tekkes The hills to the north of the latter valley are peopled by the Kalmuks, though a few scattered groups of Kazaks are met with in the Ili Valley

The Great Yulduz apparently belongs exclusively to the Kalmuks, and no Kazaks were to be seen there This occupation of territory struck me as being governed on the same principles as formerly obtained amongst the American Indians, where each tribe lived within limits settled by themselves, although inter-tribal warfare was constant

The Kazaks are gifted with no martial qualities, in this respect differing considerably from the Kalmuks, who always impressed me as having in them the stuff that makes the fighting man.

The Kazaks are an indifferent race, seeming to pass the greater part of their time in attempts to lift their neighbours' cattle, an occupation which is the chief bone of contention amongst the various tribes or sections. Those across the border in Russian territory seem to be the principal offenders, frequently appearing unawares, and driving off herds of horses from the Chinese side. One Kazak who accompanied me down the Jirgalan Valley had had 36 horses stolen out of 100, the thieves having driven them off into Russian territory, where all trace had been lost. I had a good deal of trouble with these gentry, which constantly called for the display of a determined front and a formidable Turki whip.

Again I could gather no information as to shikar in the neighbourhood, everyone's ignorance on the subject being most exasperating, and it seemed as though the long and weary trek via Kuchar and the Yulduz Valley was destined to be productive of no results. I wished I had been acquainted with the nature of the country, as, instead of marching that tremendous distance, I could have gone from Aksu to the Tekkes Valley over the Muzart Pass in ten days. I should thus have avoided much hardship and toiling through a land to a large extent uninhabited and containing little or nothing to tempt the shikari, and it was for shikar that I had embarked on the great trek from India. It was now, however, too late to regret, but one thing above all others became firmly impressed upon me, and that is, that pioneering fresh shooting grounds is a poor game, especially when pursuing it amongst a far from congenial people.

The fresh ponies for the onward journey appeared during the evening, so I was able to pay off the Kalmuks and send them back to the Yulduz. The Kazaks at this camp presented me with sheep and were generally pleasant and obliging, and I began to think they must be rather nice people, in which opinion I was, from later experience, much mistaken.

The Fame of Britain.

I started the next morning at 8 o'clock marching along the valley over undulating ground, passing many auls on the way, all inhabited by Kazaks, who apparently consider this part of the country their own. I met no Kalmuks here, and was informed the land is more or less portioned off, parts of it being considered Kalmuk preserves, and parts coming under Kazak ownership. This undoubtedly is as it should be, since were the limits of grazing grounds left undefined constant friction would result, in which warfare I should think the Kalmuks would certainly gain the upper hand.

An interesting incident occurred on to-day's march down the Tzanma Valley. I was alone, some distance ahead of the caravan, when a Kazak rode up to me, and saluted by taking off his cap—this as I have already stated being the form of salutation amongst the Kazaks and Kirghiz. He then asked me in Persian if I were a Russian. On being answered in the negative, he pressed the question, apparently to make sure I really was an Englishman, and then manifested his unfeigned delight by shaking me vigorously by the hand, saying he had, during wanderings in Russian Central Asia, heard of the might and power of the British, and had always felt a desire to meet one of them.

Seven miles down the valley I forded the Tzanma River, here thirty yards wide, and not difficult, the bed being hard and firm, and the depth of water about three feet. The track on the right bank led north, and thence debouching from a fir and pine jungle turned west up over grassy slopes. The northern side was clothed with pine trees, up to a low pass, on the far side of which I camped by some Kazak auls, the occupants being up here with their flock for the summer grazing. They spoke of the Tekkes as the great hunting ground for wapiti and ibex, so as there was nothing to be found in these parts I was more than ever anxious to reach the promised land amongst the shikar of which I had heard so much.

Camp that night was in a basin formed by the surrounding hills, the grass being everywhere luxuriant, whilst behind my tent were clumps of fir and pine, altogether a most picturesque spot. I was off again the following day at 8 o'clock, along and over grassy hills, thence down into another valley where I halted for tiffin. Some Kazaks from adjacent auls provided milk and wood, and came in large numbers to view the stranger from the outside world I was told here that horse thieves in this part of the Thian Shan were numerous, and not at all particular as to the means they employed to attain their ends I was advised to keep a sharp look out for them, their principal manœuvre being to stampede one s horses in the dead of night. As I was responsible for the ponies engaged to accompany me through to the Tekkes Valley, I determined to frustrate as far as possible any little *coups* these freebooters might contemplate Having come far and suffered much, I was not at all in the mood to be trifled with, so was quite prepared to meet any of their advances with powder and shot To show that I meant business I paraded my battery at this camp, as a hint to look out for squalls in the event of anything untoward occurring.

The next day I crossed another low range whence ensued a long descent into the valley beyond by a zigzag path completely hidden by tall grass. In the valley, here half a mile wide, we came on some Kazaks returning from the Jirgalan valley whither I now wished to proceed on my way to the Tekkes I had been unable to procure guides to indicate the nearest and best path from the last camp, as the Kazaks there knew nothing of the country, and not wishing to be lost in the mountains by inexperienced guides I preferred to pick up one *en route* I commandeered two of these men to pilot us the next day, and a hard job it was rounding them up, for they made great efforts to abscond, but being surrounded had to yield to force and bow to the inevitable To obviate the chances of their absenting themselves during the night I had all their saddlery packed in my tent and their horses tethered close by, so an escape would have been rather a sacrifice for them. I had had the camp pitched by the river bank

under some pines, and was obliged to sleep in mosquito curtains
as the insects were very numerous and trying.

This portion of the Thian Shan forms the eastern confines of the
Jirgalan Valley and is said to hold wapiti, but it could hardly be
so at this season since the ground had been stamped flat by herds
of horses and cattle belonging to the Kazaks. My plan was
therefore to move on to the Agiass Valley on the northern side
of the Tekkes, and indulge in some ibex shooting before entering

KAZAK WOMEN AND "AUL."

for the wapiti stakes during the month of September, the best
time. I could not find a single Kazak who could give any definite
idea as to the distance to the Tekkes, opinions varying considerably and no one being able to tell the same story, which is after
all very characteristic of the Oriental.

Across the Roof of the World

I pushed on the next morning and ascended the top of a high range. part of the way being through a forest of pines by a steep path On the way I met an elderly Kazak who accompanied me to the watershed between the two valleys, and I had tea with him at his "aul" situated on the far side. A pretty Kazak girl prepared the beverage made in a Russian samovar, or tea urn and served in dainty Chinese bowls The lady in question was dressed in a fur cap and flowing coat fastened at the waist, and wore high-heeled boots like the men, altogether rather a dashing damsel.

After tea I went along the ridge, past scattered groups of auls camping late in the afternoon high up on a windy peak, where I found two battered auls A heavy storm of rain came on before we arrived there drenching everyone to the skin, and reducing the paths along the mountain side to a slippery condition, so much so that the ponies were falling about and having the greatest difficulty in keeping a footing The wind blew great guns all night, and as there was only sufficient room in the auls for the pony men and servants, I had my tent pitched, a work of art under the circumstances, but which we successfully accomplished without being carried away like a balloon Towards morning the wind increased in violence, until it was blowing a perfect hurricane. The tent was on the leeside of one of the auls but at four o'clock it collapsed with a crash, much to my disgust It was all I could do to hang on to the remnants until Giyani arrived with reinforcements, which relieved the pressure I then stretched the tent over the camp bed and weighted it down with stones. creeping under to try and sleep in which I was not at all successful The wind and rain continued all day, turning the ground into quagmires of mud and water, compelling me to halt there.

The next morning dawned still and bright so I started on down the Jirgalan Valley and along the river bank. halting at mid-day for a light tiffin amongst the pines On the way I met a score of Kazak women and young girls all mounted, and dressed in the height of fashion as it obtains in the heart of Asia. They wore loose robes heavily embroidered, with top boots reaching to the knees. The majority had round fox skin caps, whilst a few affected the quaint square turban of white cloth trimmed with gold braid. The leader of this party of Amazons was an old dame well the far side of sixty summers. Her head-dress was unique inasmuch as it consisted of a huge sugar-loaf hat adorned with coral and numerous ornaments. She bestrode her mustang with the skill of an accomplished equestrienne, riding

A KAZAK BOY.

ahead like a Napoleon on the warpath. They were on the way to attend a wedding in the neighbourhood, a great event amongst the Kazaks, and a day of general rejoicing and merry-making, the whole countryside turning out.

Down in the valley of the Jirgalan there were a great many wild apple and apricot trees, the former being sweet and juicy. I camped hard by one of these natural orchards that night, and spent the evening in collecting some of the fruit. A few Kazaks were encamped in a ravine to the south and from them I obtained fresh ponies, paying off those who had journeyed with me from the Tzanma The fresh transport appeared the next morning soon after breakfast, so I travelled down the valley, crossing a side stream four miles out of camp On the other side three Kashgari merchants were located in a rough log hut they had constructed to serve as a supply store in their barterings with the nomad tribesmen I stayed there awhile to partake of tea and learnt that horse thieves were at the moment very busy lower down and likely to give trouble

I was only five miles from the junction of the Jirgalan with the Tekkes, so went ahead with a Kazak guide who knew a short cut across the hills to the left, and halted at the mouth of the valley waiting for the baggage to come up As it did not appear by 5 o'clock I rode back some distance and learnt it had gone south Despite the fact that I had pointed out the route to my Turki man, he was such an inane specimen of manhood he must in any case go wrong, so nothing was to be done but ride after the caravan, which I did through long grass, across rivers, and amongst dense forests of pines, finally discovering it at midnight I had gathered information as to its whereabouts from Kazaks at an aul I passed, as the man with me candidly confessed he did not know the lie of the land at all It was a pitch dark night, without moon or stars, so wandering about through forests and rushing rivers looking for the caravan was decidedly poor fun Once we had to get across the little Jirgalan river full of water and to such an extent that it took some time before the horses would face it Beyond this point the way led by a narrow path through pines of which we were constantly reminded by collision in the darkness The Kazak now said he thought we might find auls higher up the valley where possibly the caravan would be found, so we pushed on through alternate forest and grassy vales In places the going was treacherous, over swampy ground, and down steep hillsides where the horses blundered and stumbled in the most alarming manner,

unable to see anything in the prevailing gloom   Higher up we
sighted the glimmer of fires, and a few moments later came on a
number of cattle lying down in the long grass who, stampeding
at our approach, threatened to annihilate us by their wild dashing
about

This brought out the Kazaks from the auls close by, to ascertain the cause of the midnight disturbance   With them came a
host of dogs constituting an even greater menace than the cattle
had done, for their ferocity knows no bounds, and they are
particularly averse to prowlers round the camp, a commendable
trait in their canine characters   I found the baggage here, it
having arrived earlier in the evening   I was too disgusted to do
more than pass a few nasty remarks to the author of all the
trouble, which must have sunk deep into his Turki soul, judging
from his subsequent demeanour

A change in the route being now necessitated I decided to
proceed by the Kapsalan Pass which the Kazaks said would take
me into Kok Su, and thence down the latter to its junction with
the Tekkes   None of the people at this camp were certain as
to the ground beyond their own valley, and considerable doubt was
apparent in their minds as to the right road I ought to take   At
this juncture a lady came to my rescue in the person of the
head man's chief wife   She informed me that one, Manas Bai, a
Kazak, who lived near by would act as a reliable pilot, so I
sent off in hot haste for this individual   He duly arrived, and
loading up the baggage animals, we started up through the
forests on the opposite bank, bound this time I hoped for the
Tekkes

It was a long march that day up and down through dense
woods, and across another river on the far side of the range,
whence a long and very steep climb ensued to some auls pitched
on the edge of the forest at pine tree level   A heavy thunder-
storm came on just after we had camped, drenching everything, but as there was an abundance of firewood we soon had
them dry again

I was now close to Kok Su, in fact camp that night was on the watershed between this river and a tributary on its right bank The Kazaks here told me it would not be necessary to cross the Kapsalan Pass, but that by keeping along the ridge and across the undulating country to the west I should get down into Kok Su near its confluence with the Tekkes They were a rough-looking set, these uncouth nomads and gave me the impression of being experts at horse stealing. Hitherto I had experienced no difficulty in this respect, and as I desired to reach the shooting grounds with the least possible delay was anxious to avoid trouble with them, so took all necessary precautions at night.

I moved on in the morning over undulating country past many groups of felt tents, whose occupants came riding over on their rough ponies to gaze at us, and enquire whence we had come, and whither we were going. I halted at one of the auls and had tea and cakes fried in fat, which the ladies of the household prepared, and themselves served up They were very cheerful, and not at all inclined to vanish like a will-o'-the-wisp as is the custom generally amongst Oriental women Evidently the Kazak ladies believe in a jovial life, and are apparently not unduly worried by a high code of morals

Whilst on the march that day the pony Griyani rode threw him, and he was dragged some little distance before the animal could be pulled up I thought at first he was badly hurt, since he lay on the ground quite still, but soon recovered and pluckily remounted the wayward beast. Like all hillmen of the Himalayas, Griyani's skill as an equestrian was not of a high order, but it had at any rate the merit of possessing plenty of grit, and though he had many nasty falls during my travels they never deterred him from persevering in his attempts to become a bold sowar

I camped at five o'clock in the evening on the edge of a pine slope, and as the Kazaks in the neighbourhood had a bad reputation we kept a close watch that night lest they might attempt

the stampeding of the horses The animals, however, needed
grazing, and, despite all precautions, were stampeded and stolen
during the night

Manas Bai, the man who had accompanied me from Little
Jirgalan, was then despatched with Rahim in one direction to
round up the robbers, whilst I endeavoured to head them off
from the south, as I thought they might move in that direction,
since fewer auls were to be met with and consequently less likelihood of their being noticed Manas Bai, with Rahim and
another man, overtook them four miles away and succeeded in
getting the horses back, mainly I think through the assistance of
other Kazaks in the neighbourhood who feared reprisals on the
part of the Chinese, since they knew the latter would certainly visit
with severe punishment any outrages on Europeans As Celestial
justice is indiscriminate there was every possibility of vengeance
being wreaked on the wrong party, hence the timely recovery of
my caravan The thieves, however, captured the unfortunate
man with Manas Bai and Rahim and beat him severely When
he came into camp next day covered with bruises, I had the
headman of the district summoned, informing him I should
report the affair to the Chinese Viceroy at Kulja, which I afterwards did, with good results This delayed me considerably,
and though it was now plain sailing down into Kok Su, I did not
reach there until past noon

The Kok Su River was in full flood and we were fortunate
in not having to ford it, but crossed by a rough native bridge.
Without this we could never have got over the torrent as the
current is tremendously strong, the river bed being also full of
rocks and boulders Once over I moved west into the Tekkes
Valley There were a number of Kazak and Kirghiz auls along
the valley, and I camped that night near a group at the junction
of the Kok Terek and Tekkes River, a camp I shall ever look
back upon with feelings of the liveliest satisfaction, for after well
over a thousand miles of hard trekking from the Pamirs I had
reached the promised land.

It had indeed been a severe and trying journey, replete with much incident, whilst the caravan men with me in the earlier portion of it were a constant source of anxiety, and needed close surveillance. To get through difficult country one must have a good staff, men who are willing and plucky, and I never felt this to be more so than in the later stage of the journey from the Pamirs

It was two long marches from here to the mouth of the Agiass Valley, whence I proposed to send for Kalmuk shikaris, and settle the plan of campaign best suited to enable me to get some good shooting amongst the ibex, roe-deer, sheep, and wapiti, before moving on to the Great Altai Mountains and the *Ovis ammon* ground   All agreed that shikar in the Tekkes was of the best and I retired that night full of hope for the future, for I had arrived at the happy hunting grounds, and was at last in the far-famed Tekkes Valley

CHAPTER XII.

Sport in the Thian Shan Mountains

To the sportsman, Central Asia is known as a great hunting ground in general, and the Thian Shan in particular as the home of the big Turkistan ibex and the Asiatic wapiti. It may well be termed a happy hunting ground; but as is usual with all good things, is difficult of access. As I have shown in the preceding pages, to the shikari journeying thither from India many obstacles are presented. He must cross the mighty ranges of the Himalayas and the Hindu Kush, must march over the Pamirs, that region of awe-inspiring immensity so well termed the Roof of the World. Thence onward, ever onward, across the plains of Turkistan, dotted here and there with trees and foliage and groups of mud-built houses, the oasis in this Central Asian Sahara, until finally he reaches the Celestial Mountains. There, the goal attained and camped amidst the pine forest and grassy slopes, he forgets the toil and hardships, the stupendous ranges of mountains he has crossed, the rushing torrents he has successfully negotiated, all the perils and dangers attaching to such an undertaking, and longs only to come face to face with ibex on the rock-bound corries, and hear the wapiti calling in the dense forests which form so prominent a feature of this happy land.

Such, indeed, were my own feelings when I camped that night by the Kirghiz yurts, feelings of ineffable gratification at the thought that I was at last near the end of my journey to the Thian Shan, and amongst the ibex and wapiti.

It will here be of interest to give a description of the Tekkes, the principal river of the region in question. It takes its rise amongst the glaciers of the Thian Shan near the peak of

Khan Tengri, and having penetrated the rocky defiles below the frozen regions of its birth, emerges into a broad valley, whence it continues to flow eastward until joining the Kunges, the two streams, after unison, being known as the Ili The mighty river thus formed flows on past Kulja and into Lake Balkash, in Russian territory The Tekkes, in its course of nearly 150 miles in Chinese territory, flows through a rich pastureland, and a wonderful grass country it is

In that part of the Tekkes Valley with which I am concerned in this book, the ground rises in gentle undulations from the river. The valley is everywhere carpeted with the same rich grass, whilst the hills to the south are covered with fir and pine, and above them stretch shining glaciers and the snow-crowned summits of the main range of the Celestial Mountains, the whole comprising a scene of unsurpassed grandeur, and one that would compel the admiration of the most phlegmatic

Next day, August 12th I marched on again, fording the Kok Terek stream just after leaving camp, and thence up the left bank of the latter for two miles to some Kazak auls. Here the path branched off into the foothills, and I followed this over a very undulating country, stopping for lunch by the banks of a stream which raced down from the mountains, and then struck off into the hills There was very stiff climbing to be done, which tired the ponies so much that they kept constantly lying down on the way.

Passing through one narrow dell there was some rough ground to get over, a steep and difficult ledge leading down to the ravine There was only just sufficient room for a man to pass so we widened it as much as possible to admit of the passage of the transport One of the ponies, however, slipped when half-way down and went bumping and rolling into the river bed, fortunately without doing himself any more serious harm than a shaking. I then had things off-loaded and handed down, where we again loaded up and proceeded on our way Well up amongst the foothills were some Kazak auls, and I camped near them on the edge of the pine forest. During the night an attempt was made to stampede our horses, but it met with no success, for we pursued the would-be thieves, and they, doubtless supposing us to be armed to the teeth, took to flight, preferring not to risk an untimely fate at the hands of the exasperated ones from out of the back of beyond. All the horses were on parade the following morning, so I marched at 8 o'clock for the Agiass Valley, now only some twenty miles further east. If anything, the going was more up and down than it had been the previous day, but it was certainly very picturesque country, well stocked with pine and fir, and the usual pasturage.

A HERD OF HORSES IN THE THIAN SHAN.

I again halted for a brief tiffin by the edge of a tiny rivulet, some Kazaks in an aul near by providing milk, which Manas Bai, the man I had brought with me thus far, boiled, and I enjoyed some cocoa. I camped the night by some auls down in a nullah off the path I had been following from Kok Terek, and not far from the Muntai stream, here emerging from the hills and joining the Tekkes River out in the valley to the north. The ponies I then had with me were a poor lot, and quite done up with marching, work to which they were not accustomed at this season of the year, when the herds are usually turned out to graze.

I therefore despatched Rahim and Manas Bai to round up fresh ponies, a form of occupation at which Manas Bai was decidedly an adept. The inhabitants pay little attention to Celestial passports and the injunctions contained therein, nevertheless one can usually obtain all one requires if liberal in payment.

It did not seem worth while engaging fresh horses since the Agiass was now so close, though, judging from the appearance of those then with me, it was doubtful whether they would reach the goal. During the summer months all the Kazak and Kalmuk

A KALMUK ENCAMPMENT IN THE THIAN SHAN.

herds are grazing and have little or no exercise, so that they rapidly get out of condition and incapable of even an ordinary march without considerable preliminary training. To do, therefore, a 20-mile march with loads was certainly more than they bargained for, and must have tried their powers of endurance severely after months of a grazing life in the Tekkes, with naught to occupy them beyond cropping the rich grass.

From the high ground above camp I had a very fine view of the upper reaches of the Agiass, with its snow-crowned summits. It had all the appearance of good ibex ground and I hoped I should there find much game as a reward for the long trek from India

The Kazaks as usual displayed an ignorance as crass as it was profound one of them surpassing his brothers by declaring there were no ibex in the Agiass at all This, coming on the top of our trials, troubles and adversities, was almost more than one could be reasonably expected to stand, but I said nothing, merely regarding him with looks of pity and contempt.

I reached the Agiass River the next day, crossing it by a wooden bridge near the point where it emerges from the hills. Later in the year it is possible to ford the river when the current is less strong, but this is not feasible until well on in September, when, the greater part of the snow having melted, the volume is less. On the western side and a mile or more beyond were some auls, and a log hut, recently erected by an enterprising Sart merchant bent on doing business with the tribes in the neighbourhood Near here I camped, and the following morning sent off Rahim for Kalmuk shikaris, several of whom the local Kazaks informed me lived at Shota, some distance up the valley towards the Muzart Pass

Just after camp had been pitched I killed a snake in the long grass, a reptile 15 inches long, and, from what I could gather, poisonous The grass here was tall and thick, the local people telling me snakes were common at this season of the year

At noon the next day a Kazak Beg came to see me, and I arranged with him to supply ox transport, as the path up the Agiass was said to be a nasty one for ponies, which statement by personal experience I found out to be untrue, the valley almost throughout its entire length being practicable for them

I devoted part of the afternoon and evening to packing up kit not required on my shooting trips into the mountains, intending to store it in the merchant's log hut near by until my departure from the Thian Shan Whilst thus engaged a Turkoman appeared on horseback and dismounting, walked up to my tent, announcing himself as one named Rasul, just arrived from Kuchar, in accordance with a wish I had expressed in that town to secure his services, in place of Rahim Rasul's home was 50 miles from Kuchar, out on the road to Urumchi, at a little town called Yangi Shahr, where he kept a store and earned a precarious living. I had sent a letter through the British Ak-sakal at Kuchar asking Rasul to join me in the latter town at once the note having been despatched by the Chinese Amban. I had hoped some reasonable amount of speed might have been exerted, all things considered, but such hopes were vain amongst the apathetic Celestials It took four days to reach Rasul, but he nevertheless started at once, and followed me all through the Yulduz Valley and down into the Tekkes, finally joining me at the mouth of the Agiass He was not properly speaking a Turki, but an Argoon, that is, born of Turki and Ladakhi parents I was much gratified at this display of zeal, since he had been travelling alone in my wake for 15 days, and at once installed him as head-man, retaining Rahim to act as post runner between the Tekkes and Kulja, and to bring out supplies from time to time I also engaged another servant here as general help and to make himself useful in camp

Rasul had had a very rough time on the way from Kuchar, but, following a frequented route into the Yulduz Valley and thence onward via the Naret Pass, had escaped annihilation at the hands of outlaws He had, however, been molested by the Kazaks several times and showed me the marks of blows received in bouts with them Beyond this, however, he had suffered no serious harm. having informed the turbulent Kazaks he was proceeding to join an English traveller and that any harm befalling him would be visited on themselves by the Chinese

That night a Kalmuk shikari arrived, so the outlook became more promising. His name was Sogoon, and he informed me the best hunters were out with their flocks but would join me in a few days, having been sent for by the chief Kalmuk at Shota to whom Rahim had shown my Chinese passports

The Picturesque Agiass Valley.

Sogoon advised my moving up into the Agiass Valley, and suggested a little ibex shooting pending the arrival of the two other Kalmuks, who were well acquainted with the ground higher up and the best places for shikar

Before starting I decided to send Rahim into Kulja with a letter for the Russian Consul requesting my mail, which had been forwarded to his Consulate, and also arranged for Rahim to bring out supplies and several things of which I stood in need, and he started the following morning, August 16th I paid off Manas Bai that day, he leaving me here to return to his home in the Jugalan Valley.

From camp I had to cross a low ridge, whence a path led down into the valley The road lay up the left bank of the river, which was now a rushing torrent, fed by numerous side streams racing down from the heights on either side I camped about seven miles up, near an old disused sheep-pen, the brushwood from which provided ample firewood It was still early in the afternoon, nevertheless a branch stream which here joined the main valley was unfordable owing to the depth and force of the water, so I was obliged to wait until the morrow, when the night frosts in the regions above would restrict the volume In the evening I went out with Sogoon to look for chikor, or hill partridge, but did not come across any. A storm passed over the camp just after we returned, rather a common occurrence in this part of the world, especially late in the day, when the sky usually becomes overcast and cloudy, with falls of rain and occasionally of snow

I was much impressed with the beauty of the Agiass Valley and the fine grassy stretches flanked by high mountains through which the river flows The latter takes its rise amongst the glaciers of the Khalyk Tau Range of the Thian Shan, and has a length of some 60 miles, the first half of which is in a westerly direction, whence it flows due north until emerging into the Tekkes Valley Leading off from the main valley are numerous side nullahs and ravines, the majority of which hold ibex. The western slopes are covered with fir and pine and bear that dark and sombre aspect one associates with those stately trees   The eastern slopes run up in a succession of grassy ridges, the favourite feeding grounds of the ibex, though the latter are also found on the western side, but in limited numbers

The Ibex (*Capra siberica*) is a fine specimen of the goat family, and though he is met with in various parts of the Asiatic continent, none carry horns of such length as those to be found amidst the rock-bound corries of the Thian Shan.   Here the ibex wanders in large herds, subsisting on the succulent grass which covers the slopes, an animal ever alert and wary and one possessed of great vitality.   The Agiass Valley is a noted haunt of ibex, and its reputation in this respect had made me extremely keen to reach so good a shooting centre

From the ground high above the river banks on a fine day a delightful view is obtainable of snow-crowned peaks of the Celestial Mountains, glaciers gleaming in the sunshine, and the lovely Agiass River flowing through a valley carpeted with grass and many coloured flowers, on its way to join the waters of the Tekkes and the mighty Ili.

The following morning we were able to ford the stream, and continued up the valley for two miles, whence we turned west up a side nullah for a mile and a half, pitching camp amongst a clump of pines.   Climatic conditions were indifferent that day, with heavy rain and thick clouds, seeming to indicate a possible spell of bad weather.   Sogoon said this place was a good one for ibex, and I mentally hoped it might be, and thus contribute in some degree to reward me for all the time and labour expended in getting here.

A brief look round in the late afternoon revealed ibex high up on the mountain side in a back ravine, and I trusted they were the first of much game to be encountered   The slopes here were covered with long grass and hemlock, which made the going rather hard, as one constantly slips, more particularly in the morning, when it is damp and saturated from the dew.   There were, too, many of the horse flies about I had been troubled with further east, they commencing operations the moment the sun had warmed them into life and activity

I started early on the morning of the 18th for the ibex seen on the evening before. On the way up I came across a female ibex feeding alone down in a hollow, some considerable distance from my objective, and as we were in need of meat I shot it, sending the carcase back to camp by a young Kazak whom I had engaged as assistant to Rasul.

It was a long climb of some 1,500 feet to the main ridge, whence I hoped to work along on a level with the ibex, but for some reason they were very restless, and in addition the wind blowing from our direction caused them to disappear over the crest   I then returned to camp, intending to try the ground to the south-west on the morrow.

I was off before 5 o'clock the following morning, riding part of the way along a winding mountain track, used in spring and winter by the nomads' flocks when they come up for the pasturage

After going some distance I turned south along a bare rocky valley about four hundred yards wide, at the higher end of which we sighted two bears grazing on the eastern slopes   The wind was right and the bears in a favourable position for a stalk, so we tied up the ponies and went after them   On the way my Kalmuk, by an elaborate demonstration with clawed fingers, accompanied by sundry growling, endeavoured to illustrate to me the manner in which Bruin would act if brought to bay, so I resolved to try and account for them before they could for me   We were able to creep up to within two hundred yards and from the cover of a rock had a preliminary gaze at them   They were big beasts, one a red and the other a black bear   The Kalmuk shikari was in a great state of agitation and kept declaring they would charge us   However, I pushed the Jeffrey-Mauser forward and, covering the red one behind the shoulder, let drive.   He gave a tremendous jump and then stood still looking very sick   I rammed in another

cartridge and had a shot at the black one, though he was in a bad
position below a lot of furze bushes and I could only just see the top
of his back At the second shot both pulled themselves together
and with much ominous growling charged straight towards us.
The Kalmuk with a piercing yell took safety in precipitate flight,
leaving me to face the music, which I made some attempt to do
Unfortunately, I had that day only brought five cartridges,
hardly sufficient for the job in hand It is difficult to describe
one's feelings at such a moment as this The sight of two large
and ferocious bears sweeping down intent on tearing one to
pieces, and the critical situation thus engendered cannot be
depicted in mere words There was no time to lose I
mentally resolved to do the best and account for, at any rate,
one of the gigantic creatures with the three rounds now left to
me, in the lingering hope of being able to settle for the other
with the butt end of my rifle, truly a desperate chance Both
shots at the charging Bruins were misses, though perhaps the
firing had the desired effect, for, remarkable to relate, when within
less than ten yards they suddenly turned off and went up hill. I
sped the parting brutes with a shot at the black fellow's stern
which got him in the leg The shikari now returned and loud
were his lamentations when he learnt the ammunition had run out
It was indeed a bitter moment for me to see those fine great bears
legging it for all they were worth, and unable to stop them for
lack of cartridges The red one was certainly a very big animal
and his black companion much larger than the Himalayan species.

I returned to camp sad and silent, not unmixed with disgust,
at the brilliant opportunity I had missed of securing a unique bag

I moved lower down the valley that day and turning into
a side nullah, which led off from the right bank, camped in a
forest of pines, as this part was said by the Kalmuk to be a
likely one for ibex The ground looked promising, and in the
afternoon I went out and saw some on the high ground across
the stream to the north I could not, however, make out any
good heads so left them in peace

A Night in the Jungle.

I was anxiously awaiting the arrival of the two Kalmuks from Shota, as Sogoon did not know the ground at all well, and I was only passing the time with him pending arrival of the others, to whom the country was quite familiar

A sheep was brought up to camp to-day, so starvation, which threatened, was averted, at all events temporarily On the 20th, still feeling sick and sorry at the loss of the bears the previous day, I did not turn out very early, but at noon taking only blankets, went off and spent the night in the jungle with Sogoon and Giyani in the hope of being able to find game. We took a turn in the afternoon from the bivouac, but only saw three roe-deer, late in the evening, when it was almost dark, and even they might not have been bucks

We therefore came in and chewed maize in default of flour to make bread, the latter commodity having become exhausted and fresh supplies not yet arrived from Kulja Giyani, during my absence, had hollowed out a fine resting place under a gigantic pine, and spread my valise and bedding thereon, quite a luxuriant couch, where I slept the sleep of the just till break of dawn

After breakfast we started off into the forest, taking the ponies with us, as I had hurt my back the previous afternoon trying to lift some heavy logs for the camp fire, and walking, at any rate with me, was out of the question. We made a long tour round, but saw nothing, and as the pain in my back made any exertion a torture I came back to the main camp in the afternoon, intending to move further down the valley on the morrow.

CHAPTER XIII.

AFTER ROE-DEER AND IBEX.

On the morning of August 22 I trekked down the Agiass Valley, and on the way met Nuiah and Numgoon, the Kalmuk shikaris, coming up to join me   I was glad to see these men, for without good shikaris it is a difficult matter discovering the best ground   Nurah carried a breech-loading rifle of Russian make, and his dress comprised a black cloth shirt, leather trousers with a fiinge resembling those of the Texan cowboys, and a leather belt holding the inevitable pipe and tobacco.   His footgear consisted of skins secuied with leather thongs   Numgoon was similarly clothed, but his shirt and trousers were matted with grease and dirt which would have appalled a laundry maid.

We held a consultation and decided to go to the Mintaka for " illik " or roe-deer, thence for ibex, sheep, and wapiti.   It sounded promising and I hoped it might prove to be so, hopes destined to be duly iealised

Nurah was a famous hunter and had been with other sportsmen who had shot in the Thian Shan, but he afterwards struck me as having too good an opinion of himself   The other man, Numgoon, was a most cheery soul, extremely hard-working and keen, and in his company I passed many pleasant hours

Our reasons for moving to the " illik " ground were dictated by the impossibility of getting highei up the Agiass Valley then on account of the volume of water in the river, which would, howevei, be diminished to a considerable extent a few weeks later. We therefore made tracks for the Muntai Valley, some miles east of the Agiass.   On the way down one of the bullocks threw his load when going over a bad turn in the path, with the result that another of my yak-dans was smashed to pieces, and several things broken, including, amongst others, a good maximum and minimum thermometer.

I camped the night at the mouth of the Agiass by the Kazak auls, continuing down the Tekkes Valley next day, and then, moving up into the Muntai nullah, pitched the tents by the

NURAH.

river bank. Nurah said the country round was good roe-deer ground, and a sure find. We went out at 3 o'clock, but though we saw no roe the ground looked promising, and I came back to camp in the evening full of hope for the morrow.

The Asiatic roe (*Capreolus pygargus*) is a small species of the

215

deer family, distributed over Northern and Central Asia, and is larger than its European example. The buck stands some 30 inches at the shoulder, and the coat is of a reddish brown, changing to a lighter shade towards the winter. The horns differ somewhat from the other species of deer in that there is no brow tine, and the average length does not exceed 13 inches. There are six points, three on each horn, but occasionally seven and eight pointers are found. The habitat of roe-deer is amongst the narrow valleys and ravines of the foothills. The latter are covered with pine forest and the ground is strewn with fallen trees, dead leaves, twigs and obstacles of all descriptions, so that it is a work of art moving about without making a most exasperating noise. Along the bottoms of the ravines a growth of dense bush predominates, with tall grass running up to a height of 4 and 5 feet. There are occasional open grass plots, and on these the " illik " are generally to be found in the early morning. Whilst I was there in the month of August the grass and hemlock were very high, constituting a difficulty to successful stalking, though later in the year one is no longer troubled in this respect, as the sharp frosts cut the herbage and render the field of view less confined and restricted. The animals are not gregarious but are found in small numbers, the bucks sometimes being alone, though on occasions I encountered two together but never saw more than this number. The cry of alarm is a bark, similar to that of the Kakur, or Barking Deer of the Himalayas, and when disturbed they disappear in a succession of bounds, a mode of progression for which their length of leg admirably adapts them. Morning and evening are the best times for their pursuit, as they devote the greater part of the day to resting in the depths of the forest or in some shady glen.

On the morning of August 24th I started with Nurah soon after 4 o'clock, searching the ground to the east and north-east of camp. We went part of the way on horseback and then tying up our mounts in a clump of pines proceeded on foot to a ridge overlooking a small side ravine. There was no doubt about roe-deer being there for presently we saw one come out of some bushes. He was on the far side of the ravine, a matter of some hundred and eighty yards, but I determined to risk a shot which hit him rather far back, and he went off down below whither we followed, tracking him by the blood trail. The ground was covered with thick bush and grass jungle, and though

NUMGOON.

we saw him once he crawled into the bush and eluded us. Nurah said we should get him later on, but, as a matter of fact, we did not, although I had a glimpse of him again but not of sufficient duration to bring him down. I was sorry to lose the buck as one naturally dislikes leaving a wounded animal, the whole ethics of sportsmanship being based on its retrieve.

I returned to camp at 11 o'clock, going out again in the

evening, but saw nothing as the Kazaks had but recently left the ground I tried   There was a storm of rain late in the afternoon, not an unusual phenomenon in the Thian Shan

The following morning I went over the ground to the east of camp and saw a number of roe, but the long grass and hemlock made shikar somewhat difficult. I distinguished myself by missing two bucks badly, rather a discreditable performance, so returned to camp and spent the rest of the morning after breakfast in a search for the buck wounded the day before, but though all hands were out we failed to locate him

During the morning Rahim arrived from Kulja bringing letters and supplies, the latter very welcome as we had run out of nearly everything and were living on reduced rations Amongst my letters was one from a brother, then wandering somewhere in the wilds of British Columbia, like myself far from the madding crowd. Rahim went back to Kulja the next day, taking letters for the post and with orders to bring out fresh supplies in a fortnight to the Agiass Valley where I then expected to be

I started off at 4 o'clock on the morning of the 26th with Nurah to try the ground north of camp, keeping along the dividing ridge between two narrow valleys. This ridge trended away to the forests, higher up on the edge of which we soon sighted roe   The country below the ridge in question was undulating grass land and on a little hillock we spotted a buck at his early morning graze. We were able to move round in his direction under cover of the rounded knolls and creeping on to one of them I saw the buck still feeding and quite undisturbed, so tried a shot which knocked him over in the long grass   I thought he was done for, but when we arrived near him he suddenly dashed off, but collapsed after having gone 60 or 70 yards We followed in great haste, but he cleared off again and we lost sight of him in the dense grass   This was very annoying as I felt sure I had hit him in a vital spot, but Nurah said they had tremendous vitality and took a lot of

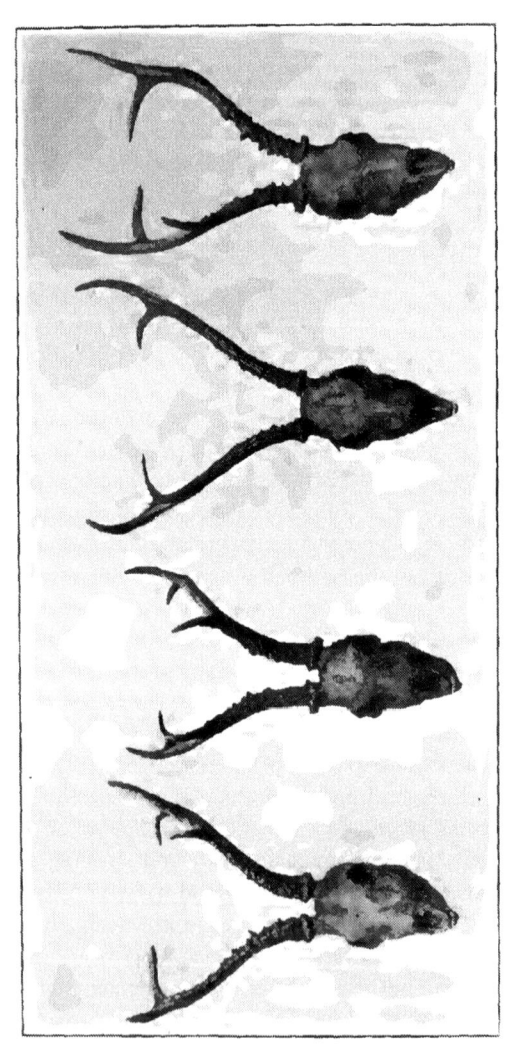

ASIATIC ROE-DEER.

killing   I resumed the chase in the afternoon and, thanks
to the tracking abilities of the Kalmuks, came up with him in
the forest to the west, a shot behind the shoulder bringing him
down.   I then discovered the shot in the morning had hit him
through the neck, which accounted for the wobbly manner in
which he held his head   It was a very nice six pointer, so that
I was getting some enjoyable shooting.

The ground to our right was much broken and covered with
bush and fallen trees   Whilst getting over these obstacles we
heard a buck barking, and presently sighted him going down
hill apparently alarmed   We dropped to earth and I then
crawled forward to the shelter of a friendly rock which commanded a good view of the quarry who was still making down
hill and slightly towards us.   Presently he stopped to look
round, just the moment I had been waiting for, and a shot
behind the shoulder rolled him over without further ado.   He
was a nice little trophy, six points. and taping over 13 inches,
quite a good average head.

On the 28th I missed a buck in the morning, rather a longish
shot from a ridge on to a grass patch below, but still not too far
had I been in form   When I came in that afternoon from
the second part of the day's shikar I found Giyani had gone off
after a stray horse.   I sent Numgoon to look for him and soon
after his departure rain set in, so I hoped both would find an
aul in which to pass the night, sheltered from the fury of
the elements.   As Giyani had not appeared by dawn and Numgoon came in at 4 o'clock in the morning without having
seen him, I took Nurah and went in search of him, sending
Numgoon along the high ground above the right bank of the
nullah   We also got on to this ground further up and I saw an
" illik," which came bounding out of the forest in our direction,
but Nurah was so excited at the sudden apparition that the
buck spotted us before I could get a shot, making off in a series
of bounds which evidenced his desire to quit such dangerous
precincts

The country to the east was a succession of rolling downs, much intersected by ravines and nullahs, the whole covered with long grass and sloping down towards the Tekkes River far out in the valley to the north. Whilst following along one of these grassy ridges I sighted Numgoon and Giyani coming along the ridge across the downs to the east, and signalling them to make for camp, Nurah and I went off to look for roe-deer. I got a shot at one across the nullah but failed to score a hit, so went back to

ROE-DEER GROUND IN THE THIAN SHAN.

breakfast. Arrived there I heard Giyani's story of his night's adventures, brought about by the runaway nag. He had pursued the elusive animal up hill and down dale with a persistency that called for my unqualified admiration, until at last he was such a long way from camp that he lost his bearings, and so spent the night beneath a fir tree, soaked to the skin by the drenching rain. At daylight he resumed the hunt and presently sighted Numgoon, so together these two rounded up the pony and brought him into camp much to Giyani's satisfaction

That afternoon I struck camp and moved further up into the Muntai Nullah, establishing my headquarters amongst the dense jungle under some giant pines. We sallied forth in the evening and prospected the ground higher up but saw nothing shootable.

On the 30th I tried the ground to the west of camp, where there were a lot of little ravines radiating from the main one, and saw a few roe. On the way back to camp, as I was moving along the side of a wooded dell, I sighted one on the opposite side about a hundred yards off My side was covered with dense bush and a few trees, the other being of much the same nature The buck was feeding on an open patch and might at any moment move into the forest where he would be quite lost to view, so using Nurah's shoulder as a rest I had a shot which struck him behind the shoulder, and he dropped in his tracks It was a good six-pointer head with particularly well-shaped horns.

In the afternoon I went off with Nurah, Numgoon and Giyani to bivouac with the object of trying ground north-west but too far distant to reach in one day from camp ; we saw a few illik on the way

I established the bivouac in a narrow ravine under some pines, and as the nights were now getting rather cool had a big camp fire, in the making of which Giyani was an expert. The entire country here was first rate illik ground, so I looked forward to obtaining some more good heads

I started off at break of dawn with Nurah, sending Numgoon and Giyani back with the kit to headquarters. We did a long round, but I could not get the chance of a shot owing to the wooded nature of the country, though we both heard illik

On my return to the main camp I decided to move into the Agiass Valley for ibex shooting, so packing up everything started in the afternoon and moved some eight miles up into the hills

We forgot to bring a cat which had appeared out of the woods at the first camp and attached itself to us, so I had now no feline companion. This cat may possibly have come from a distant nomad encampment as it was quite tame and not a wild species. I could not account for its appearance in any other way, though there were no auls within twenty-five miles. It formed an

GIYANI GATHERING FIREWOOD.

acquaintance with my expedition, taking possession of my camp bed and making itself thoroughly at home.

Whilst camped in the Muntai I had sent for and interviewed the head man of the local Kazaks, and had engaged half a dozen ponies at a fixed rate so as to be able to move anywhere and at any time. The amount included a man to look after them,

and as they eat nothing but grass, of which there is enough in the
Tekkes to supply all the cavalry in Europe, their keep costs nil.

The road into the Agiass lay through the hills and thence
over a pass at the head of the Kok Terek, leading down into the
ibex nullah   The second march out from the roe-deer ground
took us into the valley leading to the pass, and at the last Kazak
encampment I bought some sheep sufficient to last a fortnight.
I camped some distance below the "dawan" under a clump
of pines, intending to cross on the morrow   The hills around
looked good ibex ground, and as the Kazaks had moved down
into the Tekkes Valley with their flocks the game would now be
undisturbed

The next morning at 4 30 September 2nd, I went on ahead
with Numgoon, as he informed me we might possibly come
across some wild sheep near the pass and on the far side of it
The path was very rough and stony, but quite practicable for the
little caravan   We left our ponies just below the summit, and
then went on foot to look for the sheep   On the Agiass side we
sighted a herd, and after an arduous stalk lasting two hours
I bagged one

The identity of these sheep is, as far as one can ascertain,
still undetermined   Some sportsmen who have shot in the
Thian Shan incline to the belief that they are *Ovis karelini*,
but the question lacks scientific determination. They do
not run big, an average head being about 45 inches, though the
one shot by me that day was barely 40   In the Kok Bel Hills.
to the north of the Tekkes River, one gets a larger species, and
in the Jair and Saur Mountains north-east of Kulja still another.
Then in the Altai roams the big *Ovis ammon*, but the largest of
all is the *Ovis poli* found on the Pamirs   Later on I bagged
another specimen of the *Ovis karelini*, the horns of which taped
just over 40 inches

The nullah we were in was a wild and rugged side ravine,
an off-shoot of the main Agiass Valley, camp being pitched on a
rich grass sward near the water's edge   Above us stretched the

dark moraine, and then the snow-capped peaks of the Heavenly
Mountains as the Chinese have christened them. Amidst this
prospect of surpassing grandeur the ibex has his home, but
seldom disturbed by the crack of the hunter's rifle. Here he
wanders in large herds, a sight that gladdens the heart of the
shikari. During the late afternoon of my arrival in this

MY FIRST IBEX CAMP IN THE AGIASS VALLEY.

picturesque spot I had seen ibex high up on the slopes within a
mile of camp, which augured good prospects for the morrow. My
Kalmuks, however, knew still better ground on the far side of
the ridge to the east, where they said the grass was richer and
more abundant, and a favourite haunt of " tekka," the local name
for ibex.

Stalking the Wary Ibex.

We started the next morning before dawn, riding up the ravine for some little distance, and then turned into a nullah to the foot of a steep and rocky dawan, the summit of which commanded a view of the ibex ground before referred to

The pursuit of ibex entails a deal of hard work, but in the Thian Shan one can usually go part of the way on horseback, which tends to lighten the task, as there is a sufficiency of hard climbing and walking without going out of the way for it

Having tethered the horses where there was grass enough to occupy them until our return, we ascended the rock-strewn ridge to the crest line, and there taking cover searched the ground beyond with the glasses   Away to our left, and feeding on a grassy spur running out from the main range, was a herd of ibex, three or four of the bucks having good heads   The ground did not permit of a direct advance, so we had perforce to remain stationary, watching them intently through the glasses   Presently they began to move in our direction, the big bucks leading, but their progress was slow and marked by constant halts to nibble the short sweet grass   Finally they brought up beneath the shade of some rocks and there lay down for the day, so nothing could be done until they should either move further in our direction or shift quarters to more favourable ground for stalking.

By 4 o'clock the sun began to go down and a nasty cold wind sprang up but still the ibex did not move   At last, when the sun had sunk behind the hills to the west they rose and began the evening meal   This was my opportunity, for the whole herd moved slowly down into the ravine, where they were soon temporarily hidden   Dashing down the slope I reached some depressions in the terrain, the front of which commanded a view of the ravine in which the herd was swallowed up   Here we very nearly caused a disaster by coming unexpectedly on a number of female ibex some of whom spotted us before we were able to take cover and sounded their shrill whistle of alarm   The Kalmuks now counselled an abandonment of the chase for that day and returning on the morrow, when the ibex might be in a more favourable position for a stalk, so, as I did not wish to jeopardise my chances by rashly following them up, I assented

The next day was however, too bad to go out a thick driving mist preventing one seeing more than twenty yards ahead, whilst soon after dawn a drizzling rain set in, lasting throughout the greater part of the day During the night the weather cleared, so we were enabled to resume the chase setting forth at dawn *à cheval* and ascending the dawan where we had seen the ibex two days before.

Beyond the crest line we espied them feeding on the grassy slopes to the south, affording an excellent chance of a stalk, as a spur jutting out from the main ridge would give cover for an approach to close quarters On the far side of this we coasted until nearly level with the ibex and then turned into a small gully which running at right angles, continued down to the bed of the ravine Here I waited whilst Nurah went forward to reconnoitre Anxiously I watched him as he crept along from rock to rock with the stealthiness of a cat Presently he halted to peer from behind the shelter of a huge boulder, then, looking back, silently beckoned me to follow Cautiously I stole forward to join him and there beheld a joyous sight. The whole herd was concentrated on the slopes which ran down to the afore-mentioned ravine bed I singled out a big buck who was lying down facing me, a position which never gives a favourable chance Moreover it was a good 300 yards, rather a longish shot, so I determined to attempt a further advance to the cover of some large boulders ahead Arrived there in safety I drew a bead on the big buck and let drive, a lucky shot through the head He toppled over and lay where he fell, which was fortunate, for had he started rolling would have gone down a great distance, probably breaking his horns during the 1,500-foot slope which intervened between the spot and the bottom of the ravine The tape gave the horns 51½ inches, a really fine head, and a most happy beginning to my ibex shoot in the Thian Shan

IBEX (51½″).

A Good Beginning.

The rest of the herd had betaken themselves helter-skelter over the rocks, disappearing round the shoulder of the main spur I was for following them up, so, leaving Numgoon to take the skin and horns back to camp, pushed on with Nurah Late in the afternoon we again came on the herd, but they were very restless, keeping constantly on the move, so we returned to camp

The next day dawned bright and clear and we decided to try fresh ground in the nullah to the north-west having to cross a large glacier to reach the crest line, whence we descended into the depths of a rugged ravine, the eastern slopes of which were carpeted with grass Thereon we espied three bucks having their morning feed unaccompanied by the usual crowd of " madeens," or female ibex The only possible line of approach was down the bed of the stream and thence under cover of some huge boulders which strewed the lower ground where the bucks were busily cropping the luxuriant herbage My telescopic binoculars were capable of clearly defining objects at a great distance, so switching these on to the quarry I saw at once that two out of the three heads were exceptionally good ones

We had now reached the bed of the ravine and were moving along beneath the shelter of rocks cast down from above in bygone days Further down, and on a level with the ibex, was an immense slab from which I thought one might be able to get a shot, though possibly rather a long one Approach to this was a supreme effort, as we were of necessity somewhat exposed, and I feared at any moment the bucks might observe us and take refuge in precipitate flight But fortune was with me, and it looked as though the long trek from India was to receive its due reward, for we reached the cover of the slab without having been noticed It was, as I expected, a long shot, but any further advance was out of the question, so covering the biggest of the trio behind the shoulder I pulled, and—a miss resulted ! As is usually the case they paused momentarily, as if to recover from the shock of so sudden a disturbance in their native wilds, affording me time to ram in another cartridge for a second effort

This was a clean hit, from which he simply sank to the ground without further ado. I dashed on, reloading on the way in the hope of getting another shot at the next biggest now bounding over the rocks as only ibex can. Presently he stopped to survey me, a fatal mistake on his part, for I dropped behind a boulder to take a hasty aim, the shot resulting in his untimely death, though perhaps it was more of a fluke on my part than anything else, for the range was well over 350 yards. But then, does not the element of luck enter largely into shikar? Nurah and Numgoon, who now came up, were beaming with delight, whilst I was well satisfied with the day's sport, the first of the two heads taping $53\frac{3}{4}$ inches and the other $48\frac{3}{8}$ inches. Tired but very cheerful, we wound our way up the ravine to the summit of the pass, laden with the horns and skins, thence descending into the valley on the far side. We were able to toboggan most of the way down, a mode of progression requiring a certain amount of care in this particular spot to avoid an untimely fall into deep and yawning crevasses.

The ibex of the Thian Shan are larger than those of the Himalayas and somewhat darker in colour. Their number is considerable, I having seen as many as 300 in one side valley near the head waters of the Agiass. In the latter locality the ibex ground is on both sides of the river, though lower down the herds are more or less confined to the eastern slopes, but I have seen and shot ibex on the western side also. Speaking generally, the ground slopes up from the valley in a succession of grassy stretches, much broken and intersected by side ravines and gullies. Beyond this one reaches the more precipitous terrain covered with rocks and shale, amongst which the ibex usually take up their quarters after the morning feed on the grass below. The going is quite good on the whole and I should say nowhere particularly difficult or dangerous. In comparison with ibex ground in Kashmir and Chitral, where I have shot, it is easy, and during two and a half months spent in the Thian Shan I did not come across any really difficult ground.

Ibex Ground.

As far as stalking is concerned morning is undoubtedly the best time, as later in the day the wind becomes variable and often there is a fall of snow with heavy mists, which does not tend to improve matters. Generally speaking, I experienced excellent weather during the months of August, September and October, so I am inclined to the belief that these months are the best, judging from

IBEX CAMP BELOW THE KOP TEREK PASS.

the adverse reports given me by the Kalmuks as to the spring and summer.

On the 7th September I tried the ground again whereon I had bagged my first ibex, in the hope of being able to get a very fine buck I had seen amongst the herd on that occasion, but all my efforts to get in touch with him proved unavailing, mainly owing to the fact of the herd being surrounded by a cordon of madeens whose vigilance nothing could gainsay I should think his horns must have been a good 53 inches, with a very nice spread between the tips

On the 8th I had camp shifted higher up opposite the glacier, and not far from the foot of the pass leading over into Kok Terek I crossed the dawan, and worked round towards the point where I had shot on the 5th We were well up amongst the rocks and commanded a fine view of the grassy slopes below and of the pine-clad stretches on the western side of the valley My intention was to move right round via the high ground, and to cross over into the nullah again where I had established the first ibex camp, then to ride back to camp pitched higher up the ravine It meant a lot of hard climbing and some most determined scrambling over rocks and boulders, but I regarded this lightly, seeing the good shikar prospects looming largely ahead

About mid-day we came on the herd containing the big ibex I sought. They were moving away from us at the time, but seemed inclined to lie down for the day in the first favourable position offering itself Presently they crossed an intervening spur jutting out from the main range, and slowly disappeared on the far side of it. We hastened after them as well as the broken nature of the ground would admit, blundering over huge rocks and boulders in our efforts to get in close touch with them Arrived near the crest of the ridge Nurah went forward to reconnoitre and beckoned me to creep up under cover of the rocks, indicating at the same time with his finger the place where the herd was then congregated I took up my position as quickly and silently as possible, but the big ibex was in a most unfavourable spot, half hidden by rocks so I awaited developments They seemed very unsettled, the noise of our advance having probably reached their wary ears, and put them on the alert

Gradually they all moved off, heading down into the nullah, whither we followed them Here the ground was more favourable for a stalk, consisting of little depressions amongst the rocks, and tiny spurs, all leading down into the main ravine We were able to approach the herd under cover of one of these spurs and get within shooting distance but they were obviously alarmed at something, and were all on the run, so as it was getting dusk I singled out the biggest of the herd and had a shot as he was on the move The shot told, but did not bring him down at once, for he made off up into the higher rocks, with us in pursuit, and I managed to get in another shot which was a finisher The head was not the one I had wanted, for it only measured 44½ inches, a fine one for the Himalayas, but nothing wonderful for the Thian Shan, the land of big ibex

Nurah had, indeed, said before I bagged this ibex that the horns would only tape about 45 inches, true enough, though I had doubted his assertions at the time The light of after experience, however, showed me the judgment of both my Kalmuk hunters was in this respect remarkable

It was a long and weary tramp over the rocks in and out of tremendous re-entrants, and down to the foot of the old dawan, where I had arranged that the ponies should meet us We had had a very hard day's work, some 14 hours of constant going, but buoyed up with the prospects of riding back the long distance to camp, now some miles up the valley, we pushed on The ponies were not at the appointed place and we had to walk a long way before we found them, which under the circumstances was not much fun Moreover, a heavy snowstorm came on, and as it was by this time quite dark progress was difficult and laborious We discovered the ponies far down in the valley miles away from the place where they should have been, and as I was by this time somewhat angry and disgusted I read a lecture to the men on arrival in camp which they doubtless long remembered

CHAPTER XIV.

After Wapiti and Ibex

I TRIED much the same ground on September 9th, as the firing of the day before had driven the ibex towards the main valley

On the way up we passed the freshly made tracks of a big bear in the snow, and Numgoon, after examining them with a care born of long experience in the wilds, said the bear had passed that way some three hours before, and that he had been moving quite slowly, evidently on his way down to an early morning graze on the grassy slopes beneath

Bears are met with, as I have already shown, throughout the Thian Shan. They, in common with most of their tribe, hibernate during the winter after having become fat and heavy on the roots, herbs, and grass constituting their principal diet This long slumber indulged in within the recesses of a cavern or the hollow of a tree lasts until the winter months give way to spring, when the bear, thin and emaciated, emerges to regain his erstwhile plump proportions

I came one day on a small cavern in the side of a cliff fringing the upper reaches of a tributary of the Agiass It bore signs of having been occupied by a bear, for we found pieces of fur and other indications of Bruin's tenancy I thought that possibly the bear might return to his lair, but Nurah, after careful examination of the ground, said it had only used the place as a temporary abode, possibly for a day or two, and that it had doubtless left the neighbourhood, since the tufts of hair gave evidence of having lain there some time Further, Nurah's knowledge of the habits of bears was such as to clearly show that Bruin had certainly left the spot altogether

The ibex I was after were down on the grass slopes hard by the place where I had shot the big head on my first day out, so I started off with Nurah to stalk them, sending Numgoon back to camp with orders to bring everything down into the main valley to a log hut used by Kazak herdsmen in the winter months

The herd at the time was in a good position for a stalk, being amongst some broken ground with good cover to favour an advance We had to go some distance down, the slopes being steep and much intersected by gullies and waterways, all leading into the ravine which ran down into the Agiass This ravine was deep and narrow, and the herd being on the move, though at no great pace, presently disappeared into this and were lost to view We crept further on but could see nothing of them, so they must have descended into the ravine, as the upper portions. lying above us and fully exposed to view, held nothing We therefore continued down the slopes very cautiously, and soon caught sight of the herd crossing a low spur

The whole of this ground was cut up into small cliffs, gullies, and little spurs jutting out from the main ridges, and attempts to get over the terrain were rendered doubly difficult by its exposed nature, and the fact that the wind was then in the wrong direction But we held quietly on our course, arriving at last at the crest of a small ridge commanding a view of the herd, now grazing on the slopes of another spur directly in our front I had the binoculars on them and, singling out the big head, awaited the chance of a favourable shot The wind was decidedly bad and presently veered round in their direction, of which we were duly apprised by the entire herd making off in hasty flight The big ibex stopped on the top of the ridge over which the others were disappearing, and gave me a snap shot which must have told, for he stumbled heavily, and then vanished on the far side We dashed over the spur and on to the further crest, a look beyond revealing the ibex streaming down hill evidently with the intention of scaling the

opposite sides We blundered on after them and reached a
point where the ground commanded a view of the stream, on the
far side of which the herd, or rather part of it, was then gathered
There was no time to be lost, so I singled out the biggest and let
drive at him, bringing him down with a bump and crash into the
bushes lining the bank   I descended to the fallen monarch,
whose horns taped 45½ inches, and after cutting off the head and
skin proceeded to try and find the track of the wounded one,
whose horns I felt sure must be well over 50 inches   We spent
some time seeking the trail but it was difficult following the
blood tracks in the grass, as they were somewhat scanty and
not sufficient to assist us much

We then decided to resume the trail on the morrow and
started to work round the base of the hills to the point where
the Kazak log hut was situated, and where camp should by
this time have arrived   It took us some two hours of hard
up and down tramping to get there, by which time it was
almost dark   There was no sign of the caravan and no
response to our stentorian shouts only the echo amongst the
hills   As it was cold and froze at night I was not looking forward
to sleeping in the open without covering other than a shooting
suit, so we went down to the log hut and amassed all the grass
near by for a couch in the event of having to make the best of
the situation   We soon gave up hope of seeing the caravan
that night, and, uncertain how far distant it might be, and the
darkness being intense, burrowed beneath the mound of grass
collected and shivered through the night.   The grass, too, was
somewhat damp, so this did not improve matters   However
these little incidents must occur at times and one learns to take
them philosophically as one should   Neither of us had any
matches, nor had Nurah on him the usual flint and tinder
one often sees amongst the Kalmuks. and especially the Mongols.
so it was a case of no matches, no fire   It was very cold even
for Nurah and we were glad when at last Giyani appeared on the
scene at seven the following morning with the kit   He with the

others, had had a poor time of it coming down the ravine leading
into the main Agiass Valley, as the path was a bad one for ponies,
and they had not gone far before darkness came on and put
an end to their trekking.

We very soon had a fire going and made some welcome tea,
the rest of the baggage coming down an hour later. It was

"THE PONY DISAPPEARED BENEATH THE WATER."

impossible to ford the Agiass River that day owing to the volume
of water, so we were obliged to delay until the following morning
when the night's frost would restrict the flow.

Nurah and Numgoon went out in the afternoon to track the
ibex wounded the day before, and came on the place where it
had been lying down, though they did not actually see it. This

239

was a great pity as the head was undoubtedly a fine one, though I was later fortunate enough to bag others probably as good.

On the morning of the 11th we managed to ford the river, leaving part of the baggage behind in the log hut to avoid risking its loss in the angry waters, and taking only what was absolutely necessary for a few days. The task of fording the river was an exciting one. First of all Numgoon went over on his horse, a very steady creature and excellent at fording rivers, having

"HE WAS FINALLY BROUGHT TO THE OPPOSITE BANK."

with him a long rope, one end being made fast to the halter of a baggage pony, of which there were two. This animal then took to the water, being helped over by Numgoon hauling at the rope, without which assistance he would have had little chance of gaining the opposite bank. It was fortunate for us that these precautions had been taken, for the swirling current dashing on over giant boulders carried the pony off his feet, and he disappeared beneath the water, it was only by angling him in much the same way as the fisherman lands a salmon that he was finally brought to the opposite bank Our own crossing was effected in the same way, an operation rather too exciting to be pleasant. We then moved about three miles up the valley along the left bank, and pitched camp in a sheltered clump of pines with an abundance of firewood about The weather hitherto had been very good and quite conducive to successful shikar.

On the 12th we tried a nullah leading off from the left bank of the main valley, being able to ride much of the way, a pleasing part of the day's programme, since there is always sufficient walking and hard climbing A mile or so up we tethered the ponies in some brushwood and went off on foot to stalk a herd of ibex sighted towards the head of the nullah. This ground was, as usual, very broken, and intersected by small but deep side ravines, through which we now proceeded to make our way in pursuit of the herd grazing on some grass slopes beyond. We were fairly high up and the ibex low down, so that to get at them we should also have to descend, but first waited to see which way they would turn before lying down for the day Soon the herd disappeared into a fold of the ground far below us so we judged it expedient to move down and endeavour to get in touch with them This we did very cautiously, being assisted in our advance by the broken nature of the ground, creeping down over successive rises and keeping a sharp look out for the herd Suddenly Nurah dropped like a stone to earth, I following suit, as did Numgoon, who was just behind me A moment later the advance guard of the herd appeared out of the rise in the ground immediately below us, so as it was hopeless trying to get under cover we simply hung on, not daring to move, though the "madeens. who headed the column, whistled and looked all they must have felt at the strange apparition of three mighty hunters, grim and dirty, out on the warpath

I was shooting with a small 303 rifle that day, a most handy weapon, very light and easy to manipulate, and as I was in a cramped sitting posture could not afford to throw away any chances. I waited on until Nurah indicated with one of his familiar grimaces that the biggest of the herd was approaching, so I prepared for him, and when he showed up not more than 70 yards away sent him over with a shot behind the shoulder.

"WE TETHERED THE PONIES IN SOME BRUSHWOOD."

He rolled some hundreds of feet down hill, and I quite thought his horns would be smashed, but fortunately this did not happen, and when we got down to him later they were intact. This head measured $47\frac{1}{2}$ inches, so that I had now secured several good trophies.

Just after bagging this one, another ibex appeared, and I had a going-away shot, which brought him down, though a second was needed to settle him   He, too, rolled down hill into a side ravine, whither the hardy Numgoon went to skin and cut him up   The horns measured 45 inches , gathering up the spoils of the chase we returned to camp and a big fire

On the 13th I worked the ground on the eastern side of the valley, but saw nothing during the early part of the morning We then struck off into a rocky ravine, at the upper end of which the ground opened out into a basin-shape formation, and there we spotted some fifteen bucks, grazing on the grass slopes.   Three or four were big heads, but the wind that day was very uncertain, and they got it, with the result that all of them cleared off into the higher rocks where it was useless to follow as no suitable approach offered itself   So we returned to camp, intending to follow them up in the morning should they be on favourable ground   On arrival there I found Rahim had just come in from Kulja with letters and supplies, but no home papers I had anticipated.

I was busy during the morning of the 14th writing return letters for Rahim to take into Kulja, so did not go out until the afternoon, when, accompanied by Numgoon, I tried the nullah above camp on the west side, going a long way up but not seeing anything   I think the ground on the east side of the valley is undoubtedly the best, though one often comes across herds on the west, but all my big heads were shot on the eastern slopes

On the 15th we crossed the river and went up into the ravine where ibex had been seen two days before   This time we took a different route, following the ridge all the way in the hope of getting above the ibex and working down against the wind, thus obviating all chances of their scenting us.   It was a long and extremely hard climb, and near the snow line became much more so from the gigantic nature of the rocks and boulders, a climb that resulted in a blank for, despite all my efforts, the ibex got our wind and vanished   Hard luck !

On the way back to camp we picked up a head, the horns of

which measured 56¼ inches, with a spread of 38 inches between the tips, a really fine head, but much worn from exposure to wind and rain.

On the 16th I again tried the same ground, but still no luck ! There were two very big heads in this particular herd I was pursuing with such persistency, and judging from the manner in which they met and foiled all attempts to get to close quarters I presume they must have had an idea of their own importance.

NURAH AND NUMGOON LOCATING IBEX.

I was after them again on the 17th right up to the eternal snow line, and over some long slopes bare and covered with hard frozen snow, and occasional stretches of rock. Arrived at the top I had a magnificent view of the northern slopes of the Thian Shan and of the Kok Terek Valley, where I was later to enjoy some wapiti shooting. The ibex were lying out on an open patch a long way below and to my right, and the only feasible path was down a side chimney, a mass of loose rocks which clattered down making a most exasperating noise, rendering futile all efforts at silent progress. Having got down this chimney it was necessary to move at right angles up to the crest of a spur running down from the main range, whence I could get a shot, though possibly a long one. But there were too many rocks and stones about and the consequent noise warned the ibex that something was amiss, so that when Numgoon and I arrived within distant shot they were off. I had, however, a forlorn hope shot, which was a miss, the report sending the herd into the high ground, where we followed them. They went up into the rocks and disappeared round the corner of another spur, all of which ground was a mass of loose stones and shale. We pushed on to get into closer touch with them, a hard climb, but withal one that is regarded as a pleasure rather than a toil when there are good heads at hand To reach the higher ground whereon the herd was now located meant getting over some extremely rough ledges jutting out from the spur, and the noise of falling rocks loosened by us sent the herd off over into Kok Terek As it was now late in the day I reluctantly abandoned the chase and went back to camp, a long distance down the ravine and across the Agiass River, where we arrived tired but very cheerful and full of hope for the morrow.

Nurah had gone off that morning on a few days' leave in connection with family affairs, so I decided to put in another day after ibex and then trek over into the wapiti forests

Camp was moved down and Numgoon and I went off to try the ground above the right bank of the river and north-east of camp On the way up the grass slopes I killed a small snake covered with greyish blue rings along the body

We had a long round that day, almost up to the higher rocks, with some very stiff climbing in and out of steep intersecting ravines, but saw nothing, only a herd going away from us some distance above. There was no trace of the herd holding the big ibex seen some days previously, and no indication as to their exact whereabouts, so after a further reconnoitre along the top edge of the slopes, now many hundreds of feet above the valley bottom, we descended the hill, being guided to camp by the smoke curling up through the trees. We were able to ford the river on foot as the volume had decreased considerably in the last few days, and the torrent bore a greatly different aspect to what it had when I first entered the Agiass.

OVIS KARELINI.

On the 19th I moved down stream and up to the first ibex camp by way of the Kazak hut. The path was very steep but the ponies managed it successfully. On the way up to the pass leading into Kok Terek we came on a herd of wild sheep, or "gulja," as they are known amongst the natives of the Thian Shan. There were six rams, two being good heads, and they were feeding unconcernedly on the grassy slopes above us to our left. I therefore halted the ponies down in the ravine, and, taking Numgoon, started out to stalk them. The ground was steep but the whole of it being grass-covered was good going and in no way difficult or dangerous. I was able to approach under cover of a small side gully running down at right angles to the ravine, thence crept up under the lee of some rocks beyond which the sheep were feeding. They seemed inclined to work down in our direction, so I held on and they gradually drew to within 150 yards of me. I selected the biggest and gave him a shot, from the effects of which he stumbled forward on his face, but recovering himself went on after the others who had fled up hill. Some thirty yards further on he halted, and another shot brought him rolling down hill almost to the horses waiting in the ravine. The horns taped 40½ inches, but whether they were good ones I could not determine. Whilst Numgoon and I were busy taking off the head and skin, the baggage ponies went on, and camp was established higher up in the old place, whence I intended to trek again next day into Kok Terek.

The morning of the 20th dawned dull and stormy, with snow and a nasty wind, unfavourable weather for crossing the pass, which, however, was not a difficult one. It was snowing hard as we left, so taking some wood, and, halting higher up at the place where I had previously spent two days ibex shooting, lighted a fire to warm ourselves whilst loading up some heads which had been left behind there. The wind was now very strong and keen, and this, coupled with the driving snow, was not at all to the liking of a Kazak I had as attendant to the horses. He continually bewailed his hard lot, saying he would die in such weather, and spent most of his time on the way to the summit invoking the aid of Allah. The descent was steep and through knee-deep snow, soft and powdery, but offering no serious difficulties to the ponies, who were accustomed to work in these altitudes, especially in winter when the nomads move to the valleys for the pasturage with their flocks.

I went ahead with Numgoon to select a place for the camp

and prepare a fire in readiness for the others, who were numbed with the cold wind, now blowing with increased violence I camped some four miles on the Kok Terek side amongst a forest of pines, and had great hopes of the country round proving prolific in wapiti, as it gave all the appearance of being first-rate ground

The Thian Shan wapiti (*Cervus canadensis songaricus*) is one of the finest representatives of the deer family, and his antlers constitute a magnificent trophy. The ground on which he is found is mostly covered with vast pine forests intersected by deep valleys whose sides are usually steep and precipitous The best time for wapiti shooting is September, when the stags are calling, and more easily located   As a general rule the forests are densely timbered, the ground being littered with dead branches and other obstacles, so that silent movement is a matter of considerable difficulty

Tracking game is never an easy task, and this is particularly so in the case of the wapiti, who, in addition to his other attributes, is a great traveller and much on the move, sufficient argument that he is difficult to come up with

Amongst the Chinese the stag s antlers have a medicinal value when in the unformed state, so his pursuit is conducted with a persistency that will soon cause him to become as extinct as the dodo   The Chinese pay large sums for a good pair of antlers, the price varying from 50 to 140 roubles in Russian money.   The horns are reduced to powder, and then used by the Celestials for the cure of certain specific complaints, though as to whether any good results therefrom is a matter of doubt. Most of the Kazak and Kalmuk inhabitants of the Thian Shan possess rifles of sundry patterns, and unfortunately are all too successful in their quest of wapiti

The morning after our arrival in the last camp I started off down the ravine to search for wapiti, or " boga," as they are termed locally.   It had ceased snowing during the night, and the weather was quite clear and fine   I went a good way down the valley, keeping well above the left bank of the stream where the ground was mostly covered with pine forest, and open patches here and there, on which the stags are usually to be found in the early morning, but on this occasion they absented themselves.

Some distance down we came on a pony, evidently a stray that had evaded the spring round-up when the nomads move down

THE HOME OF THE ASIATIC WAPITI.

into the Tekkes. Numgoon made commendable efforts to catch it, but the animal, having doubtless tasted too long of the sweets of liberty, had no intention of being trapped, and frustrated all his attempts to corner it. I was somewhat perturbed at the sight of this pony, as I thought possibly it might tend to scare away the wapiti from the neighbourhood, but Numgoon said it had probably been here some months, so that the stags had doubtless become used to it, with which assurances I rested content

I saw one or two illik, but being bent on mightier game left them severely alone   We came into camp towards noon, as there was nothing to indicate the presence of wapiti, and it is useless trying to track them during the day, the only favourable times being morning and evening

I started again at 5 o'clock on the morning of the 22nd and went a long way down, but did not hear or see anything, nor did we come across any tracks   Three miles further on we crossed to the right bank of the stream, and went through the dense forest looking for the tracks of stag, but there was nothing to show they had been in the neighbourhood   Both sides of the ravine were thickly timbered, whilst higher up along the ridges marking the dividing line between parallel valleys the ground was more open   This is generally the best line to follow, since one gets a commanding view of the country beneath, and the stags when calling are more easily heard than down in the valley, where the noise of running water militates against any chance of locating them

As the ground here did not seem to be promising I decided to move into the next valley to the westward, as time was passing and the calling season now well advanced   Giyani and the Kazak had gone off the day before to the junction of the Kok Terek with the Tekkes River, where supplies of sheep and flour could be obtained, of which articles we stood in sore need, everything having nearly run out, owing to the voracious appetites displayed by the hungry expedition   We had turned the baggage ponies out to graze the previous night, and as only myself and Numgoon remained in camp it took four or five hours to round the brutes up, the consequence being we did not get started till past mid-day   We crossed the intervening range and over another on the far side, thence down into the valley, pitching camp on a grassy stretch by the edge of a stream. Behind rose the mountains clad with fir and pine, whilst across the rippling brook lay a rich expanse of green sward reaching to the opposite side of the valley a few hundred yards away. Giyani and the Kazak had joined us on the way to the new camp with

IN THE KOK TEREK VALLEY.

a plentiful supply of rations, so there was general rejoicing that night.

Numgoon and I were away at 3 o'clock on the 24th to the ground above camp and north thereof. We kept along the ridge, which was grass-covered, with occasional clumps of furze bush. The western sides of the ridge were covered with dense pine forests, whilst, as indicated, our side was grassy, with the

usual pines lower down   On the far side of the valley more
thick pine forest covered the slopes, and in this and all the
above-mentioned ground the wapiti were said to be   Nurah
had not yet returned from leave, so Numgoon was officiating.
As a matter of fact I much preferred him, he being a very cheery
soul and most energetic, which could hardly be said of Nurah,
who was inclined to be slack if nothing was immediately forthcoming in the way of shikar, Numgoon was never disheartened
and always ready to carry on, undaunted by adverse circumstances, ever a most commendable trait in the character of one's
shikari

We had not gone far when a stag called in the forest below,
and presently another took it up   The call of a wapiti does not
lend itself to easy description, but resembles a long-drawn-out
scream   Numgoon imitated it in camp by blowing down the
barrel of my shot gun, so this may give some idea of what it is
like.   The two stags kept calling at intervals, but not enough
for practical purposes, though Numgoon pushed on energetically,
saying he knew the place where the stags would probably come
out to feed   It was still quite dark and after slipping and
blundering over sundry stones and logs we finally reached a
point low down on the grass slopes by the edge of the forest
The wapiti was there all right, for Numgoon pointed down the
slope and in the semi-darkness I saw a big stag, though it was
all I could do to make him out, so did not fire as it was too dark
to see the sights, and I hoped for a chance at him as soon as it
became lighter

We therefore moved round ahead of the direction in which
he was going.   On the way we came unexpectedly on an illik,
a little above us.   Numgoon made a desperate effort to head
him off, but the brute bounded past us down into the forest and
there started barking and making a great shindy   This naturally
spoilt everything, and we saw no more of the wapiti.

In the afternoon we tried the same valley and the ground
nearer the head of it, but neither saw nor heard anything.   This

particular ground, in common with the whole of wapiti country, was hard to get over, being mostly vast forest and innumerable dead trees, so that coming back at night was a trying matter.

The next day I was off again by 3 o'clock in the morning, and this time Numgoon saw a wapiti just going into the forest, but I did not see it myself as I was above him at the time. None

NUMGOON IMITATING THE CALL OF WAPITI WITH THE BARREL OF MY GUN.

of the stags were on the call, so it was hopeless trying to effect anything. Unfortunately Numgoon was no hand at calling wapiti, the expert being Nurah, and I was really at a great disadvantage in this respect whilst the latter was away.

That afternoon a storm of rain, followed later by snow, came on, so that a trip into the Muntai Valley to the westward had to be abandoned Snow fell heavily during the night, but held up by five next morning, which enabled us to get away to the ground where we had heard wapiti calling two days before ; no stags, however, came out nor did we hear any. Of course one wanted Nurah as it is difficult to locate stags in that dense forest, for they only call irregularly when not answered

Numgoon considered we might do better by trying the ground north-east on the far side of the Kok Terek ravine, so I decided to bivouac for two days as the difficult terrain did not permit of the permanent camp being established there We therefore crossed the intervening range and, descending into the ravine beyond, bivouacked under a clump of towering pines. Giyani was left in charge of the main camp with the Kazak, Rasul accompanying me as cook.

As I have already said, to hunt wapiti with any success one should be able to imitate the call This can be done with the aid of a hollow reed stalk about $\frac{3}{4}$ inch in diameter, but it is difficult to do well Nurah, of course, was quite good at it, but the efforts I made could scarcely be called musical and did nothing beyond provoking much merriment amongst my cheery retainers I afterwards had other attempts at it in camp, but produced little better than a few weird sounds calculated to scare any wapiti, though it amused the Kalmuks immensely

During the afternoon Nurah arrived at the bivouac, he having come straight on from the main camp which he had reached that day from Shota, after making arrangements for the recovery of a number of his horses stolen by predatory Kazak bands

The next morning we were out before dawn, and, fording the stream, ascended the slopes on that side through a vast forest of pines At intervals Nurah would call with the aid of his blow-pipe, and, no answer being forthcoming, would trudge silently on again. Higher up we emerged on to an open stretch of grass which covered that part of the ridge To our right a small spur ran out from the main ridge, commanding a view of the forest below and of the higher reaches of the valley, towards the pass we had crossed some days previously. We halted here to take a short rest, and to listen for sounds indicating the presence of wapiti and get a response to our calls, the while I admired the magnificent panorama of mountain, forest and glacier   Presently Numgoon said he thought he heard the sound of something moving in the forest below to our right   Again Nurah called on his blowpipe, his efforts this time meeting with success, for a minute or two later a stag responded and then another and yet a third

Of the three wapiti who had taken up our call the one to the right was deemed to be the best to follow up, the Kalmuks saying that his deep-toned voice proclaimed him to be a good head   So we plunged silently into the depths of the forest, calling at intervals and proceeding with the utmost caution   On the way we came to another small opening, and taking cover behind some huge rocks awaited developments   This opening was about a hundred yards in breadth and sloped gradually down to a small hollow   From our position in rear of the rocks we commanded a view of the ground to the edge of the forest beyond   The other two stags were above and in front of us, but they seemed to be stationary, whereas the one lower down was moving in our direction in response to the calls   We were now quite close to this stag, who was calling at irregular intervals a few hundred yards away. Gradually he drew nearer until he was certainly not more than 250 yards distant, though nothing could be seen of him owing to the dense nature of the forest   From the sound of his movements we judged he would probably debouch from the forest at a point situated almost opposite to where we lay concealed   I now began to prepare for business, and awaited the advent of the monarch of the forest   He was now moving down through the woods and we caught a momentary glimpse of him heading directly towards the clearing   Presently he came out on to the edge of it and glanced round in search of his rival   As he stood there I thought what a noble picture he presented, his antlers forming a trophy worthy of the long trek from India I covered him behind the shoulder and let drive, a heavy stumble indicating a hard hit. This gave me time to put in another shot, as he seemed inclined to break back into the forest which rolled him over, bringing him with a clash into some wild currant bushes. It was a fine head, 12 points, and massive horns measuring 48 inches along the curve, and I congratulated myself on my good fortune. I lighted a big fire whilst the two Kalmuks were busy taking off the head and skin, and then we roasted the fore and hind legs, which contain excellent marrow and are most palatable to the taste

Whilst thus occupied some ibex passed across the top of the hollow a couple of hundred yards further up, and we were all greatly excited, but there being no good heads did not pursue them I was much surprised to see ibex so low down as this, practically in a forest country, but both Nurah and Numgoon said this was often the case, which proved to be correct, for I afterwards saw them much lower down in the same valley whilst engaged in roe-deer shooting

After taking off the head and skin we returned to the bivouac, fording the stream at the foot of the hill, the water being cold but otherwise quite easy We packed up the kit and went back to the main camp in the afternoon, where Giyani met us, beaming with joy at the sight of the bag

ASIATIC WAPITI (48″).

CHAPTER XV

MORE WAPITI AND IBEX

HAVING bagged one good wapiti I was now desirous of returning to the Agiass valley for some more ibex, but the Kalmuks said I ought to try the Muntai to the west, they being confident of further success in the "boga" line. I therefore decided to pursue my old tactics, and, taking only light kit, bivouac in the forests of the Muntai Valley, which, if anything, are even more dense than those of the Kok Terek

So on the morning of September 29th I started out on horseback to cross the range lying between me and the valley in question. A deal of snow had fallen during the night, and the ground was everywhere covered with it to a depth of two or three inches. On the way, and just after leaving camp, I came on the tracks of a "boga" in the freshly fallen snow, and Numgoon went off to follow it up, wildly excited when it appeared out of the biushwood and dashed off up hill. It was quite a small head, though it would have been very welcome to the Kalmuks had they been out on their own account. I descended into the Muntai Valley on the other side, bivouacking in a ravine leading off from the main valley. It was now towards the close of the calling season and I realised that if I was to get another stag there was no time to be lost

That evening we had a roaring fire of pine logs and sat around it far into the night discussing sport in the Thian Shan and the habits of the different animals, concerning which the Kalmuks have many strange beliefs. Numgoon told me that the fox is of a black colour for five hundred years, after which he changes to white for a similar period. At the close of a thousand years, having wearied of life and whiteness, he passes to that bourn whence there is no return. According to Numgoon the skin of the latter is very valuable, and the Emperor of China, who apparently has a very useful collection of furs, has only one of these, so rare are they.

IN THE PINE FORESTS OF THE THIAN SHAN.

With regard to the wapiti, if he dies a natural death, he lives for five centuries, at the end of which time he presumably quits this mortal life well stricken in years. I also asked Numgoon about the trees in the forest and his opinion on the life of the stately pine. His answer was that the fir and pine live a thousand years, always provided nothing untoward happens, after which they drop to earth and lie another thousand years till they rot!

At break of dawn we were up and away, tramping through the silent forests, a silence broken only now and again by the chirp of some bird or the falling of pine cones. In places the ground was carpeted with a rich moss, amongst which the wapiti loves to paw and scratch

Towards 8 o'clock we came out on to an open ridge, and it was whilst sitting there I espied a stag going along the sky line on the far side of the valley. We were high up in a side nullah which lower down joined another, also one of the branches of the Muntai. Our side was thick forest with open grass patches here and there, the ground on the opposite side being of a similar nature. The stag was just above pine tree level, but presently turned down into the forest, on which Nurah put up his blowpipe and produced a first rate call, to which the stag responded. Soon after this another took up the call, but he was a long way off and must have been quite a small one, judging from his tone. The open ridge where we were concealed lay high up the valley side, so that, the stag having travelled down a good way on the opposite side, we decided to descend also with a view to getting to closer quarters. We therefore went down several hundred feet through the forest. Our side of the valley, as I have mentioned, consisted of grassy stretches and irregular clumps of fir and pine, the other was very heavily timbered, with the exception of a narrow open patch close to where we had heard the stag call on our way down This one from his deep-toned voice we judged to be big, but he presently ceasing to call we lost touch with him

As the forest is very dense and the ground much broken it will be readily understood that locating a stag under the circumstances is no easy matter, the more especially as they are constantly on the move, rendering it a task of great difficulty to maintain touch with them. Soon after sighting this stag I despatched Numgoon back to the bivouac with orders to bring the kit over into the valley where

Across the Roof of the World.

we then were, and choose a suitable spot in a side ravine   I
started off with Nurah to regain touch with the wapiti, who was
calling in a half-hearted sort of way until finally he ceased
altogether   This rather puzzled me as the wind was right and
we had not made any noise, but Nurah said he had come across
some " maral " (hinds) and would not therefore budge   This
proved to be the case, for presently we got a glimpse of a few of
them   To attempt to get nearer was too risky as the place was
dense forest, the ground being covered with a débris of branches,
dry leaves and twigs of all kinds

We therefore went back up the valley for a couple of miles
and selected a spot for the bivouac, shortly after which Numgoon
and Rasul with the baggage put in an appearance and we cleared
a space under some firs

We were off again at four that afternoon, shaping a course
down the valley and then up the opposite side, finally gaining
the same ridge where the wapiti had been sighted in the morning
Patience and perseverance were rewarded, for soon we heard the
stag call quite close, though the forest was too thick for us to
get a view of him   Whilst there we heard a second one call in
the valley below, so that we were obviously on good ground
I was in high hopes one of them might move towards us, but
when it got dusk and the light too bad for shooting, even had a
chance of a shot offered itself, I decided to return to the bivouac
some distance up the valley

Both my Kalmuks were confident we should get on to the stag's
trail the following day, and as we were on undoubtedly favourable
ground I, too, was fairly sanguine   We started next morning
before 3 o'clock, going up through the forest to the crest line near
where we had heard the wapiti the previous evening   Thence we
descended a short distance and struck east through the jungle,
Nurah calling at intervals. On the way we saw a small stag a
long way off on the other side of the valley   He was with two
hinds and they were gradually working down into the valley
beneath us   Further on we saw another just going into the forest

below, but as he, too, was small I did not worry about him Soon after this we heard one call far down in the valley to our left, which, from his tone, we judged to be our friend of the evening before, so started hot on the trail. He kept on calling, so that we were able to keep in touch with him. Our way lay through the thick forest, the going being easy, the heavy moss with which the ground was carpeted deadening the sound of our movements. Lower down we reached a point where it was somewhat difficult, and broken by rocks and decidedly precipitous The Kalmuks moved round to avoid this, but I, taking a short cut, very nearly came to grief, sending down an avalanche the noise of which reverberated throughout the valley The Kalmuks said we must now stand fast and await developments, and right glad I was to presently hear the stag calling again, obviously undisturbed by a few cartloads of rock. We were still some 400 feet above the valley bottom, so descended still further. The going was now fairly good, consisting of deep soft moss, though the ground was strewn with branches and twigs.

We were now getting close to where the wapiti had last called, when suddenly we caught sight of him moving down through the forest on the opposite side He was too far off to risk a shot, besides which we only got a fleeting glimpse of him now and then as he went downward, seeming inclined to cross the stream into the forest on our side I therefore took cover behind a fallen tree trunk and awaited the chance of a favourable shot Beneath me, about a hundred yards off, was a small open patch on my side of the brook, and I was in hopes the stag might appear on this and give me a snap shot Sure enough he came on, working down through the forest, and, crossing the stream, showed up momentarily on the open grass plot. I lost no time in covering him behind the shoulder—another of my good luck shots, which was a finisher. Over he went, turning a complete somersault, whilst I dreaded his horns might be smashed When I got down to him I realised what a fine trophy I had bagged—14 points, and beautifully shaped horns taping 49 inches along the curve. One of the upper tines had been broken off, but in such a way as not to be noticeable. The two trophies of Asiatic wapiti I had now secured were big heads, measuring as they did 48 inches and 49 inches respectively, constituting fine specimens of this rare stag

Leaving Numgoon and Nurah to bring back the horns and skin I started up through the forest on the way back to camp It was a long and tiring tramp, but little I worried about that, and after a short halt and something to eat at the bivouac, rode back to the main camp where the others arrived with the trophy in the evening, being greeted with smiles of satisfaction by Giyani, who put on an enormous blaze in honour of the event which would have done credit to a Jubilee bonfire.

The next morning we held a parade of all the trophies and a pleasing lot they looked, affording me a certain amount of pardonable inward satisfaction at the sight of the reward for all I had undergone

On October 3rd I went over into Muntai again and bivouacked the night there, but saw no wapiti On the way down I badly missed an illik, which we came upon quite suddenly and who obligingly stood and posed for me, but even then I could not hit him. I was shooting with the 303, which was quite accurate, so could not account for the miss beyond bad shooting

My bivouac that night was in a side ravine, the eastern slopes being a mass of fallen timber mostly brought about by forest fires which must have occurred many years before These fires cause great damage and whole tracts of country are devastated by them, the only redeeming feature being that the grass is afterwards more sweet and succulent This is the principal cause of them in the Himalayas, where the hill people set light to the forests in order to improve the grazing. This occasionally happens in the district around Lansdowne, and during the spring the garrison has often to turn out and quell forest fires caused by some villagers who purposely ignite them

The ground here was covered with vast pine forests and in

ASIATIC WAPITI (49″).

days gone by a noted haunt of wapiti, though now their numbers have sadly diminished due, as already remarked, to the ruthless persecution by native hunters.

Whilst sitting round the camp fire that night Nurah and Numgoon related stories of earlier days spent in the pursuit of this noble stag, Nurah telling me he had once bagged twenty-four within a month, getting three in one day As a good pair of antlers commands about £10 he, during that month at any rate did more than passing well

Certain it is the day is not far distant when the Asiatic wapiti, e'en now all too rare, will have passed for ever from the forests of the Thian Shan in the same way as the bison, once found in countless herds has disappeared from the prairies of North America.

It was freezing hard, but we were fairly comfortable under the spreading pines, and as there was an abundance of firewood we had quite a good time We started off soon after daybreak, Nurah and I, to look for wapiti, illik, and boar, the flesh of the latter being greatly esteemed by the Kalmuks. There must be a number of boars about, judging from the tracks and the state of the ground where it had been ripped up by the pigs in their search for roots, which constitute their principal diet The boar only comes out at night or in the very early morning, so that anyone desirous of his blood would have to be about during those hours since he retires to the depths of the forest at dawn of day

From the high ground above the Muntai Valley I had a fine view of the Tekkes and the hills to the north. Nurah pointed out Kok Bel, which lies on the far side and is said to be a good place for *Ovis karelini*, or whatever the correct name should be for the wild sheep there found It is two marches from the Agiass, but unfortunately I could not find time to go there, as I had intended, after the ibex shoot

From this open ground I struck off into the forests again to the south and south-east, coming on some illik during the course of the morning, but I was not able to get a shot, as they were very much on the alert, in fact more so than usual. I had the ponies with me, intending to ride back to the main camp in the evening, so possibly this may have accounted for it. As a general rule a Kalmuk when hunting on his own account always goes mounted, except of course in thick forest, where it would be impracticable to proceed *à cheval*, and when any game is sighted ties up the pony prior to commencing the stalk.

A VIEW IN THE THIAN SHAN.

Towards 9 o'clock as we were going along a ridge, the dividing line between two steep valleys, we heard a wapiti call in the forest quite close, or rather I heard it, and Nurah called on his blowpipe, to which the stag responded several times. We went down hill a little way and taking up a position on a small spur jutting out from the main ridge, endeavoured to locate the stag's whereabouts as near as possible. Whilst sitting there another

wapiti called in the forest far below, but such a long way off that
we deemed it better to leave him alone and devote ourselves to
the one near at hand   There was little to choose between the
two, judging from the tone, the one nearest to us having a deep
voice indicating a big stag.   He was on the move, and his last
call showed him to be some three hundred yards off in the forest
to our front, so, the ground being littered with twigs and broken
sticks, I took off my boots, as they made too much noise, and
started off to track him   The stag responded splendidly to our
calls, but when we had got within two hundred yards it became
necessary to proceed with great caution for fear of alarming him.
The forest was very thick, and it was impossible to see more
than thirty yards ahead, so we worked on stealthily, until finally
in a more open part of the wood we saw him above us about
ninety yards off.

I could only make out the lower part of his body and was not
sure if he was a good stag, since his antlers were quite hidden by
the branches of a tree behind which he was scratching moss
Nurah, however, appeared to have no doubt on the subject, so I
crept up under cover of a pine trunk and covering him behind the
point of the shoulder pulled the trigger   He staggered heavily
and a second shot brought him down.   He proved to be only
a ten pointer, not at all a bad head but, of course, not to be
compared with those I had already bagged   One cannot distinguish objects well in this dense forest, where the trees and
brushwood preclude a favourable field of view being obtained of
the quarry.

The next day I sent all the trophies down to the mouth of the
Agiass Valley in charge of Giyani and Numgoon, there to be stored
until my return.   After starting them off I left with Rasul and
Nurah for some more ibex shooting in the Agiass, crossing the
first intervening range down into the ravine beyond, at the upper
end of which we came unexpectedly on a white bear peacefully
grazing on the hillside.   As soon as we hove in sight he dashed
off across the ravine directly in our front, and, wading the river,

disappeared round the corner of a small knoll Nurah and I followed in hot haste, blundering through the ice-cold water, and up to the crest of the knoll The bear was about two hundred yards beyond it and on the move making for the ridge, so no time was to be lost if he was to be accounted for. I could now see that he was of a greyish-white colour, the fur being thick and long; in size he was much larger than the Himalayan bear One glance was sufficient to show that he was an uncommon species of the bear family and I already imagined him as good as bagged But luck was against me, for although I had seven shots at him, all going-away ones, I did not score a hit, though, despite the distance, I ought to have got him had I been able to shoot straight Of course it is very easy to miss at these high altitudes, since the least exertion makes one puff, and as I sprinted between shots in hopes of getting nearer I suppose my aim was not much improved thereby This was indeed bad luck as the bear was undoubtedly of a type rare in the Thian Shan, since, though white bears are said to exist, and Numgoon afterwards told me he had once seen one in Kok Su, they are very uncommon and would constitute a fine trophy Personally I had never heard of the existence of white bears in Central Asia, and the meeting with this particular specimen raises an interesting natural history question

I camped that day in the ravine leading up to the Kok Terek dawan, having to cross another range to reach there It was some distance above our first wapiti camp, and in the evening I went out with Numgoon in the hopes of seeing some wild sheep we had sighted there on a previous occasion. I had a bad headache that night probably due to the combined effects of sun and snow.

The next day I crossed the pass and camped in the ravine on the Agiass side. That night there was a heavy fall of snow, signs that winter was already fast approaching, so it would not do to tarry much longer in the Thian Shan, especially in view of the extensive programme still to be carried out and the great amount of hard marching its accomplishment would involve.

A Frustrated Stalk.

We did not see any wild sheep here though it was a good place for them, but when moving the next day down the ravine into the main Agiass Valley we saw a large herd; they winded us, however, and immediately cleared off, so my efforts at a successful stalk were frustrated. I could not, however, discern any sensational heads, so perhaps did not lose anything by it.

GIYANI PREPARING BREAKFAST.

It was now my intention to march to the head of the Agiass and work the ground there, gradually moving downwards in the hope of being able to account for some big heads. The water in the river was now, of course, quite low and everywhere fordable, so the one obstacle to movement up stream no longer existed.

I camped the night of October 7th a few miles up on the left bank, but some Kalmuks had been there before me, hunting ibex for the sake of the skins and meat.

On the 8th I moved up the valley and camped near the last

jungle, the ground above to the east having all the appearance of first rate ibex country, and indicative of bumper heads. Nurah went on further up the valley to see if there were any Kalmuks shooting, as we had noted the tracks made by their horses, but he came in an hour or so later without having encountered any. He had seen two lots of ibex above and just beyond camp, so this looked promising, and I decided to stay a day or two and prospect the ground I spent the late afternoon collecting firewood in the stony bed of a side ravine, here joining the main valley, most of which had been washed down from above. That night was one of the coldest I had experienced in the Thian Shan, the thermometer dropping to eight degrees, while a keen wind did not improve matters.

On the 9th I tried the ground above camp to the east, going up over the long grass slopes, a climb lasting 4½ hours. It proved decidedly a disappointment, for the wind, having hitherto been perfect, suddenly turned the moment I came within shot of a herd numbering about 150, and before I could get a chance they were lowering all previous records. No words can depict one's disgust on occasions like this, at any rate my vocabulary was quite unequal to it Nurah was very annoyed and swore volubly in Kalmuk, which doubtless would have held its own with a Billingsgate fish porter

The ground about here certainly seemed to be a regular rendezvous for ibex, for within two hours of leaving camp I had seen well over 300 heads in four different herds It must not, however, be imagined that they all carry big horns, for out of the 300 there were certainly not more than six big heads, and they were in the herd I was after.

Of course the Thian Shan is undoubtedly the place *par excellence* for ibex, but good heads, and by good heads I mean nothing under 48 inches, are not too easily found, though they are there. Excellent shooting can be enjoyed in the Thian Shan, and once arrived one feels indeed that the reward is worthy of the toil, the many long marches, and all it takes to get there.

Camp life, too, is really delightful amidst the pine forests and grassy slopes of the Celestial Mountains, whilst the knowledge that one has such a great extent of ground to shoot over unfettered by game laws, licences, or guards, is something I leave the reader to imagine The valleys are all covered with rich grass, while those of Kok Terek and Muntai are vast forests of pines. This part of the Thian Shan is prolific in glaciers, adding considerably to the beauty and charm of the scene, as one views them above the pine tree level gleaming in the sunshine, making a very fine picture

My next day after ibex was not much better, for although I came on a herd containing about thirty bucks, one having a really good head, they were in a bad place for a stalk, being out on an open slope which commanded all the ground for at least six hundred yards around In addition there was a regular army corps of madeens near them, and another herd of ibex lower down, so after various ineffectual attempts to get near enough for a shot with some hope of scoring a hit I gave it up and went back to camp in the late afternoon.

To those who have shot ibex in the Himalayas and the Hindu Kush the numbers encountered in the Thian Shan must come as a revelation, and no slight embarrassment is caused the sportsman by reason thereof. As an instance of this I would quote some experiences on one of my days when stalking a herd above and a little to my left. Some four hundred and fifty yards straight above me was a number of madeens, and several hundred yards to my right a herd of about 150 ibex, whilst the one I was after had a cordon of madeens round it ever ready to sound their shrill whistle of alarm. Under the circumstances it was only by dint of much crawling, and endeavouring to squeeze myself into the smallest possible size, that I at last got fairly close. The bucks were, however, hidden by some rocks, approach to which was a supreme effort, but the madeens were not to be taken in, and gave warning of the approach of the gunner with the inevitable result that they girded up their loins and vanished.

On October 11th I moved camp higher up the valley some three miles above the last patch of jungle. This was near the head of the nullah, with good ibex ground on both sides, sloping up for hundreds of feet in tiers to the higher rocks I camped by a sheep pen, used by the Kazaks during the winter. constructed of brushwood, all of which we burnt during the two days spent there The Agiass Valley here divided into two branches, the western one ending in a glacier some three miles up.

On the 12th I tried the new ground and came on ibex there. We had gone a long way up almost to the top level of the grass stretches when we espied a herd of some forty bucks a good way below us, and, as usual, with a ring of madeens round them The only line of approach was down a side ravine which meant a long détour, and required careful negotiating for the ground was littered with rocks and boulders, and the noise of these as they went crashing down, when unwittingly dislodged by us, threatened to give the alarm and send the herd off in sudden flight However, we managed it all right and towards the late afternoon came within shot The herd was then on a grassy patch below us, so from our position I commanded a view of them and could single out the best head Just as I was firing at one of the biggest bucks a madeen whistled like a railway engine, which was the signal for the whole herd to get under way I singled out what appeared to be another good head and had a going-away shot, hitting him in the hindquarters and raking him fore and aft The tape gave the horns 47¾ inches—a welcome addition to the bag I then went after the one first hit, and found him lying down at the foot of a small cliff, so, resting my rifle on the edge, a shot behind the shoulder accounted for him After measuring the horns, which taped 45 inches, we gathered up both trophies and wended our way back to camp

On arriving there I was glad to find Numgoon, he having returned from his short spell of leave to Shota, after depositing the heads in the merchant's log hut at the mouth of the Agiass Valley A heavy fall of snow set in at 5 o'clock, the temperature going down almost to zero, and, as it was getting decidedly cool and the ground here did not offer much inducement for me to stay on, I trekked the following morning five miles lower down, camping in a small pine patch on the left bank of the river. It had snowed a good deal during the night, but held up before I marched. In the afternoon I went out with Numgoon to try the ground above camp on the eastern side, and saw three herds of ibex, but none contained any shootable heads.

NURAH AND NUMGOON ENJOYING A MEAL.

The following day, October 14th, it was snowing hard when I awoke, thick mists narrowing the field of view to such an extent that one could not see far, so we spent the day in cleaning masks, and moving camp a mile or so lower down to the opposite side with the object of doing the ground above.

With regard to the treatment of skins and trophies it should be remembered that wood ashes when cold and reduced to powder form an excellent preservative, and all masks, after being

275   T 2

thoroughly cleansed of flesh, should be well rubbed with this simple preparation Personally, all my masks were dealt with in this way and I found it highly satisfactory.

The weather cleared up on the morning of the 15th, so I started off with Nurah and Numgoon to the grassy slopes above Higher up we came on a herd numbering some thirty ibex, of which two were sure 50 inchers. We were on the southern side of two parallel ridges, the ground between being open and sloping gradually to a tiny stream formed from the melting snow accumulated amongst the rocks higher up. The ibex were on the northern side and some 300 yards to our front, but as the wind was in the wrong direction they very soon got it and started to move off up hill keeping along the rocky slopes on the northwestern side, and making for the crest line far above Our only possible line of advance was by the southern side, on a parallel course with the herd, which, though the valley was several hundred yards in width, was not far enough removed from their view to enable us to proceed with safety. However, there was no way out of the difficulty so letting them get well ahead, and keeping under cover of a rise in the ground we presently took up the pursuit.

When the herd had gone up some hundreds of feet they crossed an intervening range and disappeared from sight. This was our chance, so hastening to their side of the ravine we followed them up through the rocks and snow, a most tremendous climb, as the rocks and boulders with which the whole place was strewn were of gigantic size, while the quantity of loose snow made the going all the more difficult since one constantly disappeared through crevices and holes between the rocks.

When we reached the top of the ridge the ibex were lying down on the far side, near the sky line, so we sat still for two hours waiting for them to get up and give me the chance of a shot The weather was bitterly cold, freezing hard, and during the wait my boots froze as solid as a brick, so I was obliged to take them off and wrap my putties round both feet, after Numgoon and Nurah

had rubbed them and restored life.   At the end of the two hours
we could endure the cold no longer, so threw stones out from behind
our cover in the hope of shifting the ibex.   Then one of those
extraordinary turns of fortune occurred which must be experienced
to be realised, for, having shifted the ibex, a heavy mist swept
down from the top of the heights, completely obscuring them,
and when it lifted the ibex were out on the far side of the

NURAH WATCHING IBEX.

ravine a good 400 yards away! Nothing now remained but
give vent to one's feelings and then go back to camp, not an easy
matter, for my boots were frozen so hard I could not get them on
and consequently had to run down hill more or less bare-footed.

On October 16th I went after the same herd, and found them
up amongst the rocks, to reach which we had another long climb
lasting some hours, until at last we came up with our friends of the
day before.   They were out on an open slope, to which I could not

get nearer than a good 400 yards, so held a council of war and decided that Numgoon should move round lower down in an endeavour to work them out towards me   This all turned out very well, but it was a most bitter day with a cutting wind, and again freezing hard, so that by the time Numgoon had shifted them out in our direction we were both stiff and numbed.

We were lying under cover of some rocks near the top edge of the grass slopes, the ground above being mostly rock trending slightly upwards until the lower limit of the cliffs, the latter a notable feature of ibex ground in the Thian Shan   The field of view was therefore fairly favourable, and as there was every prospect of them passing between me and the foot of the cliffs I hoped to obtain a shot.   The biggest ibex passed a couple of hundred yards from me and I already regarded him as good as dead, when to crown all I had three miss-fires in succession, and by the time I had had a fourth attempt, which did go off, he was lost amongst the rocks.   It was a cruel disappointment, as I was quite sure of another record head, but luck was apparently out, and I returned to camp sad and sorrowful

The weather was now getting very cold, with hard frosts every night, and the same throughout the day on the higher ground, so that it is possible the ammunition suffered thereby.   With a view to obviating this undesirable state of affairs cartridges should be warmed before starting in the morning, and then kept in a dry pocket until they are actually required

The next day, October 17th, Nurah left for his home as he had injured his right knee, and could no longer do climbing or hard work on the hillside, so Numgoon took charge and, as usual, did very well.   I sent the camp on lower down the valley and with him did the ground above   When we had gone up a thousand feet or more we sighted some ibex coasting along the near side of a steep ravine on the crest of which we were proceeding   One of the heads was distinctly good, so I had a shot, almost a vertical one, missing handsomely.   We followed the herd over very bad ground, some of the hardest up there, so laborious in fact, that a young Kalmuk who was with me that day could not tackle it, but awaited my return on the grass slopes evidently preferring to cling to life and not risk a sudden and unceremonious tumble into eternity The herd, however, eluded us as only ibex can, so I gave it up, and then started along the top edge of the grass slopes in the hope of seeing others below

I sent the other Kalmuk back to camp with orders to have everything moved further down the valley to the entrance of a narrow ravine, at the upper end of which I had seen ibex on a previous occasion. Numgoon and I decided to work along and down to this point, a heavy day's work, but as the ponies were to meet us at the bottom of the hill it would not be necessary to walk the entire way back to camp.

Towards noon we were well up amongst the higher rocks and moving round to cross on to the next ridge by following the head of the ravine Whilst doing so we saw madeens appearing out of a rise in the ground some distance below us, so many there were and all in Indian file that I thought they would never cease coming out. At last some big bucks appeared, at any rate they looked well over 50 inches, two of them having a most extraordinary curve, even Numgoon saying they were very fine We therefore doubled up to some rocks commanding their line of advance, and awaited the advent of the big bucks During the time we had been running to take up this position we were under the observation of a few madeens, and they, watchful as ever, sounded that shrill whistle of alarm I had learnt to know so well.

I do not think I had ever seen so many ibex before, and as they kept trooping past some 150 yards away I could judge the big ones At last the two biggest appeared, the leading one being on the run. I, however, had a shot at him and missed. A little way behind him came number two, and he very kindly stopped to admire us, so I opened fire which caused him to stumble heavily but not sufficiently hard hit to bring him down He then left the herd, which had made off helter-skelter ahead, and pursued a course at right angles, being unable to tackle the steep hillside. I followed hot on his trail and presently found him lying behind a huge rock and looking very tired of life, so another shot ended the matter and I climbed down to survey him. It was not such a big head after all, the horns taping 45½ inches, with a wonderful curve, giving him the appearance of possessing a very fine pair of horns.

On the 18th I tried the ground further north and followed

CAMPED IN THE AGIASS VALLEY.

a herd of ibex, all bucks, right to the snow-line but failed to get a shot as they were uncommonly wary and gave me no chance.

I was now back at the mouth of the old nullah, opposite to which I had camped on September 11th. The next day I went up there and found the same herd, this time grazing out on the grass slopes to the north, but not in a stalkable position as there were a lot of madeens between, so I held on till the afternoon for the wind to change and the female ibex to shift to less dangerous quarters We were ensconced in rear of a ridge running half way across the upper end of the ravine, and the ibex were on the slopes to our left front, a matter of three hundred yards distant. At last the herd started grazing and gradually worked down into a hollow of the ground where they were more or less hidden, thus opening the way for an advance on our part. It was a most risky approach, as the ground was very open below and at any moment one of the officious madeens might catch sight of us, but nothing happened and we managed to gain the near side of the spur over which they had disappeared.

The herd holding the big head was just beyond, a chance that must have been a certainty, but it was again a case of miss-fires after one had drawn near enough to easily account for him. That day constituted a record for four consecutive cartridges refused to go off, though the ibex went off all right !

On the 20th I did the ground lower down the valley, the old ground I had been over when I first reached Agiass. I waited for camp to be struck and then moved to the new place with the caravan, sending off Giyani to the mouth of the valley to bring up fresh ammunition as I was heartily sick and tired of miss-fires, a continuation of which is disastrous to good shooting, the mere idea of experiencing them being quite sufficient to put one off one's aim

I pitched camp in a side ravine on the right bank of the Agiass and then went off with Numgoon to the ground above. It was a perfect day, a clear sky and not a cloud anywhere The view from the higher slopes was magnificent, ranges of snow-capped mountains, glaciers gleaming in the sunlight, and the lovely Agiass River flowing through grassy stretches far below. It made a delightful picture and a fitting one for the brush of an artist.

Arrived on the top of the ridge we saw ibex in the next dip to our left, but the ground was much too open to admit of a stalk with any chance of a successful issue. We tried hard to work round, but it was too risky and being late in the day

Numgoon counselled an adjournment till the morrow when the herd might be in a better position, so I went back to camp. There were 106 ibex in this herd and amongst them some 45 bucks, several of whom carried fine horns.

I was up there again the next morning, having ascended the ridge lower down the main valley, and found them in the depression to my right. They were only some four hundred yards distant but out on the grass slopes, and at first it did not look as

TYPICAL IBEX GROUND IN THE AGIASS VALLEY.

though I should get close enough for a chance with any hope of success. My 16-power glasses showed four of them to be bumper heads, and it can be imagined with what keenness I awaited the psychological moment. We made a move round by the higher rocks, and there, towards 2 o'clock, found a possible line of advance from above down through the rocks and snow. By sliding full length we were able to get within 200 yards to the top edge of the grass slopes We could only see six bucks who were lying down, directly below us, with a number of madeens a little to their left I was for creeping further down in order to locate the others, as of the above six only one was a really good head for the Thian Shan though, I am sure, his five companions all topped 45 inches Numgoon, however, said it was too dangerous trying any more approaching, and that we had better remain still, advising me at the same time to make sure of the big buck below But I felt this was not the biggest of the herd, so we waited lying full length amongst the stones unable to move for fear of attracting attention

At last, towards sunset, the six bucks rose and started grazing, and a few minutes later a number appeared out of a rise in the ground I turned the glasses on to them and saw a splendid buck, quite the pick of the herd There were about twenty others, all so jumbled up that I could not get a fair chance of a shot Presently the herd disappeared over the edge of the lower slope, so we crept back up hill a little way and then doubled round to a point further down and along to the edge over which they had slowly strolled This necessitated the utmost care on our part for the grass was dry and brittle, nevertheless it seemed to me we made a most disquieting noise and I fully expected to see the entire herd settling down into full flight. However, we arrived in safety, but just before reaching there a female ibex whistled like a siren and we very nearly collapsed altogether. Cautiously I peeped over the top fearing to see the entire herd in full flight. Only four bucks were visible and they appeared quite unperturbed, so I lay still and awaited developments. Presently I took another peep, and this time luck was in for there stood the big buck just about 100 yards off.

It was now or never, for the madeens had begun whistling again and were certain something was amiss, doing their utmost to put the rest of the herd on the alert and save them from the hunter I had to lean well over the edge in order to cover him, which I did as rapidly and quietly as possible, and let drive with the little ·303 I was using that day. The shot caught him behind the shoulders, but he went some little distance before finally toppling over. The horns measured 55 inches, with a spread of 31¼ inches between the tips, a really magnificent head, and a fitting termination to my ibex shoot in the Thian Shan

When the head was brought into camp I realised what a trophy I had bagged, almost a world's record The keenest joy the hunter can experience was mine, and I looked upon all the toil and trouble inseparable from ibex shooting as a pleasure, and the reward it was my good luck to gain amply compensated for the hardships and privations endured since leaving India

Of the ibex I had bagged the six best measured as follows — 55, 53⅝, 51½, 48⅜, 47⅞, 47½ inches, the measurement of the record head, as given in a standard work on big game, being 57½ inches.

The herd had gone off headlong into the next nullah, so I determined to try this ground the following day, but did not set out till noon, as we were busy cleaning the mask of the big head and taking it easy after our strenuous exertions of the past few days We followed straight up the ravine I was then camped in to near the upper end where it divided, one branch continuing eastward and the other trending away to the north It was in this latter ravine we found the herd feeding on the upper slopes and the three remaining big ibex with them.

It was a matter of great difficulty getting near enough for practical purposes, although the terrain did admit of it, being much broken with numerous little side watercourses, coming down amongst which one could proceed more or less under cover. On this occasion, however, Numgoon did not display his wonted caution, and they, sighting him, started to trek, part of the herd making for the opposite side of the ravine over some large patches of snow, thence up through the rocks and across the intervening range into the nullah beyond. The big bucks took a contrary course and moved off above the ground on which we had first seen them It was no good, so I had to return empty-handed,

IBEX (55″).

but as I had already done remarkably well I could afford to take it philosophically

On the way back to camp, whilst passing down through the ravine Numgoon saw an ermine, and told me that the Ak Badshah (the Czar of Russia) possessed many of those skins and that they were valuable, thus showing that Numgoon's knowledge in this respect was of something more than an elementary nature

The morning of October 23rd was very dull, with heavy mist and light snow, so I was unable to go out   This was unfortunate as time was now short and I ought to have been trekking on, but wished to obtain another good head, though the chances of doing it seemed poor   I put in the greater part of the day writing and arranging for the onward march, having decided to devote only one more day to ibex shooting and then push on down to the Tekkes Valley and so to Kulja.

On the 24th the weather was fine again, so I did the old nullah in the lingering hope of accounting for a big buck seen there some days before   This particular ibex carried very fine horns, Numgoon declaring they would exceed by three inches the 55-inch head I had bagged   The herd was indeed in evidence, but the wind was unfavourable and the place they were in hopeless for a stalk, in addition to which there were several female ibex above them   We therefore retired down the ravine and waited four hours for the wind to turn, which it always did towards dusk, when it blows up the nullah, contrary to the early part of the day, at which time it assumes a downward course   When we returned there were no ibex to be seen, the herd having retired into the higher rocks where all attempts to follow them were vain, so I was forced to abandon the chase and wend my way back to camp

Still undaunted I put in some terrific work the following day by ascending the ridge to the north, a long and exceedingly stiff climb over rocks and boulders at the head of the ravine wherein I was camped   This détour was undertaken in the hope of circumventing the wind, and it took me right up to the

287

snow line between the valleys of Kok Teiek and Agiass, whence I worked along the top and down through waist-deep snow into the nullah where I had so often been before. The ground was in many places fearfully steep and we slithered and blundered about on the treacherous surface, sometimes almost buried in the powdery snow, but finally getting down into the ravine on the far side. But they had vanished, goodness only knows where, and I never saw them again nor that head which was a perfect dream

It was my last day after ibex, and as I wended my way back to camp on the other side of the river amidst a clump of pines I felt the time had come when I must leave the Thian Shan, the grassy slopes and the sombre pine forests, and resume once more the trail and trek hard for the Great Altai Mountains, many hundreds of miles to the north. I had done well since my arrival in the Thian Shan, and the reward had indeed been an ample one.

It was now October 25th and I reluctantly decided to leave the Agiass Valley for Kulja and the far north. Much as I should have liked to stay on for a few more days in the hope of getting yet another record head I felt it would not do to tarry longer, since much still remained to be done and the first signs of winter had already appeared. So we put on a big blaze that night, my last camp fire in the Agiass, and the next morning, in a snowstorm and a bitter cutting wind, trekked on down the valley. The skies were heavy and overcast, and thick clouds of mist obscured the heights on the eastern side whereon I had spent many happy days in pursuit of the wary ibex

CHAPTER XVI.

Through the Ili Valley to Kulja.

It had been my intention to visit Kok Bel for some *Ovis karelini* shooting, but time would not allow of this so I went on to Kulja.

On the night of the 26th I camped by an unoccupied Kazak log hut which we partly dismantled to provide firewood. It was a

CROSSING THE TEKKES VALLEY.

bitterly cold night, freezing hard again, with a fairly strong wind, so we needed all the warmth we could muster.

I continued on down the valley the following day, the weather having improved, but still a cold wind though the sun was shining. I crossed a low spur and camped by the

merchant's hut, where I found Nurah looking quite a gay
Lothario, arrayed in new garments and having indulged in the
luxury of a shave, a striking contrast to the picture of shabby
gentility he had presented prior to leaving me , in fact, I did not
at first recognise him

I arranged for fresh transport and paid off that I had had
with me throughout my shoot in the hills   The heads had been
lodged here during my absence and I found everything in good
order, the merchant having stored them carefully on the roof of
his house, well out of harm's way, for which I handsomely rewarded him   There was a good deal of snow in the Tekkes
Valley, showing that winter had begun in earnest in addition to
which it froze hard every day

I trekked on on the morning of the 28th, but having been
able to secure only four ponies I marched on with the original
animals half way across the valley, having previously despatched
Numgoon and Giyani to hire others, and I met them a few
miles out, so changed loads and proceeded on my way.

The Tekkes Valley is here about 25 miles wide and covered
with grass to an unlimited extent   The hills flanking the valley
on its northern confines are treeless and rounded and bear a
dismal aspect compared to those on the southern side.   There
was snow in patches right across the valley the air being keen
and sharp, though the climate generally was not of the same
rigorous nature I had experienced up in the valleys.

We forded the Tekkes River late in the afternoon, the width
being some 400 feet, and the depth and strength of the current
quite moderate   Earlier in the season this river would, of
course, be impassable, but we were now entering on winter,
whose icy grip had already reduced the flow of water in every
stream.

A mile or so on the northern side of the river I camped by
some Kalmuk auls, the population on the northern side of the
valley being largely composed of them   One of the auls was put
at my disposal, but I handed it over to the servants, preferring

290

my tent, where there was less likelihood of annexing an undesirable quantity of live-stock.

Numgoon consented to come on to Kulja with me; I had
found him a useful man, but Nurah accompanied me only as
far as these auls, where I paid him off the following morning,
and we parted the best of friends.

They are good fellows the Kalmuks, but I was right glad to
see the last of the Kazaks, though this later proved to be rather

"WE FORDED THE TEKKES RIVER."

premature since I was destined to renew my acquaintance with
them further north. The latter are lazy and stupid, and their
ignorance on anything and everything is positively crass. But
withal they never miss an opportunity to best the traveller, a
strong general point in the Oriental character. I had an
amusing instance of this on the Pamirs, where I gave a man 10
rupees for just handing my letters to the post runner as the
latter passed his yurt. The former's pay was 8 rupees per month,
his duty being to pass on the post from Kashgar. When he had

pocketed the rupees he informed me I owed him something for the hire of his pony, which had carried me three miles. This took the proverbial cake and I with difficulty refrained from kicking him.

I trekked again the next day north-east along the valley, the ground being hard and firm from the frost of the previous night. On the way I passed a caravan of merchants going down from Kulja to Aksu by way of the Muzart Pass,

"I CAMPED THE NIGHT BY SOME KALMUK AULS."

situated near the peak of Khan Tengri, and the regular route between Southern Chinese Turkistan and the Ili Valley of Northern Turkistan. This is the route I should have followed after leaving Aksu on the journey from India, but it was now too late to regret.

I again camped the night by some Kalmuk auls, and had the use of another yurt in which I dined by the side of a roaring fire of pine logs, provided by the owner. Fresh horses were forthcoming here, and the remaining ones belonging to the Kazaks went back to Agiass.

The new contingent were a great improvement on the Kazak transport, and all were loaded up and away by 9 o'clock the next morning The track lay due east for some miles and thence north through a narrow ravine to the Khanakai Pass over the Ala Tau Range of the Thian Shan and into the Ili Valley The descent on the northern side was quite easy, though I encountered a considerable amount of snow on the top of the pass and for three miles on the Ili side, but not in sufficient quantities to impede progress This latter part of the route led me frequently across the stream, now frozen solid, the path in consequence being very slippery. I camped by the stream some way down, being unable to reach any auls by the time darkness had set in. The ravine was narrow but fairly well wooded, so we were able to collect a quantity of firewood, for the temperature dropped considerably immediately after sundown, the night being bitterly cold

On the morning of October 31st I moved on into the Ili Valley, a vast plain stretching away east, west and north, and halted in a small village, where the only shopkeeper placed his house at my disposal and was more than kind and obliging to the stranger at his gate

A terrific wind was in full swing when I emerged from the hills, which made progress most unpleasant, the fall in the temperature occasioned thereby being more suited to regions within the Arctic circle than the broad valleys of Central Asia.

There were many chikor in the hills, and with the object of bagging a few I had gone ahead with Numgoon, as the ground, consisting of low hills and gravelly slopes, indicated excellent prospects. I managed to shoot several, not a bad performance for me considering my capabilities with a shot-gun

I spent the evening after dinner in my quarters making myself respectable for the morrow and the entry into Kulja, an operation the importance of which may be gauged by the fact that I had not had a shave for three months, that my clothes were worn and travel-stained, the *tout ensemble* resembling a bandit chief or the Pirate King.

Everyone in the village took a vast amount of interest in us, though we were not of a species entirely unknown to them, since Kulja has a small Russian population, the presence of which and the passing of sundry European travellers has made the natives more or less acquainted with the Occident The culinary department was full of the curious-minded, intent on learning whence I had come and what were my objects in journeying hither. The idea of one undergoing so much toil and tribulation for the sake of big game shooting was quite beyond them, and, judging from their expressions of incredulity, Rasul's representations on the subject must have caused much speculation in their untutored minds.

It rained, snowed, and blew hard during the night, with the result that there was a wretched outlook on the morning of November 1st. I had been successful in hiring fresh ponies in the village and started at 9 o'clock with Numgoon and another Kalmuk, leaving the baggage to follow in charge of Giyani and Rasul It was raining hard and the wind howled as I pushed on to the ferry over the Ili River, 12 miles down the valley, cantering most of the distance

I crossed the Ili in large, flat-bottomed boats, worked by horses which have to swim the river in the execution of the task, though how they manage to endure the intense cold would be a question difficult to answer One of the ferry horses was dead on the opposite bank, frozen stiff as a plank, a silent witness to this cruel work There was much water in the river despite the lateness of the season, and on reaching the Kulja bank we had some difficulty in off-loading the horses as the big boat could not be brought sufficiently close in to allow of the animals being disembarked on to dry land The consequence was they had to be taken out of the barge into the water and then ridden ashore, a proceeding occasioning much plunging and bucking on the part of refractory steeds The wretched ferry horses who had hauled us across presented a pitiable spectacle as they stood shivering in the wind, but then there is no S P C A in this far-away corner of the world

Arrival in Kulja.

I had sent on a note overnight to the British Aksakal in Kulja, asking him to kindly prepare a house for me. and, if possible, meet me outside the city. As there are two or three entrances to the city after one leaves the ferry we missed each other, so that Numgoon and I spent a considerable time riding about streets axle-deep in mud and slush, looking for the Aksakal. Whilst thus engaged a Russian Sart (native of Russian Turkistan) came up and enquired of Numgoon if I was the European traveller expected in Kulja, and, receiving an answer in the affirmative,

A MOSQUE IN KULJA.

conducted me to the house the Aksakal had engaged and then went to apprise the latter of my arrival. The appearance of this good Samaritan was very welcome, for riding about the streets of a Central Asian town in the month of November, through extensive quagmires of mud and filth, is distinctly uninteresting, and rendered the more so by the gaze and inquisitive attention of the inhabitants.

The house was the property of the man who had accosted us in the street, and my suite therein consisted of two rooms and a large kitchen The former were heated by means of the usual Russian stove, a brickwork structure let into the wall in one corner When the fuel within is reduced to red hot ashes and all the smoke has emerged from the outlet in the chimney, the latter is closed, the heat engendered thereby warming the apartment. It takes, however, some considerable time to attain this desirable stage, so I had a small iron stove fitted in my bedroom, in which I could put on a cheery blaze at short notice.

The kit arrived at four in the afternoon, and after paying off the transport, I settled down to a stay of some days in Kulja, a "stand easy" I should appreciate after months of wandering amongst the mountains, and the hard work necessitated during my shoot in the Thian Shan

Before proceeding further it will be well to give an account of the Ili Valley and Kulja, one of the most important sections of the great area we designate under the name of Central Asia

The land watered by the three rivers, Tekkes, Kunges and Kash, is known under the general appellation of Ili, and it may be regarded as the most fertile portion of this part of the Chinese Empire It is not referred to as the Ili until after the junction of the two head streams, the Tekkes and Kunges, the former of which rises in the main range of the Thian Shan east of Lake Issik Kul, and the latter in the Boro Khoro range to the north of the main chain of the Thian Shan The two rivers after union form the Ili, which latter then flows on to empty its waters into Lake Balkash, one of the largest lakes in Central Asia The entire country watered by these rivers is known as Ili, and its rich and fertile character, coupled with the vicissitudes through which it has passed, have rendered it a noteworthy province.

The history of the region in question takes us back to the days before the Christian era when a tribe known as the Usun, occupied the Ili Valley after engaging in unsuccessful warfare with the Huns in Mongolia As time passed on the power of the Usun increased, until the date when they encountered and suffered defeat at the hands of more powerful neighbours, which brought about their further migration in the fourth century of our era, when they fell under Turkish sway Following in their wake were the Uighurs, a tribe of Turkish origin, who were succeeded by the Kara Khidans, the latter in their turn being subdued by the Mongols in the 13th century under their famous leader Jenghiz Khan. The latter extended his conquests far and wide, embracing within their limits a large portion of the great Asiatic continent. At this period of its chequered career the Ili Valley comprised, in addition to the territory along the river, the province of Dzungaria, which at the close of the reign of Jenghiz Khan was in possession of three sections of the Mongol race, who founded an alliance and were known as " Oirat," a term signifying " confederates." The events following on this alliance, which was concluded towards the end of the 14th century, tended to consolidate great power in the hands of the Oirat, until the middle of the 15th century, when they overcame the Chinese in a desperate struggle that had been of long duration Soon after this event the power and fame of the Oirat began to decay and their influence became of little account

We now pass to the close of the 17th century, when internal strife caused sections of the confederacy to secede from the alliance Dzungaria at this time was the scene of constant warfare until the advent of a chief of one branch of the Oirat who secured the aid of China in his efforts to assume the sovereignty of Dzungaria, and, being successful, thought to establish himself there as an independent ruler This was contrary to Chinese intentions, and on his becoming discontented and raising the standard of rebellion against Celestial suzerainty he was completely defeated and fled to Russian territory in the year 1755 At this time Chinese power was at a high level, and the reigning Emperor had included within his dominions Eastern Chinese Turkistan and Kashgaria, and with the object of consolidating his hold upon Dzungaria put to the sword in the year 1756 the entire population, comprising some 600,000 souls. The total depopulation thus brought about necessitated other inhabitants being introduced, and the Chinese therefore despatched colonists of the criminal and other classes from Manchuria and the western provinces of China, and brought in numbers of people from Kashgaria, termed Taranchis The latter now form a considerable proportion of the population of the Ili Valley and its vicinity. With the object of safeguarding the country forts and military posts were erected, and the seat of government appointed at Ili, or Manchu Kulja, some distance west of the present town. In 1771 occurred the famous migration of the Kalmuks from the Volga in European Russia, who had removed thither at the time of the troubles amongst the Oirat, and of which mention has been made heretofore, to the country of Dzungaria in the hope of there finding independent settlement On arrival and finding they must submit to Chinese domination they took up their quarters in the Ili Valley and recognised the ruling power

As might have been expected from a country thus peopled internal dissension became rife and the Chinese had much difficulty in subduing the rebellions which broke out amongst the various sections of the population. This culminated in 1864 in an insurrection on the part of the Tungans, who captured the city of Urumchi and massacred 130,000 Chinese and Manchus. The Chinese army sent against the rebels was defeated, and later the Taranchis, uniting with the Tungans, carried on the revolution, killing large numbers of Chinese in the fighting which followed

In 1867 these two allies disagreed, and in a battle fought near Kulja the Tungans were defeated and their leader killed. The country was in a disturbed and lawless condition, and the internal strife and bloodshed resulting therefrom, induced Russia to occupy the territory with the object of restoring order, an occupation that took place in 1871.

The advent of Russia terminated the chaotic state of affairs, and ten years later, order having been established and tranquillity reigning in the land it was restored to China on the payment of a ransom and the cession of certain territory down the Ili Valley.

As I have already stated, the Ili Valley is possessed of considerable natural resources, and only needs judicious government for it to develop into a rich and thriving province. Iron and copper are found in payable quantities, whilst a dozen miles from Kulja coal mines exist from which the inhabitants obtain what is practically the only fuel in use in the country. Here again the methods employed to exploit the coal deposits leave much to be desired, so that the advent of proper machinery and the

THE ENTRANCE TO A CHINESE TEMPLE.

establishment of the mines on a sound working basis would bring increased prosperity to an industry requiring much stimulation on practical lines.

Kulja cannot be regarded as an important trading centre, what trade there is being mostly in the hands of Russian Sarts, and confined, in so far as the imports are concerned, to a variety of cloth goods of Russian manufacture, such as calicos, linens, handkerchiefs of gaudy hue, tea, leather, trinkets of indifferent quality, horses and sheep, and some other items of insufficient importance to warrant special mention.

With regard to exports, these comprise brick tea, oil mainly used for lamps and culinary purposes, paper, skins, grain, and, what is most deplorable, wapiti horns, in the exportation of which there is a considerable trade, for, as I have said, the Chinese regard them as possessed of medicinal properties, the result being the horns command high prices.

In the more settled portions of the Ili Valley one sees evidence of the rebellions which formerly reduced the country to a state of anarchy and barbarism, and appear to have permanently affected it, since the influx of emigrants has been small, the efforts to colonise the district meeting with but slight success notwithstanding special incentives to do so held out by the Chinese authorities.

The population of Ili consists of Sarts, Taranchis, Tungans, Chinese, Kalmuks, Kazaks and Kirghiz. The first are natives of Russian Central Asia, speaking the Turki language, and with manners and customs similar to the Kashgarians, of which an account has been given in a previous chapter.

The Taranchis owe their designation to their pursuit of agriculture, or sowers of millet, the term " taran " signifying millet. They were imported from Kashgaria in 1756 as part of the new population destined to fill the devastated territories of Dzungaria after the revolution

In religion they are Mohammedan, but this has been somewhat modified from association with the Chinese Their dress consists of the flowing robes affected by the Kashgarians, with the same top boot. The head is shaven and a fur cap worn, except by the mullahs or priests, who wear the large white turban

The women are dressed similarly to those of Kashgaria, but their caps are of a stiff, cylindrical pattern, some of them being beautifully embroidered, one now in my possession constituting a fine specimen of the needlewoman's art. They are not veiled as is customary with other Mohammedan races, and enjoy a considerable amount of liberty, playing an important part in household spheres

The dwellings of the Taranchis are usually on a better scale than those in Kashgaria, windows and furniture of Russian make being often seen

The Tungans are considered by some authorities on ethnography to have sprung from the Uighurs who were settled in Kansu and Shensi, two provinces of Western China, many centuries ago They assumed the Chinese language, manners and dress, but preserved the Mohammedan religion, of which they have ever been adherents, though perhaps not very strict ones

The Tungans were also brought into Ili at the time of the rebellion of 1756, and their occupations there are confined to agriculture and trade.

In stature the Tungans are slightly above the middle height, with high foreheads and prominent cheek bones, dark hair, and meagre beards The women assume Chinese dress, but do not enclose the feet as is customary amongst the Celestial ladies

On the whole the Tungans are superior to the Chinese, and are not addicted to the opium habit, though their morals as far as trade and administration are concerned are probably on much the same level as those of their rulers

As in the case of other parts of Chinese Turkistan the Chinese element in the population is a small one, being mainly confined to a few shopkeepers and the ruling and official classes The troops are, of course, Chinese, and the Governors and high officials Manchus.

Of the Kalmuks, Kazaks and Kirghiz mention has been already made, so that nothing further need be said here respecting them.

Having given a brief description of Ili, its history and inhabitants, we come to Kulja itself. the chief town and capital of the province It consists of two towns, Old and New Kulja, the former being the one in which I stayed, and the more important of the two, from the fact that it was the centre of the last Russian administration, and such distinction as it at present enjoys from the import and export trade.

New Kulja is situated some 20 miles further west, and is the seat of the Viceroy of Ili, who exercises jurisdiction over the nomad tribes of Kirghiz and Kalmuk, and is surrounded by numerous minor officials also residing there

Old Kulja is the residence of the Taotai and the local Governor, both of whom live within a walled city distinct from the Mohammedan one   Kulja is one of the four divisions into which Chinese Turkistan is divided, the head of the administration therefore being the Taotai above referred to   The duties of this official are difficult to define, but it may be said that he is mainly responsible for the general government of the division entrusted to his charge with certain modifications in regard to military affairs.   The Viceroy of Ili differs from him in that he exercises control over the Kalmuks and Kirghiz, his authority in this direction extending to the far north of the country, while he possesses the right to correspond direct with Pekin on affairs of state.   The nomad tribes recognise him as their ruler and administrator, and the post generally would appear to be of great importance.

There is little of interest in Kulja, it being similar in all respects to any other Central Asian town   The houses are built of mud and have flat roofs, all being single-storied, and architectural beauty is conspicuous by its absence   The shops and bazaars are mainly in the hands of Taranchis and Russian Sarts, whilst there are also a few owned by Russians, where one can obtain European goods and stores of a doubtful quality   The Taranchi bazaar is the best I have seen in the course of my travels in Turkistan, the majority of the shops being provided with counters, and supplied with Russian-made goods which find a ready sale   At the time of my visit only three of the shops in Kulja were owned and administered by Russians, but as there is a good opening for enterprising

302

tradesmen no doubt their numbers will be augmented in the near future.

The streets are wider than those of Yarkand and Kashgar, and not covered in by a matting roof. Sanitary conditions are non-existent, and the thoroughfares are in a lamentable condition of dirt and disrepair, the mud in many of them being axle deep,

A KULJA LADY.

which unhappy state of affairs is intensified during the rains, when entire streets are often practically impassable owing to the mud and slush in which teams sink deep and become bogged,

The local authorities are, of course, furnished with funds for the maintenance of the streets in decent order and repair, but the pain of parting is evidently too much for them.

The only buildings worthy of note in Kulja are the Taranchi and Tungan mosques, the former situated within the citadel, and the latter without. Both are of decided Chinese design, with the corners turned up as shown in the photograph, the Tungan

GATEWAY OF A TARANCHI MOSQUE.

mosque being surmounted with a fine minaret imparting to it a handsome appearance.

On the morning after my arrival in Kulja I called on the Russian Consul-General and remained to *déjeuner* with him and his wife. Neither of them spoke English, but the conversation,

which mainly centred on my journey and the sport I had enjoyed
in the Tekkes Valley, was conducted in French. The Consul
had been 13 years in Turkistan so was well acquainted with the
country

In the afternoon I went to call on some Belgian missionaries
living near the town, Messieurs Raemdonck and Steinmann,
who received me most hospitably. They have been many years
in the country and form part of the China Inland Mission, but
as to whether their efforts to convert the heathen in this part of
the world meet with any tangible success is difficult to say. The
number of converts at present in Kulja is only 80 so that it
must indeed be uphill work for the good fathers

I stayed to supper with them, a simple meal, served in semi-
Chinese style by a Chinese servant, after which we smoked and
they imparted the news of the world, and I then drove back to
my quarters.

The next day, November 3rd, I called on the Taotai, whose
yamen is situated within the walled city He is a Manchu and
an official of high rank, and at the moment of my visit was wearing
a very fine ermine coat The little square table in the centre
of the reception room was spread with sweetmeats and
Russian cigarettes, whilst tea and a brand of Russian wine
was served, the latter of which I found to be quite good. The
conversation was confined to general topics, the Taotai being
much interested on hearing I had bagged two wapiti, enquiring
as to the length of the horns, evidently thinking I should turn
them into medicine on my return to Europe, despite my assurances to the contrary.

From the Taotai's yamen I went on to the Shingwan, or
Police Magistrate, a local Governor, who talked volubly, and
displayed a keen interest in my wanderings, though he, too, shared
the Taotai's views and could not understand why one should
endure much discomfort when there was no money to be made
out of it

Both these good people had, of course, sent their cards with the usual profuse compliments prior to my call, and the day after my visit weighed in with their presents—sheep, a sack of rice, one of oats, a good half ton of coal filling a cart, and other articles sufficient to stock a shop, to say nothing of a couple of bottles of champagne to which I did more than ample justice Evidently they know how to do the thing in Kulja.

The following day the Taotai, Shingwan, and Russian Consul-General returned my call The Taotai arrived at 10 o'clock with a retinue of armed retainers, and men bearing drums, banners and emblems in quantities sufficient to fit out a theatrical pageant I had arranged my large sitting room in suitable style, and the table groaned under sweetmeats and delicacies procured from the Russian shops in the neighbourhood, or brought with me from Kashmir and India One of the Secretaries at the Russian Consulate, to whom I had been introduced by the Consul, acted as interpreter, so that on this occasion my remarks were conveyed with greater speed and accuracy than is the case when made through the medium of a native interpreter Later the Shingwan put in an appearance, when the same ceremonies were gone through as with the Taotai

The Russian Consul-General arrived in a fine carriage, escorted by many Cossacks, and the uniform he wore and the martial appearance of his *entourage,* gave quite a brilliant colour to the otherwise sombre surroundings of my dwelling He was very kind and obliging, and later in the day sent round his Aksakal to take my orders and assist me in any way I might require

I decided to send off all my trophies by road from Kulja to the railway, and in the course of conversation with the Consul concerning the matter he informed me this would be feasible, and that there was a transport agency at Djarkend, a town some 35 miles beyond the Russo-Chinese frontier, on the way to Tashkend. The Consul arranged to take over the case of trophies from me and despatch them to Djarkend, for delivery to the agency who would then forward it to Irkutsk, there to await my arrival, whence I intended to take it on with me to Pekin,

Shanghai and India. I therefore set Numgoon to work sewing up all the heads in skins with an outer covering of felt, and they were then packed in a long case securely bound round with supports and iron bands, and rendered strong enough to withstand the great amount of knocking about it would receive before reaching the Trans-Siberian Railway. The route thereto lay through Djarkend and Vierny, and thence north to Sergiopol and Semipalatinsk to Omsk, a total distance of over 1,000 miles, entirely done by cart and sledge.

GATEWAY OF THE CHINESE CITY IN KULJA.

In the packing of trophies it should be remembered by those who may in the future visit the Thian Shan that all horns, and those of ibex especially, should be sewn up in the skin of the animals and then bound with felt, the inner covering of skin preventing the horns cracking, which I was assured they are liable to do unless so prepared. Mine were all done in this way, and when unpacked in London found to be in excellent condition, largely due to the care Numgoon displayed in Kulja.

When I was in Kashgar Captain Shuttleworth had warned me about this, citing as an instance that of some horns obtained in the Thian Shan which had not been properly sewn up in skins, and consequently had cracked to a considerable extent

On November 4th I called on the Captain Commanding the Consular escort, and stayed to lunch with him and his wife He was unable to speak English or French so my Secretary friend again filled the *rôle* of interpreter Both the Captain and his wife were very kind and hospitable, doing much to make my stay in Kulja a pleasant one

The Consular escort consisted of 80 men of the 1st Siberian Regiment of Cossacks, and though their outward appearance left much to be desired, the manner in which they managed their rough ponies was deserving of high commendation Owing to the state of the weather parades were not being held at the time of my visit so I had no opportunity of seeing them engaged in their regular exercises

At one of the gateways of the Chinese city a striking example of the drastic methods adopted by Celestial justiciars was afforded There were two malefactors, incorrigible thieves it appeared, who had become notorious and a source of considerable trouble in the city To obviate a continuance of their practices and prevent their moving about their ankles had been slit, a knife having been thrust through and the tendon cut. Thus they were crippled for life, and an effectual stop put to their evil doing, a warning not likely to be without its effect on other would-be malefactors

One evening Karovin and I went to dine with the Belgian missionaries, and spent a very pleasant time. After leaving their hospitable company we had to make our way in black darkness through the unlighted streets, proceeding with great caution to avoid being engulfed in deep and evil-smelling ditches, cess-pools, and other pitfalls so prominent in Chinese streets. Karovin was well acquainted with the topography of the town, so he went ahead to act as guide and pilot me through the maze of dirt and squalor. The only persons about were the Chinese night watchmen who now and again challenged us, to which Karovin replied. These watchmen carried a rattle which they kept sounding with the object of warning off the evil doer, and when I explained to one of these guardians of the peace, through Karovin, that we ordered things differently in England, the main object in our policemen's manœuvres being to secure those engaged in felonious pursuits, he only laughed and said it was preferable to make a noise and frighten the criminal away rather than be troubled with him and perhaps come off second best So saying he passed on, giving the rattle an extra loud turn to emphasise his views on the subject

I gave a dinner to the missionaries, and with some of the champagne presented to me by the Chinese officials and a couple of bottles of port I managed to buy in the town, it had quite a *dîner de gala* air about it We discussed most subjects, and from them I learnt a good deal, for there are probably no more intelligent observers in all Turkistan.

I also dined several times with the Cossack Captain, and he insisted on my lunching with them the day of my departure from Kulja. He had also returned my call in full uniform when I first arrived in Kulja, and appeared a fine looking figure, in the becoming dress of the Siberian Cossacks, with an Astrakhan hat of large dimensions. He was a very strict disciplinarian, and whilst I was in Kulja punished two of his men for being found intoxicated in the bazaars by an award of five hours' pack drill per day for two weeks. This must have caused them to think a little and ponder on the respective merits and demerits of having a spree when such deserts awaited them

During my stay in the town one of the Russian Aksakals, of whom there are three, was about to celebrate the marriage of his daughter, and Karovin took me to the house in order that we might view the preparations for the happy event The Aksakal's residence stood in its own grounds and was enclosed by a wall, with a large entrance gate in front On the roof of a shed at one end of the courtyard a native Turkistan band screeched forth discordant music, which had nothing to recommend it, since there was no variation in the tune, the same thing being rendered over and over again, doubtless, of course, to the delight of the guests, but worthy of being prosecuted for creating a public nuisance from the European point of view. The instruments comprised native guitars, flutes and tom-toms, the latter

THE GOVERNOR OF KULJA RETURNS MY CALL.

being banged enthusiastically on the principle of more noise more melody.

In front of the house were two tables on which strings of copper money were deposited, these being presents to the Aksakal from his numerous friends. Though the copper cash of China represents a small amount the mountains of it on those tables must have totalled up to quite a respectable sum.

The marriage was not to take place until three days later, and all the entertainments and revels then in progress were merely a preliminary canter to which the wedding day would bear no comparison. The band was the most energetic set of musicians I have ever encountered, and they commenced operations every morning soon after daybreak, continuing uninterruptedly till the evening, and without any of those intervals for refreshment so noticeable with European bandsmen.

CHAPTER XVII

Through Dzungaria towards Chuguchak

I now had to settle the details of the onward march of the expedition to the Altai and the Trans-Siberian Railway, a long and difficult trek at this season of the year with the entire country already within the icy grip of winter. I therefore decided to leave Kulja on November 12th and proceed through the Sairam Nor and Ebi Nor country due north to Chuguchak. From there I wished to strike eastwards into Mongolia and across the Black Irtish Valley to the Great Altai Mountains, thence northwards to the railway

During my stay in Kulja I had engaged the services of a Yarkandi boy, Yusuf by name. He had expressed a keen desire to accompany me and so I installed him as assistant to Rasul Yusuf hailed from Yarkand, whither he had migrated with his father a few years before. The latter had died in Kulja, and so Yusuf was left alone in the world. Before entering my service he had been employed in a Chinese restaurant, but ministering to the wants of Celestial epicures had not appealed to him, so, quitting it, decided to follow my fortunes into the unknown and learn something of the world beyond.

Rasul had agreed to accompany me as far as Kobdo in Mongolia, whence there is a caravan route which would take him back southwards to his home on the Kashgarian side of the Thian Shan. I had intended buying my own transport in Kulja, but the Aksakal and other authorities on the subject considered it far better to hire along the line of route, as at this season of the year no ponies would outlast the severe marching necessitated in covering the great distance between Kulja and the Altai

I was assured I should be able to engage ponies from place to place without difficulty, and thus be in a position to move with greater celerity than would otherwise be the case I therefore arranged for sufficient ponies to accompany me as far as the Borotala River, which flows through the country lying between the Sairam and Ebi Nor Lakes to the north-east of Kulja and distant five marches therefrom

On the morning of the 12th I sent off the kit and then went to lunch with the Cossack Captain Krepotchikov. I had engaged a tarantass with three horses, and with Giyani on the box and several tinkling bells on the troika, sailed forth accompanied by many shouts from the cheery Cossacks. It is 46 versts from Kulja to Suidun by a fair road, as the latter go in Chinese dominions, though it would scarcely bear comparison with the London to Brighton coach road, but then it was, of course, Chinese, and when one has said that one has said everything.

I arrived at Suidun at 9 o'clock that night and had some difficulty in gaining admittance to the town as the gates were closed and everyone had gone home. It was only by the most vigorous banging and thumping on the gate that I finally brought some sleepy Chinese on the scene, who proceeded to open up under protest

Three miles south of Suidun is the new town, where resides the Viceroy of Ili, the important personage I have already mentioned, who apparently to maintain the dignity of his position requires a town of his own.

In the morning I visited the Chinese quarter, as usual, distinct from the Taranchi City and surrounded by a high wall, to see one of the Belgian missionaries who has charge of this part of the diocese. He very kindly offered to put me up, so I accordingly had the baggage moved round to his place

Father Schidmt's house was a Chinese structure, with a central hall opening off on either hand into apartments, and a raised dais at the far end, on which one slept I occupied the room on the left of the hall, a stove being placed therein, so that I was most comfortably lodged

The main object of my halt in Suidun was to procure a special passport from the Chang Jung, or Viceroy of Ili, to enable me to proceed through the wild country of the Sairam Nor and Ebi Nor Lakes, and the region to the north thereof   The great man was, at the time of my visit, indisposed, and therefore unable to receive me, but the passport was duly prepared and sent over with his compliments   It was a gorgeous document, 41 by 22 inches, covered with figures of lions and tigers and strange dragons, the text being in Manchu and Chinese, so if this formidable instrument would not impress the native then I failed to see what would.

I called on the various Chinese officials in Suidun and received ceremonial visits in return.   They were much interested in the journey onward to the Trans-Siberian Railway, but, in common with other Celestials I had met before them, one's coming so far for the sake of sport was an inexplicable problem, and they could not understand why one should undergo so much when there was no monetary benefit accruing, their views in this respect coinciding with those of the Kulja Amban

The Officer Commanding the troops at Suidun also enquired if I converted the horns into medicine, this, according to his view, being the only possible use to which the trophies could be put, and being obviously dissatisfied with my reply asked if I had been sent into this distant land of mountains and shikar to learn how to shoot!   This was the limit in questions, even for a Chinese one.

Father Schidmt acted as interpreter for me, his knowledge of the Chinese language having been acquired from a residence of many years in Turkistan.   The hospitable father wore Chinese dress and lived in the Celestial style, and was very assiduous in his attentions to the colony of converts he had established. There was a Chinese boys' school behind our quarters and from the roof of the house we occasionally watched them at their drills, conducted on the Swedish model

A Land of Corruption.

There is little of interest to see in Suidun, the Chinese city containing nothing worthy of note, the houses being of the usual flat-roofed type, and the Chinese shops adorned in front with many signboards covered with strange hieroglyphics.

The general state of dirt and decay was indicative of the need for reform in the system of administration, which is the root of all the evil. In this land of sin and corruption everyone robs and

A STREET IN SUIDUN.

cheats, and those who are not past masters at the art of bribing stand no chance in the competition for posts. There is the case of a certain Amban of a large city whose defalcations were something enormous, he having, amongst other things, maintained a force of 500 men on his books as the strength of the local garrison, and continued to draw pay, rations and equipment for this number, when in reality he kept but 42. This lasted for 12 years, at the end of which time he must have been passing rich, but it was

not sufficient for a Chinaman   In the end matters reached such
a stage he was dismissed and sent to offer explanations to the
Governor-General   This must have been effected to their mutual
satisfaction for he is now back again in his former post.

At Suidun I was informed that shortly before my arrival the
Amban in Charge of the troops had been directed from Pekin to
submit a report on the musketry training of those under his
command   He therefore paraded the garrison in the courtyard
of his Yamen, where the gallant soldiery blazed off their ammunition in the air, the while his Excellency sat down and smoked
the pipe of peace   At the close of this instructive course of
training the latest thing in musketry returns went in and an
indent for more ammunition !

The country north of Suidun through Borotala, and past the
great Ebi Nor to Chuguchak is more or less uninhabited, with the
exception of the nomad Kazaks, who are found in the sheltered
valleys to the north of the Ebi Nor   It therefore became necessary to lay in a stock of stores and provisions to suffice until I
should reach Chuguchak, since there would be nothing obtainable
in the interim   These consisted of vegetables, tea, sugar, rice,
dried fruits, and various other articles together with Turkistan
bread made of white flour, which, when hard, makes good eating
and can be carried great distances without deterioration

Everything having been satisfactorily arranged I left Suidun
on November 17th, and marched 15 miles to Lutsukou   The
Chinese and Russian roads run together for the first four miles
when they branch off, the former continuing on past Lake Sairam
and eastward to Urumchi, Hami and Pekin, the latter to Khargos,
on the Russo-Chinese frontier, Vierny and Tashkend   The
Chinese road, the one I followed as far as the Sairam Nor, is in
a fair state of repair, and there are karauls, or guard houses at
intervals, where the small escort accompanying one is changed

I put up in a small house outside the village of Lutsakou,
and in the evening sallied forth to look for duck, of which there
was said to be a few on some ponds near by.   I discovered duck

there but they were very wary, in addition to which the sheets of water were fringed with tall rushes preventing one seeing much. Whilst manœuvring round one of the ponds, hoping for a shot as the duck rose, I noticed a Chinaman directly opposite carrying a murderous looking weapon. This he was

A GATEWAY NEAR THE SAIRAM NOR.

preparing to loose off, for me a timely discovery and one that obviated the chances of my receiving the charge of shot and shell from his ancient fowling piece instead of the duck.

Whilst the caravan was busy loading up the following morning I went over to watch some Chinese cavalry engaged in riding

317

and other exercises on the plain near the house. There were 18 cavaliers under the command of an officer, and the parade was distinctly an original one. They each galloped in turn along a trench about 3 feet deep and 4½ feet wide, firing at three little mud targets placed on the parapet at intervals of 120 yards. The majority of these gallant cavalrymen were too busy hanging on to their mounts to trouble about shooting straight   They contented themselves with blazing away yards beyond the target, doubtless hoping to get out of it alive   Some of them did not fire at all at the first target, which amused the Officer Commanding immensely, he apparently regarding the morning's work as a huge joke, and the mere fact of no one scoring a hit did not seem to worry him in the least   The performance having terminated they formed up and rode away, with colours and banners flying and all the panoply of war, well satisfied with the result of the day's labours, no checking of targets, cleaning of rifles, or any such essential details troubling them.   Military training in Chinese Turkistan is obviously conducted on original lines

Eight miles beyond Lutsakou the road enters the hills and then runs through a narrow valley to the village of Atai, beyond which I camped the night   It was bitterly cold, with a keen searching wind that did not improve matters, but we were lucky to discover a quantity of logs cut for purposes of bridge building, with which we made quite a respectable fire, although as it was freezing hard, life in the open was not enviable.

On the 19th I continued up the ravine to the Talki Pass on the northern side of which lies the Lake of Sairam Nor   The ascent from Atai began at once, leading through the cleft in the hills, crossing and re-crossing the river a number of times by substantial bridges of Chinese construction.   The mountains now bore a desolate and cheerless aspect, the profusion of foliage and vegetation which in summer clothes their sides having been all cut down by the frost and severe cold, the only note of colour being the dark and sombre pines   Half-way up the defile I passed a Chinese guard-house, the occupants of which were probably hibernating for the winter since not a soul was visible

Beyond this point the road assumes a steeper gradient until I reached the top of the Talki Pass, at an altitude of about 8,000 feet. Beneath the summit of the "dawan" lies the Sairam Nor, a vast sheet of blue water about 20 miles long by 15 broad, and surrounded by high mountains, the view of snowy peaks in Russian Turkistan to the north-west being magnificent The water of the lake is brackish and therefore undrinkable, and fish are also said to be unknown in it, but it is marvellously clear and one can see to a considerable depth. The banks slope away precipitously from the water's edge, giving rise to the belief that the lake is of immense depth I saw several duck, but without a boat it would be hopeless trying to do anything amongst them. Just below the pass, on the southern shore of the lake, is another Chinese fort, garrisoned by a few unhappy soldiers, whose existence in this cold and windy spot must indeed be a dull and cheerless one

The road follows the southern shore of the lake to Santai, situated at the eastern extremity, a small village with a serai, in the courtyard of which we camped

A march east of Santai there were reputed to be gazelle in great numbers, the Chinese term them "hwang yang," or yellow sheep, and I think they are a near relation of the Yarkand Gazelle (*Gazella subgutturosa yarcandensis*). I therefore sent on part of the caravan north-east through the hills to the Borotala River, and went myself with Numgoon, Giyani and one servant to endeavour to bag a specimen of the gazelle, thence intending to cut through the hills to Borotala

We started on the 20th, along the main road, the Imperial route to Pekin, and over which trade from Central China is conducted This trade probably assumes fair proportions for on the way we met a caravan of 180 camels going down to Kulja laden with tea and other commodities.

I put up in the serai at the tiny hamlet of Setai, 20 miles east, where there were only a few Chinese, deep-dyed scoundrels, one of whom, an old rascal, black with the dirt of ages, tried to swindle me heavily over some grass for the ponies, by demanding a price that would have purchased a haystack But I had travelled too far to be so easily done Unfortunately he could only speak Chinese so that all my polite language was lost upon him

I found numbers of gazelle round Setai, but the ground is quite bare and open, merely a stony plain with withered grass here and there, affording no cover whatever for stalking

This gazelle is much akin to the Indian Chinkara (*Gazella bennetti*), only from my experience the average horn measurement does not exceed 10 inches It is of a slightly different species to those found in Southern Turkistan and exceedingly difficult to stalk I found it hopeless trying to get near enough for a shot, as they begin jumping when one is a good 400 to 500 yards off

I was after them again on the 21st, and must have encountered 50 or 60 during the course of the day, but the stalking was a hard proposition I had two long shots, but missed each time I should much like to have secured a specimen of the gazelle, but in two days one could not expect to do much Probably had I remained a little longer 1 might have secured one by a fluke, for I could see no other way of doing it, taking into consideration their extreme wariness and the difficult nature of the ground they inhabit

I could not afford any more time in their pursuit so reluctantly packed up on the 22nd, and, striking across the wide and stony valley, marched through the Borokhoro Hills on the northern side of which flows the Borotala River

The Borokhoro are barren mountains, rock and gravel strewn, with here and there wormwood and low-stunted scrub in the ravines and narrow valleys by which they are intersected. On the northern side of the range the road debouches on to an immense plain stretching away to the Borotala River and the mountains in Russian Turkistan to the north-west I followed the track across this plain for several miles, trying unsuccessfully to stalk some "jeran," or gazelle, on the way, until reaching the Borotala River, on the other side of which there is a settlement of Kalmuks and Taranchis The ford through the river was quite passable, for at this season of the year all the streams contained little water.

I found the rest of the caravan installed in a house prepared for my reception, an attention that was all the more welcome by reason of the bitter cold without. The majority of the people here were Kalmuks, the head man in charge of the district being also a Kalmuk, acting under the orders of the Chang Jung at Suidun He called on me and I arranged for the hire of fresh transport in accordance with the orders contained in the formidable looking document the Viceroy had furnisht . me with All details being satisfactorily settled I decided t' move again the next day and north-east to the great Ebi Nor Lake

I had heard from various sources of a variety of argali of the great Argali sheep of Central Asia existing in the hills to the north of the Ebi Nor, so with the object of testing the information determined to devote a few days in the hope of securing what is undoubtedly an undetermined species

I was also informed at Borotala that ibex roamed the hills bordering on Russian Turkistan to the north-west, but little information was available as to their numbers and size of horns, none of the Kalmuks having apparently ever shot them, so I deemed it scarcely worth while going off the line of my route on what might have easily proved a wild goose chase

On the morning of November 23rd I started out from Borotala, taking a direction north-east across the plain, entering some low undulating country 12 miles further on The sheep ground was said to be east of this on the shores of the mighty Ebi Nor, and a Kalmuk shikari I had picked up in Borotala informed me he had often encountered them there. It did not, however, impress me as being wild sheep ground at all, as the hills were very low, only rising some 50 to 100 feet above the level of the plain, and not at all indicative of their haunts

After a march of 18 miles I reached a karaul where there was a small post of Mongol soldiers, put there as the outward and visible sign of Chinese occupancy. These men were armed with old-fashioned guns, dirt and rust eaten, but they were a jolly set of people and presented me with a sheep, besides assisting to pitch camp

The Mongols inhabiting this part of Asia, so far removed beyond the pale of civilisation, are primitive to a degree, paying no attention to the outer world and the mighty questions convulsing it Their astonishment at my kit was great, for they told me they had never seen such articles before, and the production of patent camp furniture and cooking appliances completely passed their understanding

I started on the morning of November 24th for the argali ground, accompanied by the Mongol shikari and a man from the karaul. Our way led through low lying hills covered with stunted scrub and wormwood. From the ridges of these hills one could get a good idea of the surrounding country which resembles a sea of rounded knolls of an average height of 50 to 100 feet, intersected by little valleys, ravines and open stretches There was scarcely any grass, the surface of the hills being strewn with rock and gravel I camped some 12 miles out in the bed of an ancient stream which in days gone by must have been a large waterway but was now merely a stony level covered sparsely with brushwood to a height of three or four feet.

In the late afternoon I went out in the hope of seeing some of the sheep, and did, to my considerable surprise, come across a very fair ram. During the march that day we had not seen tracks nor any sign whatever that they were in the neighbourhood, so I consequently had begun to think their existence was a phantom one.

I Encounter Wild Horses.

I followed up the ram in question, but the ground was very low, only averaging some 50 to 70 feet above the general level, and intersected by innumerable little valleys and ravines, so that locating the quarry was extremely difficult work.

That the sheep exist there is no doubt, although their numbers must be quite small. The ram sighted was with two ewes, and his horns would have measured about 35 inches,

"THEIR ASTONISHMENT AT MY KIT WAS GREAT."

the tips coming close in at the lower jaw and then turning slightly outwards. The thickness at the base and along the horns did not appear large, and the bulk of the ram was much below that of the sheep I had shot in the Thian Shan, averaging perhaps 36 inches at the shoulder.

I was away the next morning before 8 o'clock, being mounted as the ground admitted of the use of ponies. Moreover the locality I was to try that day lay some distance to the north-east, hard by the shores of the Ebi Nor.

The route lay through an undulating country covered with gravel and withered grass, and from the summit of some high

ground a mile or more from camp I obtained a fine view of the
Ebi Nor Lake, which is about 40 miles long and of an average
breadth of 25 miles The shores to the south and west are flat
and covered in places with a salty deposit From the distance
the lake had the appearance of a vast inland sea

I had a long round that day but only saw three ewes, so
the sheep are evidently very rare The entire country bore a
deserted and desolate aspect, and the array of gravel-strewn
hills, bare of any foliage, gave one the impression of being at the
ends of the earth, to which the Ebi Nor, lying a few miles away,
a tremendous stretch of water disappearing into the east, lent
additional colour

The country on the northern shores of this great lake contains
wild horses and Gindan, my shikari, informed me we should see
some, but that to get into close touch with them would be a
matter of great difficulty, as the animals were exceedingly shy
and wary and would take to instant flight on scenting the least
danger.

The wild horse was first discovered in Mongolia by the
famous Russian explorer Prejevalski, after whom it is named
(*Equus prejevalski*) Those I encountered stood some 13
hands and carried shaggy coats and long manes; they
appeared eminently suitable for a strenuous life in these barren
lands where the scanty vegetation would reduce other and less
hardy animals to starvation I found it impossible to get nearer
than 450 yards, or thereabouts, for their powers of scent and
hearing are developed to a remarkable extent.

In the afternoon I tried fresh ground to the west in search of
argali, but there was no sign of life though we scoured the
country for miles around

On returning to camp and a consultation with the shikari,
I realised that to bag a specimen of the sheep would necessitate my devoting more time than I could now afford I
was still many hundreds of miles distant from the Altai, and
the closing in of winter warned me that to hope for a chance

at the *Ovis ammon,* I should have to trek on with all possible speed.

I therefore decided to move the next day and work through the sheep country, which would in the evening bring me to the western shores of the Ebi Nor, where I hoped to find the rest of my caravan.

It froze hard during the night but was warmer on the morning of the 26th, so I started off through the hills, sending the baggage by a more direct route, but all we came across were some old horns, one pair measuring 40 inches, which Gindan assured me

· THE EBI NOR LAKE, WHERE I FOUND WILD HORSES.

was a good head. From here we worked on through innumerable little valleys and ravines, the country being much broken, a sea of hillocks, all with the same desolate appearance, on the eastern side of which we debouched on to the shores of the Ebi Nor Lake, and then marched round to its western extremity where I found the caravan had already arrived, having secured fresh ponies.

The Mongols called this part of the district Kizil Tus, and its principal characteristics were flat stretches covered with long grass in the central parts, and boggy and swampy near the lake shores.

To the north of camp were ranges of mountains, part of the Ala Tau system, whilst to the south were the undulating hills through which I had marched during the day The plain on which the tents were pitched stretched away to the west into Russian territory, and to the east lay the lake, its still waters unbroken by a single ripple

My camp was not far from the Russo-Chinese frontier, and the Mongols informed me the country around was infested with robbers and raiders of all descriptions , in this respect resembling our own North-west frontier of India where battle, murder and sudden death are of all too frequent occurrence

The bandits of the Ebi Nor region come over from Russian territory, rob any passing caravan, and then return across the frontier whither the Mongol levies cannot follow them A few days prior to my arrival in this lawless spot, two unfortunate merchants returning from a bartering journey amongst the nomad tribes to the north, had been waylaid and robbed of their goods and chattels, their throats being cut by the raiders who had then disappeared across the border. I therefore had my battery ready, and should not have hesitated to use it had these gentry attempted anything upon us, as I was informed they would endeavour to do

The entire country from the Sairam Nor to Chuguchak is full of horse thieves and raiders since the route, as stated, lying along the frontier, enables them to indulge their raiding propensities practically unchecked

The night I encamped at Kizil Tus two Kazaks joined me from the Borotala saying they wished to proceed two marches further north, where the tribe to which they belonged were established for winter quarters, but were chary of doing so alone owing to the disturbed nature of the country I was not quite sure that they were all they represented themselves to be, and for aught I knew might well have been in league with the rogues and rascals of the neighbourhood I however decided to risk that, feeling sure of being able to hold my own in case of trouble, so acceded to their request to be allowed to accompany me

A Desolate March.

I struck camp at Kizil Tus early on the morning of the 27th, and marched north-east across the plain, the grass thereon being now withered and dry. Six miles took me into low undulating country, a land of desolation, gravel and sand covered. Some miles beyond this undulating country the track leads into a more enclosed country, occasionally open ravines and again narrow rocky ones devoid of vegetation, with only scant brushwood in places.

There were reported to be Kazak encampments in the hills to the north, and the two Kazaks with me stated I could reach there in one day but that it would necessitate a long march.

"TWO KAZAKS JOINED ME FROM THE BOROTALA."

I continued on all day through a monotonous land comprising bare rock-strewn ravines with intermittent open stretches covered with a meagre showing of coarse grass.

At 7 o'clock, as we were still apparently a long way from the Kazak encampment and it was already pitch dark, the nights closing now at five, I halted in a rocky ravine and pitched camp. The cold was intense and everything frozen hard, so that the cow dung fire, of which commodity we had brought a certain quantity from the last camp, did not contribute much towards a cheery blaze, though we made the best of it and were passably jolly under the circumstances.

I was accompanied by an escort of Mongol soldiers who were responsible for my well-being, and before leaving Kizil Tus in the morning I had despatched Rasul ahead, with two of these worthies and another man, giving him orders to locate the Kazak encampment and hire fresh horses from the Zung, or head man ; this would enable me to move on to Chuguchak with all possible haste, as provided with relays of horses one can march much further than would otherwise be the case

I always found the Kalmuks, and usually the Kazaks, very willing to supply horses, as they did well out of it, both in cash and presents, and moreover I was armed with the passport from the Viceroy which the nomads would hardly dare to ignore.

There was no water obtainable here so we improvised a sufficient quantity by boiling some snow in the kettle, but it took a most exasperating time to get hot over the cow dung fire, at which Giyani and I worked with unremitting attention. We none of us obtained much sleep that night for the thermometer was several degrees below zero, and a nasty cold wind howling through the ravine nearly reduced us to the state of mummies, despite unlimited blankets and " razais "

I was glad to get away the following morning before 8 o'clock, the route lying through a further succession of rocky ravines of an average height of 200 feet Three or four miles out I crossed a long open plateau, and descended on the far side into a fairly broad valley bare of trees but with a greater showing of grass than in the country previously traversed Here I found a number of Kazak auls, and arriving near them some of the inhabitants came riding over to see us. From them I enquired as to the whereabouts of Rasul, but as none of them had apparently seen him, he had no doubt gone elsewhere All these men were clothed in furs, with fur caps reaching down over the nape of the neck and the ears, and affording excellent protection from the rigours of the Northern winter They told me there were more auls further up the valley, so I decided to push on, and at 4 o'clock in the afternoon reached them, but there was no sign of Rasul or his party, so I began to get anxious and sent men off in search of him

I had an aul brought down to cook in, which also served as a dining room, as it was too cold in the tent. This aul was carried down by all the old ladies and girls in the place, their ages varying

328

from fifteen to fifty, a band as merry as the famous Wives of Windsor.

There was a fair supply here of camel and horse dung, so that Giyani was able to initiate quite a respectable fire, though the pungent fumes at times almost drove me forth into the frosty night.

After dinner, a very smoky affair, I spent the evening in writing up my diary and commencing a long letter to a

A MONGOL KARAUL.

brother officer which I hoped to despatch from Chuguchak. It took some time to thaw out the ink, though it had been carefully packed away in one of the yak dans, and at intervals in writing I had to pause and warm my hands over the dung fire, as they were simply numb from the intense cold, which must be experienced to be adequately realised.

CHAPTER XVIII.

In Chuguchak, Western Mongolia

THE country I was now marching through, and which continues up to Chuguchak, several days' journey to the north, is a most desolate land, nothing but low rocky hills, without a sign of bush or grass, or a stick to light a fire.

I was much impressed with the dreariness and entire absence of life here, not a bird, not an animal, nothing to temper the sensation of loneliness and utter desolation The silence of these vast solitudes is indeed oppressive, and in November, when the land lies locked in the grip of an inexorable winter, the feeling of loneliness is accentuated. One only occasionally meets with auls of the nomad tribesmen, who during the winter are more or less stationary, preferring then to remain settled rather than endure the hardship and privation entailed in moving about.

The days were rapidly closing in now, and the moment the sun disappeared beneath the horizon the temperature would go down with a run, whilst frequently at dusk the bitter cold wind, instead of subsiding, would continue with unabated vigour throughout the night

It is indeed a bleak and inhospitable land, and during November and December, when I was marching through it, a snow-covered wilderness, across which the wind shrieks and howls as it only can on the steppes of Central Asia

There were said to be no argali here, and, judging from the appearance of the country, it certainly looked anything but a happy hunting ground

I was obliged to halt for a day on November 29th as I could still obtain no news of Rasul, and could not imagine where he had gone I did not suspect foul play as he was accompanied by two of the levies, and the Kazaks, though a distinctly lawless set of people, would hardly dare to molest him, seeing I possessed written authorities from the Viceroy and other high officials which would certainly cause stringent enquiries to be instituted should anything untoward occur The Chinese are slow at the best of times, but once the wheels of justice are set moving the results are inclined to be a little indiscriminate, a possible eventuality of which the nomads were doubtless well aware

I sent off two more of the levies during the day with a mission to try and discover Rasul, but I had reason to believe they merely went to the next group of auls and sat tight until the evening, when they returned with the report that no trace could be found of the missing ones I was not certain that they had not gone forth properly as instructed, but my suspicions were based on good grounds, though, not wishing to upset them in any way, I wisely refrained from making any observations on the subject, and reserved any sarcastic remarks for a later date

There was nothing to do during the day, so to prevent myself becoming stiff and frozen, I strolled forth with a sack and collected fuel, the *bois de vache* as it is known in Switzerland, a lively occupation for a mighty hunter !

On the morning of November 30th, as there was still no sign of Rasul, I decided to go on with the same lot of horses at any rate as far as Yamatu, which is situated on the main road running from Urumchi to Chuguchak, and the route by which communication is maintained with the northern part of Dzungaria and Chinese Turkistan. There, should Rasul not have by that time rejoined me, I intended conducting a search, leaving the caravan to await my return

Yamatu lay in a north-easterly direction through the low-lying hills, though the exact track thereto was unknown to any of us, so it became necessary to obtain a guide, which, after an immense amount of trouble, I succeeded in doing, engaging the services of a young Kazak who professed to know the road

It was nearly noon before I got away, and after travelling a few miles the guide informed me he wished to return to his aul, as he was not acquainted with the topography of the country. This was nothing more than I had expected, but was determined he should not leave me in the lurch, so compelled him to come on and I marched till 6 o'clock when I camped in a sheltered dip in the hills. Soon after snow began to fall, so, making a square of the kit, we collected all the cow dung fuel available and proceeded to ignite it, not at all a cheerful pastime, as a strong wind was in full swing, and this, coupled with the falling snow and the low temperature, made it difficult to get the fire started. If one really wishes to taste of the sweets of life one should try lighting a cow dung fire in a snowstorm. It is a most exhilarating pastime, how exhilarating only the initiated know!

It continued snowing steadily throughout the night, and when I awoke next morning there were several inches on the ground. The Kazak guide had decamped and got clear away, which he must have done some hours previously, for there was no trace of his horse's tracks in the snow. It was foolish of him not to play straight with me, as it would have been entirely to his advantage, and I should have rewarded him handsomely for his trouble in piloting me through this hopeless land. But, of course, he was a Kazak, and one could not expect anything better from a representative of this race. I had thought to have seen the last of the Kazaks in the Thian Shan as they are a very undesirable tribe, and though I saw and came a great deal in contact with them during my shoot in Ili and the Tekkes Valley I did not note many redeeming features in their characters.

We had considerable difficulty that morning, the first day of December, in loading up the baggage, as the ropes were all frozen solid and our hands were so numbed with the cold that it was consequently a long drawn out operation.

Soon after I had started Rasul appeared in the distance and in a few minutes came up saying he had been searching

all over the country, and that finally the head man of the
Kazaks had found him and indicated the road I had taken. It
appeared Rasul and the two levies had gone to another encampment of Kazaks to the west of the one I had encountered, and had
arranged for fresh ponies which the Kazaks were willing to supply.
Rasul had there awaited my arrival, but not seeing anything of us
the next day had sent off one of the levies to ascertain our whereabouts. This man came back and reported he could learn nothing,

ACROSS THE WIND-SWEPT PLAINS OF MONGOLIA.

so that Rasul, much perturbed, had then started off himself
with the two soldiers and scoured the country, finally meeting the
head man who told him the direction of my march.

Yamatu is a tiny settlement on the main road and consists
of a guard-house and a few forlorn Chinese soldiery, a serai, and
half-a-dozen mud huts wherein dwell the only inhabitants of the
place beyond the military element. By main road one no doubt

conjures up imaginations of the Grand Trunk in India or the great Continental *chaussées*. But no, it is not so at all. On the contrary it is real Chinese and an example of the earliest word in road construction

There is a telegraph line connecting Urumchi and Shikho with Chuguchak, but it is an indifferent one. The poles are of all heights and the wire is sometimes carried on the top of them and anon lower down, the relative positions no doubt depending on the amount of energy the constructors felt capable of exerting at the time the wire was put up. Still, the fact of it being there at all is something of which the Celestial may justly be proud, for he cannot by the widest stretch of imagination be considered an up-to-date creature The wire is very slack in places, so much so that one can easily touch it when on horseback. Soon after leaving Yamatu I passed one of the poles lying on the ground, it having been evidently uprooted by the wind, with the result that the wire there was dangerously taut, though no one seemed to object and it would probably be spring before the Celest al operators worried their heads about attending to its repair. No reasonable man would expect them to turn out in such weather to raise a fallen pole !

As there was an hour or two of daylight when we reached Yamatu I went on to another settlement called Thul, 10 miles further north, and was lucky enough to get quarters in the serai in the shape of a small room boasting a stove. Giyani filled the latter with wood and very nearly burnt me out, but I nevertheless enjoyed it after the cheerless bivouacs of the past few days

The morning of December 2nd dawned black and forbidding, thick clouds rolling across the skies and giving every indication of unsettled weather At 9 o'clock I set out in a biting wind and heavy snowstorm which, however, moderated a trifle towards noon On the way I passed the ruins of a village, the mud huts presenting a dreary aspect with the roofs falling in and walls crumbling, due to the ravages of time. No one knew the cause of its

334

abandonment, which must have occurred many years before judging from appearances.

Soon after, as the wind blew with renewed vigour, I was glad to take refuge in a filthy Chinese inn at the little village of Sari Khulsin, where I had at any rate the satisfaction of being sheltered from the fury of the elements and the driving snow

The inn consisted of a central courtyard with rooms along the four sides, evil-smelling dens fit only to be compared to the Black Hole of Calcutta. My room was on the northern face of the courtyard, entrance to it being gained by a door of ancient make on creaky hinges, and through a narrow central hall The interior of the room was in complete darkness, as the one opening in the wall had been covered with paper to prevent the snow blowing in A few holes thrust through this improvised shutter admitted a limited quantity of light, enabling me to see across the room On one side was the " kang," or raised sleeping place, built of mud and stones, with the upper surface smoothed off and the interior hollow to admit of a fire From its appearance the room had not been occupied for months, and needed the attentions of a broom to divest it of some of its undesirable accumulation of filth I tried lighting a fire but it was not a success, for the fumes from the damp wood created dense volumes of smoke which put even Giyani's lungs to a severe test.

I trekked again the next day away from this Chamber of Horrors, across the plain to the north-west, not following the direct road running to Kurte and Durbuljin but striking across country to Chuguchak by way of the Emil River.

The country here is a vast depression in the surrounding mountain ranges, and lies at a low elevation, Sari Khulsin being about 1,200 feet above sea level. To the north stretch the snowy range of the Tarbagatai, whilst to the east the broad valley continues, being shut in on the south by the Urkashar Range, which joins the outlying spurs of the Saur Mountains

The country to the west is open and resembles an immense rolling plain, and hills to the southward constitute its limit in this direction. I marched across the plain encountering occasional encampments of nomads who came to stare at the stranger from the unknown, and satisfy their unbounded curiosity as to what we could be I forded a small stream *en route* a branch of the Emil River, which was not quite frozen over, the central portion, where the current was swift, being clear of ice.

Six miles further on I crossed the Emil River itself, here about 30 yards broad and with a moderate current, the depth of the water reaching to the horses' knees. This river rises in the Tarbagatai range to the north-east of Chuguchak, and flows westward through Chinese territory to Lake Sassik Kul, into which it empties its waters, a total distance of about 170 miles

On the north side of the Emil River is situated a small hamlet called Setar, now in ruins and long since deserted, the causes of which I endeavoured to ascertain but could gather no information on the subject. Just beyond the ruins I met some herdsmen driving in flocks of sheep and cattle to their auls for the night, and they told me of the existence of another village further on which could be reached by nightfall I therefore pushed on, despatching Rasul ahead with one of the Kalmuks to secure a suitable house in the village and prepare it for us.

It was freezing hard and very cold work riding, so when 5 o'clock brought pitch darkness, and no sign of house or aul, I began to think we should never reach there at all We, however, struggled on, shouting at intervals in the hope of getting a response to indicate the presence of habitations We continued on till half-past seven, and then heard distant shouts in reply to our own stentorian calls. Presently Rasul loomed up in the darkness and piloted us to a Chinese hut in which he had secured a small room and another for cooking in, or rather sharing the same kitchen with the inmates Mine had a stove in it and a stack of dried cowdung in one corner so there was no lack of fuel The owner of the hut was a Chinaman who evidently regarded me as a perambulating bank by demanding, when we packed up the next morning, a price for our night's lodging worthy of a West End hostelry. However, as my ideas on the subject differed considerably from his, the little *coup* did not succeed.

The Chinese met with in this part of the Celestial Empire are of a low class, a large proportion being of the criminal caste and

THE GREAT GATE OF CHUGUCHAK.

those who have been ejected from China proper to settle in Turkistan where their presence is less likely to be a public danger than in civilised parts. It is the same with the soldiery who are sent into Turkistan to form the garrisons of the different towns, the majority being enlisted from the scum of the bazaars and the sweepings of gaols, and sent out to do duty in distant provinces of the Empire. The higher officials are, of course, in the

337   z

majority of cases, Manchus and Chinese of high rank, but with the lower classes it is quite different

I had sent Rasul on in the early morning to Chuguchak to make arrangements for quarters in the town and to convey my caid to the Chinese Governor with the passports, which one has to do on arrival in a town.

I went ahead of the caravan with Giyani the next morning and arrived outside the walls of Chuguchak at mid-day

Chuguchak stands on a level plain at the foot of the Tarbagatai Mountains, here rising to a height of 3,000 feet. The Russian Consul had despatched a mounted orderly to meet me, an individual wearing a big white fur cap and a sword like unto the two-handed weapon of Richard Cœur de Lion. The Chinese Governor had also sent a retainer to convey his respects and good wishes and welcome me in his name to the capital, as is the custom in this land. Rasul was with these people, and, thus escorted, I rode on through the great gate of the city to the Sart quarter, where I found two rooms prepared for me in a house belonging to a native of Russian Turkistan. The latter was more or less civilised, in fact almost a Russian, his dwelling being furnished in the Russian style and bearing quite a pleasant aspect. He and his wife, a young lady of ample proportions, I found to be hospitable people, unlike the ordinary Sart, and most attentive to one's wants and creature comforts

Chuguchak lies within 12 miles of the Russo-Chinese frontier, and is a fortified town of some importance From it routes lead north-west to Sergiopol and Semipalatinsk in Russian territory, and northward across the Tarbagatai Range to Zaisan, near the great Lake Zaisan, as also eastward into Mongolia, the Altai Mountains and Kobdo. The population has increased considerably of recent years owing to the more settled state of the country, the establishment of a telegraph line and the construction of a road connecting it with Urumchi and the Ili country. The town is in many respects superior to Kulja and the cities of Kashgaria, the streets being wider and cleaner, and bridges,

338

wherever they are required, being substantially built and maintained in good order. Compared with Aksu and Kulja the walls of the city are also in a passable state of repair, and do not display the same tumble-down aspect one notices so much in Southern Chinese Turkistan.

There is a fair trade in cloth goods and other manufactures of a similar nature, the majority coming from Russia, there being a Russian custom-house at Bakhti, on the frontier, presided over

THE GOVERNOR OF TARBAGATAI AND HIS STAFF.

by an official charged with the supervision of all imports introduced. A very considerable trade is carried on in brick tea; indeed it forms one of the chief imports into Mongolia from China proper.

The day after arrival I donned my uniform and drove in a tarantass, accompanied by Giyani and others, to call on the Tchja, or Military Governor of Tarbagatai who resides in a spacious Yamen and has a number of well-dressed retainers.

On reaching the official residence the great gates were thrown open and I marched through lines of uniformed retainers to the end of the inner courtyard where the Tchja was waiting to receive me. We then passed into the reception room, comfortably furnished in semi-European style, with armchairs, settees, tables and other articles of Western furniture. The conversation was conducted in Turki and Hindustani, the Tchja being well acquainted with the former tongue, a pleasant surprise after my experiences of former Ambans and the laborious methods of interpretation necessitated by their ignorance of the language. The Tchja astonished me by his geographical knowledge, acquired during journeys made to Moscow and St. Petersburg and over the Trans-Siberian Railway, whilst he was also looking forward to visiting the Continent and England. The conversation centred mostly on my expedition and the route ahead, the Tchja stating he would provide me with a special passport in Chinese, Mongol and Turki, so that I should have no difficulty on the road. He expressed the hope that I would often visit him during my stay as he was fond of European society and had not met many English before.

From the yamen I proceeded to call on the Russian Consul, who is charged with the task of safeguarding the interests of the Russian colony in Tarbagatai and to foster trade between the two Empires.

The Consulate stands in its own grounds and is a large building painted white, the interior being well furnished, with a number of Chinese ornaments distributed about the rooms. The Vice-Consul was at the time in charge, and he received me hospitably, inviting me to dine with him every day during my stay in Chuguchak. The appearance of his young wife, dressed in a dainty Parisian costume, was a revelation to me after months of wandering amongst shaggy and unkempt nomads. The chief of the Russian Customs on the frontier was also present at dinner that day, but, as he could only speak Russian, conversation with him was not very animated.

M Loutchitch, the Vice-Consul, informed me the route through the Altai, Mongolia, Kobdo, Uliassutai and Kiakhta to Irkutsk was an exceedingly hard one in winter, and doubted my being able to follow it owing to the severity of the cold on the Mongolian steppes. The alternative route, and the one I might have to follow, lay through Siberia and presented less physical difficulties than the other

On the 6th the Tchja returned my call, arriving in a smart tarantass with a Russian coachman in cocked hat, and a host of mounted retainers bearing the various flags and banners emblematical of his greatness I received the Tchja at the entrance to my apartments and ushered him in. Tea was served, and we then proceeded to discuss my journey and the sport I had enjoyed in the Thian Shan as well as the projected route across the Mongolian steppes. I was much impressed with the general knowledge displayed by the Tchja, and his unfeigned admiration of things European, which indicated a marked desire to come more into touch with Western civilisation

He announced his intention of giving a dinner in my honour on the 8th, and also desired to show me a wapiti stag, and a red bear, in the Yamen grounds, which invitation I cordially accepted

Soon after the Tchja's departure the Huei Tai (Officer Commanding the garrison) and the Ti-fang-wan (an official in charge of municipal affairs) arrived   The latter was an old man and had been 30 years in Turkistan, being formerly stationed in Yarkand and Kashgar, so was acquainted with the country I had passed through, that is as much as one can expect Chinese officials to be with the land committed to their charge. He was bent with age, and did not do much beyond putting an occasional question, preferring to smoke his pipe in silence, doubtless pondering on the motives which prompted my being on the trek at this season of the year

My other visitor, the Hsei Tai, had been 34 years in Chinese Turkistan, and possessed the reputation of being a proper and honest person, certainly rare qualities in this wayward land   I afterwards heard he was not on good terms with the Tchja, which was, however, not the case with the old Ti-fang-wan, who was rather a favourite, probably on account of his quiet and inoffensive manner

At the conclusion of these visits I went off to dine with Loutchitch, and stayed there till seven in the evening, much enjoying his genial company   He was a Chinese scholar of no mean order, and through his instrumentality I was enabled to purchase some hand-painted glass snuff bottles, several ancient scrolls, and a number of hand-painted pictures of flowers containing quotations from the ancient Chinese classics. I also acquired a number of figures worked in silk and some pictures on silk paper representing scenes from Chinese life

On December 7th I returned the calls of the Hsei Tai and the Ti-fang-wan, and Shingwan, in their respective Yamens, being regaled with tea, sweetmeats and the usual polite conversation, always a strong feature at ceremonies of this kind   After these visits I drove through the bazaars and was much struck with the superior aspect of the place and the air of thriving importance it bore, a state of affairs no doubt largely due to its approximation to the Russian frontier

At noon three of the leading merchants, Russian subjects, called to pay their respects   The principal one was engaged in the skin trade, and at his invitation I visited his shop where he showed me large numbers of fine sable and other skins being prepared for exportation to European Russia.

When these people had departed the Russian Consul came to return my call, arriving in full uniform, seated in a smart tarantass escorted by Cossacks, the whole making a very brilliant show, well calculated to impress the crowds in the bazaars with the might and power of the great White Czar   The Consul was kind enough to apologise for not having called before due to a case, on which he was engaged, taking up much of his time

At 2 o'clock I drove to the Consulate to dinner, spending a

pleasant afternoon there   We discussed various topics, Loutchitch relating some good stories of his experiences in China.

On December 8th I dined with the Tchja, the banquet taking place in one of the reception rooms at the Yamen, and timed for 12 o'clock   Loutchitch was already there when I arrived, as well as the Chinese guests, of whom there were about a dozen We had a preliminary conversation during which tea was served, and the Tchja showed some fine maps of the Chinese Empire and Siberia he had obtained from Russia

We then adjourned to inspect the private zoological gardens, which comprised a full grown Altai wapiti stag, a red bear and one or two other animals, as well as a number of excellent Siberian, Chinese and Manchurian ponies, of which our host was justly proud.   He pressed me to accept the wapiti as a present, an offering I declined with many thanks, though I should like to have tendered it to the Zoological Society had not the expense of transportation been prohibitive

At dinner the customary delicacies gracing a Chinese table were served, including roast sucking pig, sharks' fins, sea slugs, stewed celery, stags' tendons, duck's brains, ligaments, and eggs preserved in chalk, the latter distinguished by their age and antiquity, from which standpoint their edibility is regarded by Chinese *gourmets*   There were a great variety of other dishes, and, as I had the honour of being the principal guest, I was assailed with snacks from them all by my hosts who desired to show their unremitting attention, the acme of Celestial polite- ness   The salads made of radishes and cucumbers were ex- tremely good, in fact the cooking of all the dishes left nothing to be desired, although the ingredients of which they are composed in many cases severely tries one, so that the ordeal is not altogether an unmixed blessing

During dinner the Tchja was particularly gracious and charming, asking many questions concerning England, which country he seemed very desirous of visiting   He informed me he had arranged a dinner and duck shoot to take place at a mill outside the city on the 10th, and I accepted the invitation, expressing my sincere thanks through Loutchitch. After dinner tea was served and then the Tchja saw us off, the Consul making a fine show in his tarantass with a number of outriders in white fur caps and long blue coats

I spent the next day in looking round the town and the Russian colony, the latter of growing proportions, owing to the facilities for trade which accrue from the situation of Chuguchak. There were a number of Chinese soldiers in the bazaars, armed with old and rusty weapons, the manipulation of which must be an art difficult of acquirement   Some of them carried smooth bore rifles, suffering from the same complaint   They reminded me of a story Krepotchikov had told me in Kulja regarding his experiences of the Chinese Tommy Atkins   Information had reached Kulja that a force of 40 Chinese soldiers was then congregated on the Russo-Chinese frontier to the north-west of Kulja   With the object of ascertaining their motives the Cossack Captain had been sent up there with a detachment of his men. The Chinese were, it appears, in pursuit of some robbers who had escaped across the border, and carried firearms, one of which Krepotchikov examined and found to be loaded. On drawing the owner's attention to the fact the latter coolly explained that six months before, whilst out on the plains, he had sighted a fox and had endeavoured to secure it, but the fox having other views gave him no chance. The operation of unloading had escaped his memory until reminded of it by the Cossack Captain examining the rifle out of curiosity, which showed their neglect in the care of arms

On the 10th the great duck shoot and dinner at the mill took place, to which, besides myself, the Russian officials and the leading Chinese residents had been invited   I drove thither in my tarantass, accompanied by Giyani, and armed with gun and cartridges   The entertainment was well organised except that there were no duck, which however, did not seem to unduly worry the host   We first of all assembled in a large log hut at the mill tastefully decorated and furnished for the occasion so that it bore quite a gala air. There wines and liqueurs were served, this I assuming to be preliminary to the duck battue. After the drinking of healths and all the guests had arrived, a move was made to inspect the mill, the duck being apparently quite a secondary consideration. This accomplished the Tchja suggested we might go down to the river and look for duck, so we proceeded thither in carriages and on

GUESTS AT THE SHOOTING PARTY.

horseback, a distance of half a mile. But the duck had evidently taken a day off, for none were visible, so the host with the benign smile of satisfaction said we would return and shoot the dinner, a suggestion meeting with the cordial approval of the Russian guests to whom a well-laden table was more congenial than chasing duck on a cold December day.

The dinner was not a purely Celestial one but a mixture of Russian and Chinese, the result being rather pleasing, while the wines which accompanied it were of good quality, all the best brands obtainable in the town being displayed on the festive board. This was a very comforting item in the day's programme, and the absence of the evil-smelling Chinese brandy, the memories of which were still fresh within my mind, gave rise to much inward satisfaction.

The wife of the Russian Consul was also amongst the guests and looked very becoming in the Caucasian Cossack dress, consisting of a long scarlet robe reaching to the knees and fastened at the waist with a girdle, with places across the breast for cartridges Top boots, a large white fur cap and a riding whip completed this warrior costume, the whole giving the wearer a distinctly martial air and bearing

Another important guest at the feast was the Tchja's young and prepossessing daughter attended by a diminutive Chinese maid The lady's feet were not encased and disfigured as is the custom with Chinese women. Amongst the Manchus this practice does not obtain, and their women are thus able to walk with ease and grace instead of hobbling along on stumps as is the case with the unfortunate Chinese ladies

During an interval in the dinner I took a photograph of the assembled guests, and after further parley, the drinking of many healths and the pledging of each other, we dispersed, some driving back in Russian carriages and others proceeding *à cheval.*

CHAPTER XIX

ACROSS THE MONGOLIAN STEPPES

WHILST in Chuguchak I settled the details in connection with the route to the Great Altai Mountains and onwards through Mongolia It had been my intention, when I set out from India, to proceed from the Thian Shan, through Dzungaria and Mongolia, to the Altai, which I hoped to cross north of the Black Irtish Valley and thence get down on to the Ammon ground, situated on the northern slopes of the mountains in question The exact geographical position of the region for which I was now heading lies between the Russian frontier at Kosh Agach and the main chain of the Altai

It was in Chuguchak that I first began to realise great difficulty would be experienced in carrying out this programme in its entirety. As to whether the passes over the Altai were practicable at this season of the year no precise information could be obtained, but all agreed it would be an undertaking attended by the gravest danger, and meet with certain disaster if attempted I, however, determined to essay the task since the main object of the expedition was centred on the Altai, and the hopes of being successful in bagging some specimens of the grand sheep who there has his home were sufficient incentives to me to push on in spite of heavy odds From the Ammon ground I purposed proceeding east to Kobdo, Uliassutai and Urga, and thence northward to Kiakhta and Irkutsk, and so to Pekin, Shanghai and India

The day after the dinner I called at the Russian Consulate to get my Russian passport *viséed*, as the official regulations on the subject require that all travellers entering the Russian

Empire from Chinese territory shall have the *visée* of the Consulate nearest to the frontier. I also obtained a passport for Giyani enabling him to enter Russian territory, without which he would have been detained by the authorities

The Tchja had detailed two Kalmuks to accompany me as far as the Kesil Bach Lake, nine days' journey to the east, in Western Mongolia, also providing me with a special passport for the country under his jurisdiction, so I set forth from Chuguchak on the morning of December 12th, the baggage having preceded me earlier in the day I sent a note to the Russian Consul to thank him again for his kindness and hospitality during my stay and then rode on through the city and out by the great gate I took the road lying to the north, intending to follow this along beneath the Tarbagatai Range The country here is a vast plain stretching away for 50 miles to the east, where the mountains then close in, and the path then lies through the latter until the more open country round the Mongol settlement of Wong is reached two days' journey west of the Kesil Bach Lake Fortunately the weather was fine, but sharp and cold, all the streams being frozen solid.

Along the main road running from Chuguchak to Durbuljin are habitations at intervals, but this route was to the south of the one I was on That I traversed was a flat and dreary plain, the grass brown and withered, with no sign of bush or tree throughout all its desolate extent

I pushed on for 18 miles, crossing many streams running down from the Tarbagatai Mountains to the north, all frozen firm and smooth, on which the ponies slipped and blundered in lamentable fashion. I camped at a Chinese peasant's hut, the owner placing one of his two rooms at my disposal, in which I rigged up a stove bought in Chuguchak, one of the best investments I had ever made. The room set aside for my occupation had a large window of lattice work, pasted over with sheets of paper, but full of holes, and to such an extent that it resembled life in an air shaft The door was large and ponderous, likewise having a plethora of holes and cracks, through which a couple of cats bounded at intervals, chasing each other round and round presumably to get warm and prevent themselves being mummified into frozen examples of the feline race.

Despite the fact that I had the stove going there were 31 degrees of frost in my room, and as I discussed my frugal dinner I thought of cheerier places to pass the night in. The servants shared the other room with the proprietor, and were also provided with a stove; but there was no outlet for the smoke which would have stifled an army of bees. Giyani was making

A HALT ON THE MONGOLIAN STEPPES.

desperate efforts to open an ancient window and lessen the evil, in which he finally succeeded. It was too cold to write so I retired to bed and read Boswell's " Life of Johnson," trying to imagine I, too, was in the more congenial neighbourhood of Piccadilly and the Strand.

On awaking next morning I peeped forth into the gloom, the air being keen and the thermometer at 15 degrees below zero to still further temper the atmosphere. Yusuf came in soon after and set the stove going, but even at its best we could not bring the thermometer higher than something below the freezing point.

I dressed thinking of pleasanter occupations than a trek across Asia in December, and wondering what it would be like in the dreary month of January. We loaded up the baggage and started at 9 o'clock across the same desolate plain, with nothing to relieve the monotony beyond the occasional passing of a frozen stream, across which it was a work of art getting the ponies.

At mid-day I halted to adjust the loads and give the animals a rest near the ruins of a deserted village. What had caused its abandonment no one could tell, but Bháta, the Mongol Beg who accompanied me, said the country around was lawless, and that in former years bandits and freebooters infested the neighbourhood, robbing passing caravans and terrorising the district to such an extent that the inhabitants lived in a state of constant dread, never knowing when they might be raided and their property and cattle stolen.

I camped the night in another Chinese hut forming part of a tiny settlement, the only sign of human habitation we had seen that day. The occupants were not of the usual type of surly Chinese one finds in this distant corner, but on the contrary received us cordially and placed a room at my disposal. In the latter was a gigantic tub full of cabbage in the process of being pickled, but being frozen solid it was not actively offensive. The room possessed a stove and as there was a supply of cow-dung, the only fuel in use here, I was passably comfortable.

The owner of the hut was an old Chinaman who had lived here for many years, and was in consequence fairly well acquainted with the district bordering on his home. He could not understand why I should be marching through the country at this season of the year, a question I found sufficiently difficult to answer myself, he adding that the Chinese practically slept all through the winter, only sallying forth when necessary, preferring the warmth of bed and blankets to the Arctic rigour without, in which they showed a certain amount of wisdom.

The land I was now passing through consisted of gravel soil, covered with a scanty crop of short grass, and not affording any

pasturage worthy of mention. The aspect of the country is a
desolate and inhospitable one, as indeed is that of all the steppes
of Central Asia and Mongolia.

On December 14th I resumed the trek, continuing over a
country which gradually assumed a more undulating character,
and towards noon led us into low hills, bare and now shorn of
whatever grass they might possess in the summer months. The
Kazak guides accompanying me were not sure of the proper
route so I decided to march due east, a route leading us through
a succession of rounded hills to a Kazak encampment. The

"I HALTED NEAR THE RUINS OF A DESERTED VILLAGE."

occupants came out to stare at us, as usual, and to wonder
what could induce my being on the move in such weather.
They were a wild ill-mannered crowd of nomads, some fifty
in number, and their felt auls were enclosed in walls of reed
and brushwood brought from great distances to serve as a shelter
against the winds which rage in this part of the world as they
probably do in no other.

All the nomads remain stationary during the winter months
and their dwellings are constructed on the same principle as the one

above described, whilst those who inhabit a wooded country build log huts for occupation during the winter, for even the best of auls cannot keep out the terrific cold The danger does not, however, lie in the rise or fall of the thermometer, but in the searching wind which knows no obstacle and spares no man. The mere fact of the temperature sinking to 30 and 40 degrees below zero is not in itself a great hardship. It is when accompanied by the cruel and relentless winds that constitute it an element against which all efforts are futile

The Kazaks informed me there was a karaul of Mongol soldiers some distance to the east, which I should encounter on my way, so in order not to miss it I pressed in two unwilling souls to act as guides and pilot us thither.

I crossed a low range of hills and then followed the course of a river, which the Kazaks called the Ulungkoi, until late in the afternoon The hills to the north were rounded and undulating, those to the south being more rugged and serrated, forming the outlying spurs of the Tarbagatai, while the width of the valley was some four miles

At 5 o'clock it was quite dark, and one of the Kazak guides told me the karaul lay to the south so I started off in that direction to search for it I might have known that the karaul was probably a phantom one, and that it was asking too much to expect a Kazak to tell the truth It was freezing hard, so that wandering about over the bleak steppe at night looking for karauls was not at all to my liking When we finally brought up in a sheltered dip of the hills I decided to camp the night there, and gave orders accordingly

There was a small stream close by from which, after breaking the ice, we were able to get water for tea. The Kazak guide had vanished in the darkness, having succeeded in stranding us in the unknown, but we made the best of it though I think the night was certainly one of the coldest I have ever spent. There was a good deal of stunted scrub, and I amused myself by igniting it and producing temporary warmth, by which the caravan was enabled to thaw itself out   The pony men had a number of sheep-skins and fur coats in which they enveloped themselves, all huddled together in a gigantic heap, an enclosure none stirred from till break of dawn, and it was tolerably hard work inducing them to do so even then

In summer it might be passably interesting to trek through this country, but under winter conditions, and in the teeth of the wind for which Mongolia is noted, is decidedly uninviting What inducements it might hold out to the sportsman during summer I am unable to say, but in December it is certainly a land to avoid, with its total absence of wood, and a wind I imagine that must resemble those blizzards down at the South Pole.

The light of after experience has demonstrated to me the impossibility of including the Pamirs, the Thian Shan, and the Great Altai Mountains in one's shooting programme when restricted to twelve months, and then going on to the Trans-Siberian Railway

As I have shown in the preceding pages the best season to visit the Pamirs is June and July, at the close of which period one can move to the Thian Shan and reach the wapiti and ibex ground at the right time, which, in the case of the stag, is September, and the ibex the latter part of August and October At the conclusion of one's shoot in the Thian Shan the first signs of winter have already appeared, and the distance lying between the latter mountains and the Great Altai render it a task of great difficulty reaching there in time for the *Ovis ammon* before the weather renders it a matter of impossibility.   One must, therefore, winter *en route*, either in Kulja or in Chuguchak, the former for preference since there is more to do and see though perhaps that is not saying much   To endeavour, therefore, to carry out the full programme in the limited space of twelve months is out of the question, as the cold weather renders travelling an undertaking of great hardship coupled with the fact that one cannot shoot during the Mongolian winter, as, apart from the intense cold, the depth of snow effectually bars all movement

Across the Roof of the World

When I looked out on the morning of the 15th it was bitterly cold, while the remains of last night's tea were frozen into a solid block in the kettle standing by the fire Breakfast was an icy affair, after discussing which I lighted the small bushes and grass around the camp to warm us all a little The ponies presented a picture of abject misery, being simply perished in the cold, their still forms, silhouetted against the sky, betraying no sign of life

Loading up was always our worst task as the night's frost reduces everything to a state of rigidity and makes the work a trebly hard one Every piece of metal seared the hands if touched, so it was always necessary to halt some distance out and re-adjust loads and tighten the ropes, which we then were better able to do, since the temperature was less Arctic than in the early morning.

My route that day lay through the undulating hill country due east till nearly noon, when I turned south-east, in the direction of a karaul said to be situated in the hills These karauls are established along the frontier line and at some distance from it as the outward and visible sign of Celestial occupancy, and are held by a few Mongol levies armed with weapons ancient and rusty The karauls are merely a collection of two or three auls in a sheltered position in the hills, the levies being occupied with their flocks during the summer months and remaining stationary throughout the winter I was glad to reach the karaul in the evening, for a biting wind had set in soon after marching that morning and increased in force as the day wore on

The karaul lay in a sheltered side ravine hard by the Russian frontier, on the southern slopes of the Saur Mountains, wherein is found a specimen of the wild sheep of Central Asia This range here forms the dividing line between the two Empires, and at this particular point runs to a height of about 5,000 feet There were four auls at this karaul, with a strong contingent of dogs, the inhabitants being Mongols, a cheery, interesting race of people They prepared one of the auls for me,

354

and when installed therein I was as comfortable as could reasonably be expected under the circumstances

During the night the wind abated considerably, and the morning of December 16th dawned fine and bright I rewarded the Mongol inhabitants for their hospitality to us, and then set forth again through the same low hills for three miles, whence I turned east and continued along a narrow valley to the summit of a small dawan This was crowned by a cairn, to which my Mongols added a few stones, I following suit, much to their delight They said it would bring luck, a commodity I was willing to go to any lengths to obtain

There was a long and gradual descent through a narrow valley bordered by low rounded hills, which impressed me as being good wild sheep ground, and the Mongol soldiers who accompanied me stated sheep were certainly to be found there, but in limited numbers The argali, according to their account, existed in the Saur Mountains to the north, though the best places, they said, were within the limits of Russian jurisdiction Eight or nine miles up this valley I reached another karaul, halting there for a frugal lunch and to take on fresh guides to a post said to be about twelve miles across the plains to the east

From the karaul the route lay through the hills for a mile and then led down on to a stony plain with mountains to the north and south at a distance of ten or eleven miles To-day's march was destined to be one of the longest I had done since leaving Kulja, for the next karaul was at a much greater distance than I had imagined.

Away across the stony plain I again struck undulating country, a rolling prairie, of seemingly boundless extent When the shades of darkness closed in and I was still as far off as ever I began to foresee the possibilities of another night in the open without fuel for a fire, or indeed any such luxuries. After several hours of forging ahead, numbed in the piercing wind, and unable to see more than a few yards ahead, we heard the distant barking of dogs, a sound that was as music to the ears, and the sweetest that can greet the traveller when trekking across the bleak and arid steppes of Mongolia. We pushed on in that direction and soon reached the karaul, situated on the far side of a tiny hillock and completely walled in by a palisading of brushwood as a protection against the bitter winds. This karaul was similar in size to the one I had passed the night before, and had a force of six Mongols stationed there.

Soon after I had arrived Bhata came into my aul stating that as I was only a day's march from Wong it would be better for him and Rasul to go on ahead in the early morning and give the young Mongol chief notice of my coming, to which proposition I agreed. Rasul and he therefore started the following morning at 5 o'clock, taking with them my Chinese passports. I left later, striking across the plain, which was stony with a scant display of grass.

Away to the north and south were ranges of mountains, whilst to the east the plain stretched away like a limitless ocean. I had never passed through a more desolate and uninteresting country, its whole aspect oppresses one with its bleak and arid wastes, no trees to lend a touch of colour to the scene, no bright foliage to charm the eye after days of rock and gravel, nothing but the same seemingly endless wilderness, and the silence of the vast prairies which, when not swept by Arctic blasts, are unbroken by a single sound and undisturbed by the note of a single bird.

Towards 3 o'clock I came in sight of Wong, the Mongol settlement, and shortly after Bhata, and a number of Lamas and other Mongols came riding out to meet and conduct me to a hut they had prepared for my occupation.

CHAPTER XX.

From Wong to the Kesil Bach Lake.

Wong—two marches to the west of the Kesil Bach Lake—is the principal settlement and residence of the chief of this part of Western Mongolia. The latter is a young man of 24, living in a hut of wood and plaster.

Mongolia forms part of the Chinese Empire and is bounded on the east by Manchuria, on the south by Chinese Turkistan

LAMAS AT WONG WHO CAME OUT TO MEET THE EXPEDITION.

and China proper, and on the west and north by Siberia. Its area exceeds 1,250,000 square miles, the greater part comprising barren and sterile land, of which the desert of Gobi or Shamo is the best known.

Across the Roof of the World

North-western Mongolia is mountainous, and included amongst its ranges is the Great Altai, one of the principal mountain chains of Asia It stretches eastward along the northern side of the Gobi Desert and westward into Siberia Gold is mined to some extent within its limits, and indications of auriferous wealth are much in evidence .

The climate of Mongolia is noted for its extremes of temperature, ranging from great heat in the summer to intense cold in the winter, and accompanied by terrific storms of wind, rendering life on the steppes one of great hardship It is, however, dry and invigorating, a fact largely responsible for the hardy race of nomads who constitute the population. No precise estimate of the numbers inhabiting the country is available, but it probably does not exceed one and a half million

The Mongols are of average height, with flat features, high and prominent cheek bones, and almond eyes, while their hair is worn in pigtails similar to the Chinese

The women also plait their hair, but with the difference that it is worn in two cords hanging down in front of either shoulder They also affect ornaments of silver or coral according to the wearer's station in life

The Mongol dress comprises a long blue coat of Chinese cloth, closely resembling dungaree, trousers of a like material or leather, and Chinese boots reaching above the ankles The hat is of a round shape, like an inverted bowl, or else similar to that worn by the Chinese In winter fur coats and sheepskin trousers are worn, as also a fur cap with ear flaps which can be turned back and fastened over the top The long coat is secured by a girdle, from which depend pipe, flint and tinder, and a pouch for carrying tobacco

Their dwellings are the felt tent or aul, the movable habitation peculiar to the nomad tribes of Central Asia

The Mongol is a fine horseman and never moves anywhere, however short a distance, unless mounted He sits forward in the saddle and manages his wild rough pony cleverly The saddlery is decorated with gaudy trappings, and, in the case of the wealthy, boasts much silver plate and other adornment

The food of the Mongol comprises mutton, milk and brick tea, grain being to them an unknown quantity Brick tea forms one of the chief imports from China, and the Mongols use large quantities of it The tea, in the form of bricks or slabs, is sliced off with a knife in the same way as one would take chips from a plank It is made in water to which salt is added, and the beverage, mixed with milk or cream, is then stirred and boiled The iron pot is only cleaned at long intervals, and then very cursorily, so that the resultant mixture is of a doubtful quality

Meat when eaten is boiled or sometimes roasted over the fire, chunks of it being thrust into the camel or cow dung furnace, contact with the latter giving it a tastiness it would lack were it prepared in less primitive fashion "Kumis" is also a drink much in favour amongst the Mongols, and a form of cheese made from clotted cream is met with in nearly every aul

A Mongol does not trouble much about washing, so that he, too, evidently pays scant attention to the old adage that cleanliness is next to godliness The operations of eating are performed with the fingers, on the principle that the latter were made before forks At the close of the meal he wipes his hands on the skirt of his robe, the use of finger bowls and serviettes being dispensed with.

The men are lazy and indolent and leave most of the work to be done by the women, who prepare the meals, manufacture the kumis, and contribute a large share to the task of herding the flocks and securing them at night after their return from the grazing grounds. The men watch the flocks mounted on their sturdy ponies, and when not thus engaged spend their time gossiping or visiting other auls with the same object

Horse racing is much indulged in, a pastime at which the Mongol shows to great advantage

Those of them inhabiting the more mountainous portions of the country excel as shikaris and hunters, being keen, good on the hillside—as is the case with the Kalmuks—and possessed of the attributes going to make up the ideal shikari

Their notions of distance are based entirely on the time taken to proceed from one given spot to another, and in answering enquiries thereon they reply that it will take a day, or two nights and one day, according to the situation of the objective There are two ways by which distance with them may be calculated, i e , they will tell one that if one goes fast—trotting and cantering —it can be done in such and such a time, or if slowly, double the period will be required

The religion of the Mongols is Lamaism, or Buddhism, and the clergy, or lamas, constitute more than half the population It is not within the province of this book to discuss the rise of Buddhism, but reference may well be made to its leading features. The advent of Buddha occurred five centuries before the birth of Christ, when he believed himself to be invested with a divine mission This culminated in the promulgation of the religion which spread through a large part of the Asiatic continent The fundamental principle of Buddhism is contemplation, and among its precepts was the ordaining of celibacy, which caused the establishment of monastic orders composed of both monks and nuns In the days of their inception these monasteries were undoubtedly the seats of learning and religion, but in course of time their influence exerted an adverse effect upon the people, and the tyranny of the priests and inequality of castes—to overcome which Buddha had striven—became reinstated The spiritual and temporal head of Lamaism is found in the person of the Grand Lama of Lhasa, the centre of Buddhism, which, until the recent British political expedition there, had for years remained a sealed book to the outer world

There is a temple in Wong, to which were attached over 300 lamas, all dressed in the customary robes of red and yellow. Their heads are shaven and they pass the day in prayer and reciting the incantations peculiar to Buddhism. Although celibacy is enjoined, immorality is rife amongst them, and from

all accounts the lives of the greater portion are not on such
chaste lines as their calling would demand

I visited the temple and the buildings in connection therewith the day after my arrival in Wong, as I was unable to continue
the march owing to bad weather and a hurricane which howled
across the plain from the north-east   The temple was large and
built of solid beams and mud plastering, the hall measuring
about 80 feet square   At the far end a low flight of steps led
up to a smaller chamber, containing relics brought from Lhasa,
and beautifully carved bells of copper workmanship   The
head lama, who showed me over, was a man of about 30 years of
age, with a villainous cast of countenance, a shaven pate and
grimy paws, his robes no longer the same bright colours they
once were   Over his right shoulder he carried an old blanket,
matted with the accumulated grease and dirt of generations, as
some additional protection against the inclemency of the weather.
Altogether this high priest did not possess that air of sanctity
one usually associates with the religious orders, nor did he
impress me as being one to whom to apply when in need of
spiritual relief

When I left this inner temple the lamas were engaged in
chanting their hymns, ranged in rows along the platforms, all
kneeling, and mumbling so rapidly that one could not catch any
of the words   The call to prayer is sounded on a conch shell,
a summons that is frequently heard, commencing with the
break of dawn, so that whatever their bad points are they
must perforce be early risers

During my short stay at Wong I went to see the lama's
kitchen   This was in a large room with beaten mud flooring,
having at one end a circular fireplace, constructed likewise of
mud, of a height of about 3 feet   On the top of this was fixed
a huge iron cauldron, the space beneath being filled with
camel dung and such brushwood as is obtainable in the form
of " burtsa."   The cauldron was filled with water, chunks of
meat were thrown into it, and the whole then seasoned with

lumps of salt and periodically stirred   Cleaning and washing out appeared unnecessary details, so that the edges all round the cauldron were lined with scum and filth, which were duly merged into the contents of the pot from the vigorous stirring by an unwashed lama   The other end of the room was furnished with a similar fireplace, over which another large cauldron for making tea was secured   Water was brought in in wooden buckets and poured into the cauldron, brick tea was then reduced to chips and cast into the murky liquid and salt added   The mixture was then allowed to boil, when a bucketful of milk was added and the tea thus concocted ladled out into the wooden buckets and taken away by fatigue parties of lamas. The chef was not particular as to a little flavour from the floor being added to the tea, for now and again he would put down the ladle on the dung-covered ground and move to the further end to stir the Irish stew in course of preparation there Presently he would return to take up the ladle with its coating of dirt and undesirables and plunge it into the cauldron, to the complete indifference of those for whom the beverage was intended

The morning after arrival in Wong I went to call on the young chief, and he received me at the door of his house, surrounded by his retinue, ushering me into the one apartment, which had a brickwork stove built in one corner   The nomadic instincts were strong within him, for inside the courtyard were pitched two large auls, wherein the primitive Mongol is much more at home than when surrounded by four walls   The young chief served tea in glasses, and was very polite and attentive, prominent traits in the Mongolian character   He told me there were wild sheep in the hills to the north, but that it would be impossible to hunt them now owing to the depth of snow and intense cold in the valleys

He enquired as to how many days' journey it would be to England if one went on horseback, a question that was a poser, but which I answered by replying it would take at least one hundred, which seemed to astonish him considerably.   I therefore followed it up by informing him it could be done in less time if one went by sledge and rail, but his knowledge of the iron horse was nil, so this did not convey much I endeavoured to explain what a wonderful thing the railway is, but he became so mystified that I concluded it better to change the subject rather than endanger my reputation for veracity

In reply to further questions on the matter of my wealth and worldly position he expressed great surprise on hearing I possessed no sheep or cattle, and failed to comprehend how I could possibly exist in this universe without a strong contingent of lambs and kine My explanations on the subject being obviously considered unsatisfactory I refrained from further comment, but the future traveller in Mongolia will do well to pose as a shepherd and owner of stock on a big scale if he wishes to be numbered amongst the high and mighty

Later in the day he returned my call and I showed him my Goerz-Anschutz camera, in which he was greatly interested, and when I took a photograph wanted to open the dark slide and see the picture My rifles and guns were a source of keen enjoyment to him, and for any of the latter he offered me as much silver as I cared to name, but I declined

After his departure he sent a present of a roll of Chinese silk, of a brilliant red colour, more suitable for the wardrobe of a *danseuse* than that of a wandering shikari He also despatched to my quarters a variety of dishes made by the cooks of his household, which my servants, ably seconded by the Tchja's attendants, disposed of

On the 19th, with fresh horses hired here, I resumed the onward march, striking north across the plain and over the western limits of the Saur Range It was a dull and gloomy day, with much snow and a hard frost The entire population, including the lamas, came out to see my departure, such an occurrence being something they could not miss

The country was still a vast plain, similar in all respects to that traversed from Chuguchak. To the north stretched the

range of mountains already referred to, a high snow-covered
chain running east and west, the greater part being within the
confines of the Russian Empire The openness of the terrain
gave full scope to the wind, which blew with great force,
rendering travelling a matter of extreme hardship, not unmixed
with danger, for therein lies the risk of trekking in the winter
months, the wind often overwhelming the luckless traveller in
its icy grip

A steady march of eight miles took me into the hills and along
the course of a small river flowing through the ravine I had
entered   The stream was frozen firm and solid, and in places
the ravine was so narrow that we were obliged to proceed on
the ice, a mode of progression not at all conducive to easy
going for the horses, who slipped and fell constantly on the
treacherous surface

Higher up, in a side ravine which led off from the right
bank, I reached a karaul at three in the afternoon, and, as
it was too far to the next habitation I decided to camp
the night there   One of the three auls was prepared by the
owners for me, and another for the servants, shelters of which
we were all very glad to take advantage, in view of the wind
and snow without   Mine was quite a small one, constructed
of the usual felt, but long since discoloured to a deep black from
constant use and the effects of fire and smoke on its erstwhile
white surface   The interior was hung with ancient and
gaudy trappings, whilst in one corner rested bowls and platters
of wood, from which the occupants eat their frugal meals   A
box hewn out of a tree-trunk and a low table on legs some eight
inches in height, modelled in primitive fashion, completed the
furniture of this dwelling on the Mongolian uplands   Here was
an illustration of the simple life, which, contrasted with that of
the Western and civilised world, stood out as an object lesson
that could not fail to impress the traveller. I watched some of
the Mongols dining that night—thrusting chunks of meat and
legs of mutton into the camel-dung fire, and anon turning them

round in the pungent fuel. When finally cooked, they dislodged the undesirable accumulation from the burning argols, and tore off the smoking flesh with their teeth, seemingly to thoroughly enjoy this savage meal. At such a sight my thoughts travelled across the mighty continent to far away England and a civilised dinner with all its delights, to fully understand and appreciate which one must travel amongst these primitive people and watch them in all their humble and untutored lives.

THROUGH A LAND OF ICE AND SNOW.

The night was intensely cold, the thermometer registering 51 degrees of frost, and my aul, being old and full of rents, was very draughty. The Mongols are, however, a hardy race and able to withstand the rigours of such a climate, of which I had an apt example when I looked out in the morning. Close by— enveloped in skins, the hides of sheep—were two children, of ages not above six and eight years, enjoying a peaceful sleep with 19 degrees below zero. It is such an upbringing that makes the Mongols what they are—a sturdy race of nomads inured to hardship.

Across the Roof of the World.

As it was a long way to Gum, where lived the chief of the Kazaks inhabiting this part of Mongolia, I marched before 8 o'clock through a narrow and stony valley, crossing and re-crossing the frozen stream several times. Thence I continued on over a broad snow-covered plateau, a mighty wilderness, ice-bound and locked in the grip of a hard and relentless winter. Beyond this plateau, I descended into sheltered valleys, or more correctly rounded hollows in the hills, where dwelt a few nomads who seemed astonished beyond measure at our appearance.

The auls occupied secluded nooks in these bare and desolate valleys, and with their flocks the nomads would remain until the first signs of spring enabled them to move to the higher ground and fresh pastures. Past these auls I entered once more on to another stretch of plateau, from which a view of the surrounding country was obtainable.

To the north, across the Black Irtish Valley, I obtained my first glimpse of the Great Altai, an imposing chain of snow-capped mountains, which form one of the principal ranges of Asia.

Descending from this plateau I reached an undulating plain stretching away ten miles to east, west and north. Gum, the home of the Kazak chief, was on its eastern confines, and towards this haven I marched till dark. On arriving there, I found a settlement comprising a log hut with four rooms—the residence of the head-man—and a few auls wherein lived his attendants. The chief received me hospitably and placed one of the largest rooms in his hut at my disposal, in return for which I gave him a shawl as a present for his wife on departing next morning. My quarters were plentifully bespread with rugs and felt numdahs, and there was also a stove with an ample quantity of scrub, similar to the "burtsa" one finds on the Pamirs. At one end was a raised dais constructed of mud, to serve as a sleeping place, and in the walls were driven huge pegs on which were hung clothes and various articles of a household nature. The chief presented me with a "dasturkhan" of dried fruits and Russian made sweets, of which we partook in company, the while he imparted information on the Altai and the country bordering on the Black Irtish Valley, which districts constitute the main pasture grounds of his people

The latter were divided into ten sections of 1,000 auls, the head of each section being responsible for the good behaviour and conduct thereof   In the summer months the nomads move up into the higher ground amidst the valleys on the southern slopes of the Altai, but during the winter they remain in the Black Irtish Valley and the country contiguous to it.

The Kazaks own nominal allegiance to the Chinese, but it is of a sketchy nature.

East of Gum, at a distance of about twenty miles, is situated the great Kesil Bach Nor. The chief told me there were now no Kazaks there, but that many were in the habit of visiting the pasture grounds round the lake during the spring

I arranged to hire horses for my trek northwards to the Altai and the new town of Shara Sumbe, which lay four days' march further on—judging from the information I gleaned from the chief

The wind blew hard during the night, but it died down a little at daylight. The weather was, however, dull and gloomy, and the outlook not a pleasant one. We were, of course, used to such climatic conditions, but hoped the wind would rest quiet and not add to our difficulties

I paid off the Mongols from Wong, and engaged a fresh band of Kazaks through the instrumentality of the chief, to proceed with me as far as the Black Irtish Valley, or, at any rate, I trusted they would do so, though quite prepared for their absconding without previous notice

I said good-bye to the hospitable chief and then struck east through some low hills out on to a vast plain sloping gradually downward to a wide open valley—where dwelt a few Kazaks in auls encircled by walls of brushwood to keep off the wind—west of the Kesil Bach Lake, which here forms the principal feature

CHAPTER XXI

Across the Black Irtish Vallfy to the Great Altai Mountains

The Kesil Bach Lake is the largest in Western Mongolia and situated south of the Altai   Its length is about sixty miles and the width averages twenty   Its western shores are flat and lead on to the broad open valley I had passed through   The pasturage is limited, the country for the most part being barren and sterile, with a meagre crop of grass, insufficient for the needs of the nomad's flocks, who consequently frequent the region of the Black Irtish Valley and the land to the north thereof, where they have greater facilities for the support of their large herds

After viewing the lake, noting its western and south-western shores, and taking some photographs, I pushed on through the hills to the north, to reach which I crossed the wide valley, here covered with low stunted scrub, the soil being sand and gravel, but in the hills giving place to a rock and sterile deposit.   The country to the north of these hills leads to the Black Irtish Valley, though the river itself is not encountered for a good thirty miles further north, but the natives term the country " Irtish," in much the same way as the nomads of the Tekkes, Jirgalan and Kunges Valleys, refer to that region under the general name of Ili

It was severe trekking that day and told heavily on the ponies, as the plateaux are covered with deep soft snow, through which the going is exceedingly laborious and trying   North of the Kesil Bach Lake it is an up and down country, through many little dips in the hills, which proved hard work for the ponies, so much so that long before I camped that night two of them were quite done up and unable to proceed further.

The Kazaks I had met near the lake told me there were some auls situated on the northern slopes of the range, but though I pushed on energetically till past seven I saw no sign of human habitation. It was dark soon after four, which was the signal for the thermometer to go down with a run, and by the time I decided to give up looking for the auls and camp it was 15 or 16 degrees below zero—not the night to be on the move. The two ponies fallen out by the wayside were abandoned, and their

THE SHORES OF THE KESIL BACH LAKE.

loads transferred to spare mounts I had with me. They would be picked up later on when the Kazaks returned to Gum. I expressed considerable surprise at their being left in this way and probably stolen by predatory bands, but the Kazaks said there was no fear of this, since the weather was far too severe for any prowlers to be about on the off chance of securing plunder.

During the night the thermometer dropped to 25 degrees below zero, cold enough even for a Kazak, which a strong wind

whistling down the valley did not tend to lessen It was too
cold to pitch the tent, and the ground being much warmer we
made a barricade of the baggage, spreading our blankets
within the enclosure thus formed The servants were provided
with an abundance of " razais " (large quilts stuffed with cotton
wool to a thickness of half an inch), woollen blankets, and fur
coats made of the thickest sheepskin I had been able to secure
in Kulja, so we passed a comparatively comfortable night,
if such be possible in the open with 57 degrees of frost There
was very little brushwood, merely the stunted scrub and some
" burtsa "and wormwood, though we managed to collect sufficient
for a fire to make tea from snow-water, as the real article was not
procurable in the neighbourhood Some Turki bread I had brought
from Chuguchak, now frozen as solid as a rock, completed
our frugal meal, since it was too Arctic to expect any cooking on
a more elaborate scale

I left this cheerless bivouac at 8 o'clock on the morning of
December 22nd, and marched through low hills over a sand and
gravel soil, which supports nothing more than the scrub one
sees so much of

Four miles beyond camp the country was more undulating, and
the route led over broad and rounded hills of no greater height
than 50 to 100 feet I was now in the Black Irtish Valley,
which stretched away to the Altai Mountains, the latter forming
a snowy wall along its northern boundary The Irtish rises in
the Altai south-west of the town of Kobdo, whence it flows west
through Mongolia, and into the Zaisan Lake in Russian territory
From here it assumes a wider and more important aspect, being
navigable through Siberia, past the town of Omsk on the Siberian
Railway, up to the Arctic Ocean, into which it pours its waters
after a course of 2,500 miles from its source

The Black Irtish Valley, at the point where I crossed it, is
about 40 miles wide and everywhere covered with grass, especially
in the central parts, where it is high and dense Here there are
trees and brushwood, affording an ample quantity of firewood.

During the winter some of the Kazaks live in log huts as being warmer and more comfortable than the aul, particularly in mid-winter, when blizzards are the rule rather than the exception.

Once down in the valley level I reached a grass country, interspersed with birch and willow jungle. Here is excellent pasturage for large herds of cattle and horses, and a great many of the Kazaks remain there throughout the winter. I reached a number of auls at noon at a spot called Khurdia, hard by the Irtish River, and halted there for a brief rest before continuing across the valley.

"WE CROSSED THE BLACK IRTISH RIVER, A SOLID SHEET OF ICE WHICH WOULD HAVE BORNE A SIEGE TRAIN."

The chief of the Kazaks in this part lived in a rough log hut at Khurdia, and from him I obtained fresh horses for the onward march. In the one room of which the log hut was composed I noticed a combination calendar, clock and thermometer, of Russian make, and on my enquiring as to where he had obtained it the chief told me that the year before a Russian traveller had visited the country from Uliassutai and had made him a present of it. He said the traveller in question had come with a small escort of Cossacks, so I concluded it must have been the Russian Consul who resides at Uliassutai, a town some 200 miles to the east of Kobdo, in the heart of Mongolia

Outside the hut and hanging on a palisade which protected the doorway was a very fine red bear skin, which had been bagged about six weeks before on the southern slopes of the Altai I had never seen a finer specimen of the red bear, the fur being particularly long and woolly. The Kazak chief informed me there were a great many in the forests of the Altai, and that he had often seen and shot them I take it to be a variety of the Himalayan Snow Bear (*Ursus arctus isabellinus*), but, of course, very much bigger than the latter

Soon after leaving Khuidia we crossed the Black Irtish River, a solid sheet of ice which would have borne a siege train The width at this point, some 100 miles from its source, was eighty paces, but at flood time, during the months of June, July and August, when all the tributary streams are rushing torrents, the volume is greatly increased and the river frequently overflows its banks, flooding the surrounding country

My suspicions regarding the Kazaks now with me and their evident desire to avoid accompanying me to the north side of the valley were confirmed in the conduct of the man in charge, who had been deputed by the chief to go as far as the point in question It was past 4 o'clock when we were across the river, whence for several miles a course due east had to be pursued owing to the ground immediately to the north being swampy and impassable He was a very truculent individual, constantly saying I should not reach any auls that night, as the next encampment was situated a great distance away I was desirous, however, of pushing on, with the object of getting to Shara Sumbe on the morrow, so gave orders that the march was to be continued and camp pitched by the first group of auls in the centre of the valley So I held on through the grass jungle, and everything went well until past six, by which time it was pitch dark, with a bitterly cold temperature, such a night as makes marching purgatory and camp a torture

Signs of discontent and lawlessness were now visible amongst the caravan men, the climax being reached when they came to a sudden halt and the ringleader declared they would go no further. The latter leaped from his horse, and, shouting and gesticulating, commenced to throw the loads off, uttering various threats against myself and servants. But the Kazak is a coward at heart, and were instant action taken I felt the situation could be saved. So, in desperation, I waded in with my long whip and administered a thrashing to the blustering bully who thought to

CARAVAN MEN WHO MUTINIED IN THE BLACK IRTISH VALLEY.

overawe me, an action that galvanised the rest of my party into activity. This turned the tide of events, and the Kazaks, in whom the yellow streak is evident, wavered, and then went on.

Soon after 8 o'clock we heard the barking of dogs to our left, and a few minutes later saw the lights of some auls in that direction. They proved to be part of a Kazak encampment of a semi-permanent nature, one of the five dwellings being a log hut and the others built round with substantial walls of wooden palings and brushwood   The Kazaks here told me it was only a day's march to Shara Sumbe, the town in the foothills of the Altai, and that I could reach there the following day before sunset

Although it was nine o'clock before I camped I resumed the journey next day at eight, marching a couple of miles before getting out of the bush, whence I entered on a plain with gentle undulations, stretching away for a distance of ten miles   The route then lay through low rounded hills and across another plain for ten miles, beyond which I struck due west by an indifferent cart road in the outer foothills to Shara Sumbe, situated in a dip in the hills and somewhat scattered

I rode on up the road leading to the town into the main street, at the top of which I halted at the entrance to a house and shop that appeared to belong to a native of Turkistan   I enquired of him the address of one Ismail Bai, to whom I had been recommended by the Kazak chief at Khurdia as being a Kashgari merchant engaged in trade in the Altai   The man I was addressing proved to be the Kashgari merchant I sought, and was known in the town as the Shangi

Ismail Bai was a Mohammedan and hailed from Kashgar, whither he had migrated some years before to Kulja and later to Chuguchak   Thence he and his family had moved on to Zaisan, in Russian territory, a town situated five marches to the north-east of Chuguchak, and where, hearing of the possibilities of the Chinese Altai and Mongolia from a trading point of view, he had decided on transferring his headquarters.   At the time of my arrival he had been resident in Shara Sumbe five years, having during that period opened a branch at Kobdo, the Mongolian town on the north-eastern confines of the Altai, lying on the direct road between the Russian frontier, Uliasutai, and Urga

Ismail Bai's trade was mostly restricted to cloth cotton goods, and the purchase of skins from the Mongol trappers in the Altai, though he also did a considerable business in brick tea

374

which forms the main article of trade in Mongolia. Ismail Bai and his brother received me most hospitably, and gave over one of the rooms in their house for my use, where I was comfortably installed.

As I have said, Shara Sumbe lies in the foothills of the Great Altai, at an elevation of 2,850 feet above sea level. The town is

ISMAIL BAI.

founded on the site of an ancient monastery wherein formerly dwelt many red and yellow robed lamas, but the monastery has now given place to the new town established by the Chinese with a view to consolidating their hold on Western Mongolia and the Altai region. The population consists of Mongols and Chinese, the majority of the shops being in Chinese

375

hands, though there are also a number of Sart merchants engaged in business in a small way. The Altai Mountains to the north of the town are crossed by a pass leading down on to the northern slopes, and east to Kobdo, which can be reached by this route in eight days from Shara Sumbe. The pass in question is, however, not an easy one, and is only open for a few months in the year, the alternative route lying along the southern side of the range through the Black Irtish Valley and over the eastern shoulder of the Altai into Kobdo, a journey involving a march of from 16 to 20 days.

On December 24th I called on the Ching Sai, or Governor of the Altai. He did not seem to enjoy being in this distant outpost of Empire, and with a sigh of regret remarked that it was a long way from anywhere, adding that though he had ordered some films for a camera from Pekin the year before, they had not yet arrived. He held up his hands in horror at the idea of my attempting to cross the Altai at this season of the year, and said I should certainly die in the attempt, a not very comforting assurance.

At 3 o'clock he returned my call, arriving in a small tarantass, which Haji Ismail Bai had presented to him two years before. His visit lasted nearly two hours, he being very talkative and seemingly pleased to have an opportunity of meeting an Englishman. He imparted much information on Mongolia and the Altai, and Chinese intentions with regard thereto, at intervals bewailing his hard lot in being stationed here. No doubt so small a place would afford little scope for his activities, but he looked forward to the time when it would develop into a busy centre, bringing with it an era of prosperity and an increased exchequer. He was much interested in my rifles and shot gun, asking several questions, also sending for his own battery, which comprised a rifle and gun, both of German make, for my inspection. We then discussed the Boxer troubles of 1900, in which he took part, showing me a bayonet wound he had received in the forehead from one of the rebels during the fighting before

Pekin. His remarks on the various contingents engaged were very amusing. He eulogised the British, American and Japanese contingents, and extolled their marching and campaigning abilities as of a high order.

I spent Christmas Eve quietly, glad of the rest and relaxation from marching through this ice-bound country, although not free from worry, for Giyani had been ailing since the 21st, and was now in the throes of bodily aches and pains, so I had taken

KAZAK WOMEN IN THE MONGOLIAN ALTAI.

him into my room to nurse him back to health. Again my lack of medical knowledge prevented a diagnosis of his case with any degree of certainty. He complained of severe pains in the stomach and head, so I dosed him with chlorodyne and other suitable medicines, which gave some relief, though it was an anxious time for another three days with his temperature rising and falling in the most perplexing manner.

Christmas Day dawned bright and clear to the wanderer in these bleak and windy wilds, far from the madding crowd. In the morning I called on the Hsei Tai, or officer commanding the garrison, at his Yamen situated in a dip of the hills a mile to the north-west He had a small body of his troops drawn up to receive me, the bugler blowing a fanfare on an old trumpet of German make, a discordant noise certainly, but still a fanfare

The Hsei Tai greeted me cordially, and we adjourned to the reception room, where a table was laid with tea and sweetmeats and a supply of Russian cigarettes He told me he had only recently arrived from Pekin, having been appointed to the command here, and since his arrival had completed a tour of the district Whilst thus engaged a report had spread amongst the Kazaks that they were to be pressed for service as irregular cavalry by the Chinese, which so alarmed them that they all cleared out of the neighbourhood, bag and baggage, martial ambition obviously being at a low ebb amongst them

The Hsei Tai returned my call in the afternoon, not appearing in a " mapa," or Chinese cart, but on horseback, accompanied by some of his unkempt soldiery They all rode into the little courtyard of my quarters and dismounted, the Hsei Tai, followed by his interpreter and pipe bearer, being received by me at the door The conversation was on general lines, my shoot in the Thian Shan being the topic that interested him most, especially the wapiti horns My negative replies to his questions as to whether I had put the latter up for auction seemed to completely mystify him, and he evidently thought I had lost a good chance, so that doubtless his opinion of my money-making abilities was not high

With the Hsei Tai's departure were concluded the ceremonial visits incumbent on one after arrival in a Chinese town, so that I could now devote myself to the problem of reaching the far side of the Altai and getting down on to the *Ovis ammon* ground, in search of which I had come so far and endured so much

On December 26th the amount of snow on the ground had been considerably augmented by a heavy fall during the previous night, so that climatic conditions had still further changed for

378

the worse, and prospects of crossing the formidable range of mountains seemed but slight

Mongolia is noted for the variety of wild sheep found within its limits, the finest of which is located in the Great Altai Mountains Here is found the true ammon (*Ovis ammon typica*), of the great Argali sheep, for which North Central Asia is noted Its habitat is the range of mountains in question and the highlands of North-western Mongolia In appearance it resembles the *Ovis poli* of the Pamirs, but the length of horn is not so great as in the latter case, the record for an *Ovis ammon* head being 63½ inches, whilst that of the *Ovis poli* is 75 inches

It frequents the bare uplands on the northern slopes of the Altai, and moves in herds of from ten to twenty Like its Pamir congener the ammon is a difficult animal to stalk, being extremely wary and hard to approach, but when secured the horns constitute a magnificent trophy, and one of the finest that could grace a sportsman's collection.

CHAPTER XXII

In the Great Altai Mountains

I HAD decided when starting north from the Thian Shan to go on to the Altai in the hope of securing some specimens of the *Ovis ammon*. My original programme, drawn up before leaving Lansdowne, had included the Altai, though prospects of ultimately reaching there were dependent on considerations of leave and the amount of time at my disposal in which to carry out the expedition in full

With my arrival in Kulja I began to realise the difficulties confronting me, and the possibility of being unable to negotiate the formidable passes leading from the Black Irtish Valley on to the wild sheep ground on the northern slopes of the Altai mountains. It was after leaving Chuguchak, a month later, that I foresaw it would be a hard proposition to attempt the crossing of the Altai so late in the year, for the intense cold and depth of snow would probably bar my movements. I trekked on, however, hoping against hope that I should be able to manage it, and thus achieve the main object of the expedition, to accomplish which I had trekked many hundreds of miles through a desolate country in the depth of winter, when all nature is locked in an icy grip and the vast steppes are bare and bleak, swept by an Arctic blast that defies resistance.

The nullah leading to the pass which crosses the main range of the Altai north of Shara Sumbe, at an altitude of just under 10,000 feet, was blocked with snow, and higher up became more than ever impassable. To take ponies over by this route was clearly out of the question, so on returning that night

I reviewed the situation and finally resolved to move up the
Black Irtish Valley and across the eastern shoulder of the Altai
into the town of Kobdo The latter is situated on a plateau, a
distance of fifteen to twenty days' trekking, the actual length of
time taken being dependent on the state of the weather and
the probability of being held up by other adverse conditions

From Kobdo I purposed continuing either eastward through
Mongolia to Uliasutai, Urga and Kiakhta, or northwards past
the Ubsa Nor Lake to the Siberian-Mongolian frontier, and
down the Yenisei River to Krasnoyarsk, on the Trans-Siberian
Railway

There are no ammon on the southern slopes of the Altai,
but in long conversations I had with Haji Ismail Bai and
Mongols acquainted with the country, I learnt there were Altai
Wapiti (*Cervus canadensis asiaticus*) on this side

The Siberian roe-deer (*Capreolus pygargus*) is found, too, in
the Altai, but its habitat is the same as that of the Thian Shan—
the foothills and fairly open forest country on the northern slopes

Red bear of the variety I had heard of in the Black Irtish
Valley also exist on the southern slopes, and, judging from skins
I saw, they must be very fine specimens, the coats being large
and extremely furry

The 27th was dull and threatening, heavy clouds obscuring
the sky, with a steady fall of snow throughout the day, causing
me much misgiving for the forward trek   In the afternoon I had
another look round, and then went to take tea with the Chinese
Officer Instructor of the troops, who hailed from Pekin and was
acquainted with Europeans and desirous of seeing radical
changes introduced into China's military forces

I had arranged in Shara Sumbe for 14 ponies and four men as
drivers to accompany me to Kobdo by the southern route, and
the Ching Sai had also detailed a Mongol Beg, or small official,
with two levies to escort me thus far.   He had furnished me with
a special passport for the territory within his charge so that the
nomad Mongols and Kazaks might see I was travelling with the

full licence and authority of the representatives of the Son of Heaven

Giyani had improved and was now much better, so I fixed my departure for the 28th on my way to Kobdo, the first march out from Shara Sumbe being Burtakhoi, in the Irtish Valley, some 25 miles south The morning dawned fairly bright, and though it had snowed heavily the previous day and during the night had ceased before daybreak The outlook was as cheery as could be expected in the Mongolian uplands at the end of December, though there was deep snow everywhere and the cold was intense During the night the thermometer never dropped to less than 25 to 30 degrees below zero, in itself not a serious menace, but, accompanied by the winds for which Mongolia is noted, it spells death to all who are luckless enough to be overtaken by it

After bidding good-bye to the hospitable Haji, I rode forth with the caravan out on to the frozen wastes to the south It was useless halting longer in Shara Sumbe so I determined to make the attempt to reach Kobdo, as further delay could not have improved the position but would rather have added to the difficulties already sufficiently formidable From Shara Sumbe, on across the plain stretching away to the centre of the Black Irtish Valley the country is entirely open, there being no shelter available from the winds which sweep it at this period of the year

About eighteen miles out one enters a bush and scrub jungle inhabited here and there by scattered groups of Kazaks who rest quietly within the shelter of their auls, herding the flocks near by, and passing the time until spring releases the land from its wintry grasp and renders movement a matter of possibility and safety Until this central part of the valley is reached there is nothing to relieve the eye but a bleak and snow-covered wilderness, and it is one I could not help contrasting with pleasanter places I had known in various parts of the world

I had been warned of the possibility of encountering a blizzard, so had seen all the loads firmly fastened and everything rendered as secure as possible, in order to avoid unnecessary work at reloading on the way when every moment might be of importance

I had also foreseen the likelihood of frost bite being an enemy to cope with and had therefore carefully instructed Giyani, Rasul and Yusuf, to come to me the moment they felt any part of the body getting into a state of numbness, when I could check the effects of it by vigorous rubbing with snow Strange as it may seem this treatment appeared to them the last thing that should be done, and this well-known and only cure for frost bite, when the parts affected are not too far gone, seemed to the Oriental way of reasoning a fallacious remedy In the light of after events had Giyani but obeyed my injunctions much that was to eventuate might easily have been avoided

Despite all my precautions to lessen the fatigue of the animals and make the march as easy as possible, the deep snow and consequent heavy going told severely on the animals, and the progress of the caravan was constantly checked as ponies became exhausted and unable to struggle ahead without pro-longed resting The cold was extreme, whilst at intervals the whistle of an Arctic blast foretold the approach of rough weather Some idea of the rate of progress may be drawn from the fact that forging along in this way it was late in the afternoon before we were half way to Burtakhoi, the Kazak encampment situated amongst the bush jungle in the central part of the Irtish. Once there all dangers and difficulties would be practically over, at any rate for that day

But we were not to escape so easily, for at 4 o'clock a blizzard came on, the strength and force of which was terrific, driving the snow along in dense clouds so that the ponies, unable to stand such a battle of the elements, turned round and refused to face the blast It seemed impossible that anything human or animal could withstand that appalling wind, and it was only with the

greatest exertions the animals were urged on again The
Kazaks in charge of the ponies were not the men upon whom
one could rely at such a juncture, since they lacked the instinct
and courage necessary to extricate themselves from a difficult
and dangerous situation, and wished only to submit to what
they regarded as inevitable fate

Assisted, however, by Rasul I drove the caravan forward
like a flock of sheep in the direction of the auls I hoped we
should reach before dark The wind increased in force and all
our beards and moustaches were a mass of icicles and encrusted
snow, my own mouth and nose being completely enveloped in
ice which accumulated as the result of respiration, the breath
being instantly frozen into solid icicles

Never in Canada or British Columbia had I experienced even
a semblance of the rigours of such a climate, one against which all
the warming influences of fur coats, fur waistcoats, sweaters
and eight-foot woollen scarves bought in Kulja were futile One
must be made of iron to stand it—such weather as is only met
with in northern latitudes By 5 o'clock the feeble light had
already disappeared and night came on apace as it ever does
in these regions

Whilst we endeavoured to make headway against the icy
hurricane the snow whirled up by the wind blinded us and prevented our advance, forming on all sides a white sheet whose
folds encircled us and hampered our every movement I could
feel my hands and wrists, despite thick fur gloves, becoming
numbed, the first indications of frost bite, whilst the caravan
men were in a similar plight In the black darkness it was
impossible to see ahead, we could only struggle forward,
urging on the animals, and force them to maintain a heading
against the wind and prevent their lying down, an eventuality
I had to guard against since I knew the caravan men would
rapidly follow suit

Several of the drivers complained loudly in an agony of
despair that they were frost-bitten, and that their ears and noses

384

were hard and yielded no sign of life when pinched The crucial moment was at hand, a moment in one's life when disaster seems inevitable, and no line of escape presents itself It is then one becomes desperate and strikes out against the danger fast folding one in its sinister embrace Not a minute was to be lost ! Shelter must be reached, for without it none would live to tell the tale of that terrible march

It was only with the most strenuous exertions that progress could be maintained, struggling against odds which no words could ever portray At last, towards 6 o'clock, we reached a hut inhabited by some Chinese brickmakers, who said there was a Kazak encampment close by on the other side of the river which ran near the hut, so we crossed it and gained the shelter of the friendly auls

Glad indeed we were to reach such a haven of refuge, for our plight, after several hours at the mercy of a pitiless blizzard, was really lamentable

The settlement in question consisted of two auls and a small log hut, and there I had time to survey the scene and note what had happened. The cases of frost bite included frozen ears, noses, cheeks and hands, a ring of distressed humanity, all apparently looking to me as a panacea for every ill and a sure cure for frost bite, such is the faith of the Oriental in the powers of the European Whilst thus engaged Rasul came in and informed me that Giyani's hands were in a bad state, so I at once examined them He appeared looking very despondent and shamefaced, and in reply to my questions said he had been trying to warm his hands over the fire as they were quite numb and possessed no life or feeling, but that the warmth had not affected them and they seemed worse rather than better ! ! It was then too late to attempt any massage, for the moment I touched them the skin peeled off his fingers I therefore bandaged them as well as possible, and made up a bed for him in my hut, too sick at heart to censure him for not obeying my instructions to report at once in the first instance. I had

saved my own hands and nose by vigorous rubbing, as also
Yusuf's left cheek, which, though horribly swollen, was still
sound and not permanently affected

I did not pass a pleasant night with all the sick and sorry
ones around me, worries that assumed greater proportions when
I contemplated the possibility of Giyani losing both hands
Poor little man, he was in a sad way, but the warrior spirit within
him went far to lessen the strenuousness of the occasion

All hope of reaching Kobdo and traversing the country north
of the Altai had now to be abandoned, and I resolved to make for
Zaisan, a small Russian military post on the Russo-Mongolian
frontier, where I knew medical aid would be available

That night the turning point in the expedition was reached,
for I realised to the full it was no longer possible to entertain
the hope of going on through Mongolia, or of obtaining any
shooting in the Altai, and that the game was a lost one.
Nothing, therefore, now remained to be done except reach
Zaisan as rapidly as possible, and thence trek on to the Trans-
Siberian Railway and civilisation

The blizzard continued with undiminished fury throughout
the night, and on the morning of the 29th was still blowing
great guns, bitterly cold as usual, and a dismal, gloomy day

It was now necessary for me to go back to Shara Sumbe to see
the Chinese Governor and obtain a passport to traverse the
country down the Irtish Valley into Russian territory, since
the one I possessed only covered the land between that town
and Kobdo I knew that unless I was provided with proper
credentials I should meet with difficulties on the way, besides
which the caravan men refused point blank to go on to Zaisan
I therefore set out with Rasul and the Mongol Beg, after tending
Giyani and making him comfortable, to make fresh arrangements
in accordance with the alteration in the programme necessitated
by the circumstances

That day was one I would feign forget and relegate to the
limbo of the past, but the memory of it will always remain Half-

way across the plain the Mongol rode up to me and said his chin was as hard as a stone, the appearance of it being a ghastly white, a sure indication of frost-bite

We were riding due north and therefore experienced the full force of the wind blowing from the mountains, so it became more than ever necessary to reach Shara Sumbe quickly before becoming frozen as stiff as planks   The deep snow and hard going, however, militated against any attempt to force the pace and it was nearly 4 o'clock before we arrived at the welcome shelter of Haji Ismail Bai's house

On the way I had felt my hands, legs and feet becoming numbed and devoid of all life, despite huge top boots and several pairs of felt and woollen stockings, two pairs of trousers and a fur coat amongst other articles of raiment.

Gradually the feeling of numbness wore off which, had I known it, was the critical moment when instant action should have been taken, but the combined effect of driving snow and the desire to get out of it alive, and that right soon, caused me to forget the imminent danger, and to postpone treatment until beyond the piercing wind   It was not until I had dismounted in the court-yard of Ismail Bai's house—or rather, had been helped out of the saddle—that I saw I had been badly frost-bitten in the right leg and more particularly the knee   My hands, too, were in a parlous condition, and so were Rasul's, as well as his face   We indulged in some tremendous rubbing with snow, and in the end saved the situation, all except my leg, which was too far gone to yield to treatment   I rubbed it with snow as I had never rubbed before, and when blood began to ooze out and the parts to soften I hoped it might not prove to be a bad case.

Ismail Bai produced a Chinese doctor from the town, who came armed with weird plasters and poultices composed of some doubtful looking mixtures, to the application of which I submitted, though not at all sanguine as to the good results the Chinese medico assured me would eventuate   I passed a comparatively quiet night, but in the morning the affected parts had swollen considerably and were full of a yellowish watery matter, which I was able to release with the aid of a needle the good Bai brought me

In the meantime I had to complete arrangements for reaching Zaisan, so sent my card to the Ching Sai's Yamen with a polite request that he would provide me with a passport covering the country between Shara Sumbe and the Siberian frontier, as although the Peking passport enabled me to travel anywhere within the boundaries of the Chinese Empire, further credentials from the leading Chinese authority of that portion of the Empire were essential, since Peking is far distant to the nomad way of thinking, and he has respect only for those in immediate authority over him

I was, of course, unable to ride, so arranged with Haji Ismail Bai to hire an old Russian tarantass he possessed for the journey to Zaisan, and also purchased horses and engaged a man as driver The tarantass was in a bad state of repair, old and creaky, and it took two days to prepare it for the rough roads it would have to traverse to the Siberian frontier

The Chinese doctor visited me again before I left and seemed much hurt on learning his remedies had had no effect, whilst I daresay my remarks as to his medical skill were not such as to send him away elated at his professional skill   The frost-bitten parts were in a very bad state, and layers of cotton wool had to be constantly applied to absorb the yellowish water and matter percolating therefrom

CHAPTER XXIII.

DOWN THE BLACK IRTISH VALLEY TO THE SIBERIAN FRONTIER

ON January 1st, everything being ready, I started for Zaisan, having sent a man two days before to bring in news of Giyani He had arrived the previous night with information that the latter was better It was late in the morning of New Year's Day before I left Shara Sumbe, and the two horses could only with great difficulty struggle through the deep snow When darkness fell we were still several miles from the encampment, and it looked as though we should be compelled to spend the night on the bleak and windswept plain Once in going over a steep sandbank my crazy vehicle collapsed and, rolling down hill, turned completely over, myself underneath, the horses kicking and struggling, altogether not a pleasant experience for one frost bitten and unable to move hand or foot Luckily I escaped with nothing more than a severe shaking. Rasul and the others were able to patch the tarantass up, and we went on for another two miles when it broke down again in a deep ditch and threw me out Still undaunted the noble army of martyrs got to work again and with rope tied up the front axle, which had split in the centre I started once more but within less than another half hour it smashed again with a sickening bump in a deep depression in the ground, which the darkness had prevented the driver seeing. I had had quite enough of it for one day so compassed the rest of the distance to the Kazak encampment on foot supported between Rasul and one of the Mongol soldiers

Across the plain we had heard answering calls in response to our shouts and presently saw the flicker of a light which gradually drew nearer and proved to be Yusuf carrying an old horn lantern The camp was not more than a mile distant, which I managed to do at the cost of much pain and many halts, more glad than can be imagined to reach the hut at last after such a strenuous day

Giyani was better, but the skin of his hands had peeled and the nails were loose, in addition to which he was unable to move the joints at all, so there was no time to be lost in getting to Zaisan.

I was, however, obliged to halt here the next day whilst my chariot was being repaired and made ready for the horribly rough going down the Irtish Valley.

January 3rd was dull and cold, with the thermometer 28 degrees below zero at seven in the morning, and the air keen and sharp. The road led through scattered jungle and grass country, with groups of auls here and there, and herds of horses and cattle. Parts of the valley are covered with high and dense grass, reaching in many places to six feet and more On the way I passed a Kazak cemetery, the few graves possess ng no ornamentation, being simply mud built and placed far from any habitation as is the custom amongst these people Graves of the wealthier are surrounded by a wall of mud and in other ways made to look more imposing.

It was a long and desperately weary march that day, for the tarantass broke down five times, and we exhausted our supply of rope in patching up the front axle which was the root of all the evil and refused to be put right. The pace was terribly slow after the first breakdown, as every time we reached any ditches or uneven parts of the track it was necessary to proceed with the greatest care to avoid a sudden and unceremonious collapse.

Soon after 4 o'clock darkness supervened, and the inky blackness, unrelieved by moon or stars, made it doubly hard work to find our way through the long grass and reeds which cover the Irtish Valley here We must, however, have done a good 25 miles that day, finally arriving at a Kazak encampment on the banks of the Irtish where there was wood in abundance, which enabled us to indulge in a fire as some sort of solace to the toils of the day.

Mortification of the frost-bitten parts had now set in, and the operation of dressing my wounds and disposing of the gangrene resulting therefrom was indeed a painful task I found a solution of carbolic, from some tabloids I carried, very good for this, and continued the treatment twice daily, despite the pain occasioned by it, until arrival at Zaisan.

TREKKING THROUGH THE BLACK IRTISH VALLEY.

I was obliged to halt another day on the banks of the Irtish River, pending repairs to the wretched tarantass being completed. The front axle was hopelessly broken down the centre, but we managed to patch it up by binding a piece of iron round the woodwork, not perhaps a brilliant specimen of the blacksmith's art, but good enough for the occasion.   .

On January 5th we resumed the march, rather a sorrowful band, as Yusuf was now very bad with a swollen face, due to frost-bite, to allay which I could do nothing beyond bandaging it and seating him on a camel, where he wept steadily from pain and anguish for three whole days, at the end of which time matters improved and his face gradually resumed its normal and erstwhile plump appearance.

This part of the Black Irtish valley through which we were now passing was a good grass country, though now, of course, covered with snow, with patches of jungle here and there, amongst which were to be seen groups of Kazak auls These people would come out to meet me, intently watching my every movement and examining with great eagerness the camp furniture and other articles, as they were placed in any of the auls for the night. Such things were entirely foreign to them and savoured, I suppose, of the miraculous.

I halted that night at a group of Kazak auls where was a log hut, the dwelling of a Zung, or head man The chief Kazak of the district, a Khurdia, or one who has authority over 1,000 auls, came to see me soon after arrival, a fine looking man about 50 years of age, with high cheekbones and an ample black beard His cap of fox-skin reached down over the ears and nape of the neck, and was fastened under the chin by richly embroidered ribands. His dress comprised the usual " khalat," or silk robe, lined with cotton wool, over which was worn a heavy fur coat having an ample collar, and secured at the waist by a girdle of beautiful workmanship. Dark cloth pyjamas, lined with wool, and stuck into leather boots reaching to the knees completed his costume The sleeves of the coat are made very long so that they come down over the hands and thus take the place of gloves

The Khurdia told me that formerly the country round was very lawless, but since the Russians had exerted greater authority along the frontier line raids were less frequent and bands of robbers had now little scope for their activities In the district I was then passing through were some 250 auls, and a large number of sheep, horses and cattle

On the 6th I resumed the march to the Siberian frontier in a gale of wind, which sent the snow along in clouds and the thermometer down to many degrees below zero The country was an undulating sandy stretch covered with stunted bush and a few trees.

Four miles beyond camp I crossed the Irtish River again on to an open grass-covered plain which continued uninterrupted until a range of low hills was reached at about 19 miles, truly a bare and desolate land. Some three miles through these hills I debouched on to the plain once more, where I hoped to find some auls in which to camp the night, as the wind was blowing

KAZAK WOMEN AND CHILD IN MONGOLIA.

with great force, while the dense clouds of driven snow prevented our seeing more than a few yards ahead. These "burans," or storms, for which the steppes are noted, spring up with appalling suddenness, and often travellers, overtaken by them and unable to find shelter, are frozen to death. Fortunately the Kazak guides with me knew the correct route, a good point in their favour, so we held on our course, until the wind dropped considerably with the approach of darkness, and by 6 o'clock ceased altogether It was unpleasant as long as it lasted, while the prospects of another disaster and further cases of frost bite amongst the caravan were not agreeable to contemplate All were, however, well clothed and provided with ample furs, gloves and scarves, and thus able to resist the fury of the storm which, though not so bad as that experienced on December 28th, was still a formidable specimen of the dreaded " buran."

I reached a Kazak camp of 20 auls at 8 o'clock, after a forced march of fully 30 miles, necessitated by the fact of there being no intermediate stage I was always glad to reach the shelter of these auls as the pain of travelling and the terrific bumping over stones, hillocks, and numberless other obstacles was just about the limit of human endurance.

There were at least 100 Kazaks at this camp, the auls being surrounded with walls of grass and bullrush palisades to protect them from the force of the wind which blows with great violence over these bleak and arid steppes

I have before described the dwellings of the nomads, and the aul has ere now become familiar to the reader The furniture and appointments of these movable homes are of the simplest description. Mine that night resembled a butcher's shop, for in the central part over the fireplace hung many joints of meat being smoked for future use , it was therefore a matter of much difficulty moving about without risk of capsizing sundry sirloins and shoulders, not, indeed, of mutton but horse, for the dweller of the steppes finds horseflesh a great delicacy, and it ever forms a prominent feature of the bill of fare. Around the sides were several boxes of Russian make, ornamented with gaudy tinsel work and layers of brass, a form of embellishment dear to the nomad's heart. Within these boxes were pieces of silk and cloth, constituting the finery of the ladies of the family and for wear on state occasions, such as a wedding or some equally important event

Prominent in the aul was the leathern " kumis" bottle, that doubtful beverage of which an account has already been given.

The Kazaks drink large quantities of it, and its manufacture is one of the principal occupations of the women in early spring Stuck into the rods, forming the framework of the aul, are wooden bowls and spoons, black and grimy, from which everyone eats indiscriminately, the only washing they receive being a rinse with water at rare intervals. Numdahs or carpets of felt were spread upon the floor and also round the fire which blazed cheerily in the centre, thus completing the furniture of this primitive homestead

The Kazaks were much astonished on hearing from Rasul that I performed my own medical dressings, and the head man amongst them came to ask my advice as to the curing of sundry ailments with which members of his band were afflicted

Their faith in the healing powers of the European is remarkable, they apparently thinking it only necessary to bring forward the sufferer for an immediate cure to be effected. This is often embarrassing, since one's reputation is at stake, and to get out of the trouble with safety is a matter calling for a considerable display of skill and circumspection

The following day another long and agonising march ensued to Uliassutou, on the Siberian frontier, due west of the Zaisan Lake. The latter is an immense sheet of water into which the Irtish River runs, and, issuing from the western shore, flows through the province of Semipalatinsk, past Omsk, and northward to the Arctic Ocean It was 28 miles to Uliassutou, all rough going, mostly over plain cut up by innumerable ruts and hillocks, in which the wheels of the tarantass bumped and jolted with sickening persistency, though luckily for me without coming to grief

I reached the frontier late at night, camping in an old log hut there belonging to a Kazak It was an indescribably filthy abode, low pitched, dark and gloomy, with no outlet for the accumulated stench of long years, and only a tiny door to enter by, so one had to bend down and crawl through into the inky darkness beyond

Across the Roof of the World.

At break of dawn I despatched Rasul in search of a fresh tarantass, or a sledge, to take me into Zaisan, 56 versts distant He returned towards 8 o'clock accompanied by two Siberians, one being the official appointed to supervise the skin trade and examine hides entering Russian territory, there being a considerable business in skins amongst the Kazaks, who dispose of them in large numbers to Russian traders

These men were very respectful, and when I enquired if they could supply sledges for the journey to Zaisan, replied in the affirmative, but stated the cost would be 50 roubles for two sledges. This I knew to be an outrageous swindle, and promptly told them so, and they finally reduced their demands to 30 roubles, nearly four times the just amount, though as I felt too ill to indulge in further remonstrance with them, and was naturally anxious to reach Zaisan without further delay I agreed for this sum   The sledges were duly brought round, and at 10 o'clock, having loaded up and dressed everyone's wounds, I set forth, crossing the frontier into Siberia, a few hundred yards further down

I had been steadily discarding various articles since leaving Shara Sumbe, having no further use for them, and now disposed of some more, including a stove of good iron work I had brought from Chuguchak   I presented this to the Kazak owner of the log hut, much to his delight, and when I left he was setting it up, giving to this Black Hole on the Mongolian Steppes quite an air of importance

Just beyond the frontier, here determined by a little river, the northern banks of which are in Chinese territory and the southern within Russian jurisdiction, was a neatly built log hut covered with white plaster, the residence of the official detailed to watch the skin import trade and from whom I had hired the sledges   When I passed in my sledge he came out with his family and invited me to partake of a cold collation, a repast where vodka predominated.   Having swindled me heavily over the hire of the sledges, I suppose he thought something ought to be done to bring his rapacity less prominently into light, hence the lunch and the vodka   I stayed there about an hour and then bidding him farewell set out again.

As soon as we were comfortably installed in the sledges the horses bounded forward at the touch of the yemschik's whip over the hard and firm snow, the sledge gliding swiftly along with no sensation of movement or discomfort, an exhilarating mode of progression peculiar to such travelling   The country was a barren undulating steppe covered with a white layer of snow, and monotonous in the immensity of its extent

It was my first march within the mighty Russian Empire, my first acquaintance with the Siberian Steppes, which stretch away to the shores of the Arctic Ocean   I had crossed the dividing line between the dominions of the Flowery Kingdom and those of the Northern Colossus, not without a feeling of relief, for the journey had now reached a stage where it was no longer a matter of keeping warm but a stern question of keeping alive

It was onward, ever onward, across the vast and silent steppes with the land locked in the icy grip of winter, the aspect of dreariness and desolation being oppressive and gloomy in the extreme

Twenty-four versts from the frontier I reached a village and drove up to the post-house, a wooden building of two rooms, in one of which the family lived, the other being set apart for me.

That day, January 8th, was a Russian feast day, and the inhabitants were exchanging visits and parading through the streets in sledges, singing carols and drinking healths at intervals

The old man in charge of the post-house and his wrinkled wife were in a hilarious state of mind, having imbibed not wisely but too well, so that business for the nonce was attended to by the son, a lad of sixteen, who looked bored with life and moved about as though he had lost a 10-rouble piece and picked up a kopeck

After my travels through the desperate country just quitted, the furniture of the post-house, meagre though it was, came as a revelation to me, and, despite the pain and suffering, I passed a fairly comfortable night amid surroundings to which I had for many months been totally unaccustomed

The walls of my room were decorated with prints of fiery colour, prominent amongst them being portraits of the Emperor and Empress

At 8 o'clock the following morning horses and sledges were brought round and I entered on the drive of 26 versts into Zaisan It was still the same barren and snow-covered steppe country over which we mostly galloped, and then finally breasting a low ridge, we discerned the little town of Zaisan several miles distant, and lying at the foot of a range of hills The only exciting incident on the way occurred when the rearmost sledge, taking a corner too rapidly, overturned and shot the baggage and occupants out unceremoniously, but the snow was too deep and soft for any harm to be done.

On arrival in Zaisan I drove to the post-house, and there installed, sent off letters to the Russian authorities and to an officer in the 3rd Siberian Cossacks to whom I had been given a note of introduction in Kulja in case I should pass that way. In course of time they appeared and after a stay of a few days in the post-house, where I received medical attention at the hands of the surgeon in charge of the hospital, I was removed to the latter building there to undergo operations for the grafting of new skin and be more directly under the care of the doctor than I could have been in the little post-house

Giyani, too, received every attention at their hands, and to the care and skill displayed by the Russian doctor and the great kindness shown him, as well as me, in our unfortunate contretemps, he owes the complete restoration of his hands to their normal condition

Before resuming the narrative of the last stage of the journey to the Trans-Siberian Railway, it may be interesting to give some account of this far away outpost of the Czar's Empire on the borders of Mongolia and Siberia

A Month in Hospital.

Zaisan is a small Russian military post, 56 versts from the Mongolian frontier, and hard by the great Zaisan Lake. To the south lie the mountains of the Saur range, wherein a variety of wild sheep is to be found, as also a large red bear, which is doubtless of the same species as that encountered in the Altai.

There is a considerable nomad population in the Zaisan district, and during the summer months trade in horses and cattle

THE AUTHOR AND TWO RUSSIAN OFFICERS.

is carried on. The Zaisan Lake holds fish, and many are disposed of in the settlement. Small river boats now ply on the lake and down the Irtish River to Omsk in summer, so that the little frontier post is connected by water with the more populous part of Siberia along the great railway.

During the time I spent in hospital there was little to do beyond reading the few books remaining with me, and indulging in long conversations with Russian officers who called and assisted to make my enforced detention as pleasant as possible, a kindness I shall ever look back upon with unfeigned gratitude.

When sufficiently convalescent to venture into the open I availed myself of several invitations to dine with my genial Russian acquaintances, whose efforts to render my lot happy were still further evidenced.

MY ORDERLY AND A SIBERIAN SOLDIER OUTSIDE THE HOSPITAL AT ZAISAN.

Before leaving Zaisan I paid off Rasul and Yusuf, giving them money, clothes and rations, together with a horse and sledge, to take them to Urumchi, in company with a caravan then starting for Chinese Tartary, on the way to their far-distant homes.

Rasul had served me well, so it was with feelings of sorrow and regret that I bade him farewell and severed the last link between me and Southern Turkistan and the happy lands of the Thian Shan.

Through the kindness and personal interest shown me by His Majesty's Ambassador in St. Petersburg, I was provided with permits by the Governor-General of Western Siberia, acting on instructions from the Russian Government. The latter communicated with the local authorities at Zaisan and along the line of my route to the Trans-Siberian Railway, 800 miles to the north, with the result that many difficulties were removed and I was enabled to travel at greater speed than would have been the case were I less powerfully accredited

CHAPTER XXIV.

BY SLEDGE ACROSS THE SIBERIAN STEPPES.

WHEN I first arrived in Zaisan the doctors advised my proceeding with all possible haste to Omsk for the purpose of undergoing treatment in the military hospital there, but on further consultation this was considered impracticable in view of the state of the frostbitten parts. The surgeons therefore communicated with the Russian authorities in St. Petersburg, through the Governor-General, in a despatch, stating that the removal should not be attempted for at least another fortnight.

SUMMER VIEW OF A STREET IN ZAISAN.

By the beginning of February I was in a fit condition to undertake the long sledge journey to the Trans-Siberian Railway, and therefore fixed the date of my departure for the night of February 6th, completing all arrangements accordingly.

During that afternoon I paid a number of farewell calls, being now able to don my full-dress uniform. Everyone had been more than kind and hospitable to myself and Giyani during our sojourn in Zaisan, and we owed them a debt of gratitude it would indeed be difficult to repay.

Sledging Through Siberia.

In the evening I supped with my genial friend, Captain Chytanoff, of the 3rd Siberian Cossacks, and his wife, and we pledged each other in good cognac, expressing mutual hopes that some day we might again meet to renew our acquaintance under happier auspices.

I had ordered the sledges for 10 o'clock, as the mails had arrived during the day, and fresh horses for the outward journey would not be available earlier. There was considerable delay, it being 2 o'clock on the morning of the 7th before I finally started. A number of Russian soldiers, patients in the hospital, came to witness my departure, and when I personally inspected Giyani and tightened his coats and mufflers they could not withhold exclamations of astonishment. I enquired of Khatimski the cause, and he informed me a Russian officer would never dream of taking such trouble with his men, and that to serve under the British must indeed be happiness itself.

KIRGHIZ AND CAMEL CART.

From Zaisan the route I followed to the Trans-Siberian Railway lies through Kokbekti, Ustkhamengorsk, Zaminagorsk, Barnaul and down the Ob River to Novo Nicholaevsk, a small town on the railway south of the city of Tomsk, the capital of Western Siberia. It is a total distance of nearly 800 miles, and the road between Kokbekti and Ustkhamengorsk skirts the western slopes of the Altai, some outlying spurs of which it crosses.

In summer travelling is done by means of the tarantass, a four-wheeled vehicle, but in winter sledges are in vogue. The traveller can purchase his own sledge and thus obviate the trouble of removing his baggage and himself at every stage, as the post sledges only run on the stage to which they belong. It is thus preferable to have one's own sledge, and avoid the inconvenience of turning out at all hours of the day and night to change vehicles, especially in the winter, when movement in the open is anything but pleasant

A good sledge can be purchased for from 40 to 60 roubles and re-sold at one's destination, often for as much or more than was paid for it, particularly in the winter when they are in great demand

The roads are maintained by Government, but require little attention in winter as the track runs over the broad steppe on a layer of snow usually several feet in thickness   The stages are at distances varying from 15 to 35 versts, the intervals depending on the nature of the country and the state of the roads to be traversed

As I was unable to purchase a satisfactory sledge in Zaisan, I took the post vehicles which necessitated sixty changes *en route*—in mid-winter very poor fun   These post sledges are marvellously strong, and they need to be to withstand the terrific bumping experienced over rough parts of the road

Sledge travelling in Siberia is not expensive, the charges for horses and vehicles being 3 kopecks per horse per verst, and a further tax of 10 kopecks per horse per stage levied by the Government   There is also a charge of 12 kopecks per sledge per stage.   Considering the nature of the country and the conditions prevailing, especially in the winter, these charges are by no means excessive

A receipt is given at every stage for the hire, and in each post-house is affixed a notice detailing the number of versts to the next station, so that one can calculate the amount to be paid over, and obviate the chances of being swindled.

The horsing of the sledges is, as a rule, distinctly good, so that in winter, on well-frozen tracks, one can maintain a high rate of speed

The traveller, on application to the local authorities and the production of his passport, can obtain a permit entitling him to

404

horses and vehicles *en route* at the fixed rates, but the holding
of this permit gives no priority of claim, and should any officials
be travelling at the same time he only receives horses after the
latter have been supplied. There is, however, another class of

GIYANI IN SIBERIAN DRESS.

permit, a courier's pass, the possession of which entitles the
holder to horses without delay, and should there be none
available at the post stations others must be procured locally.
This permit is a difficult one to obtain and is only given in

405

exceptional cases and when one is furnished with powerful credentials

It is usually limited to couriers and others proceeding on business of importance that will brook no delay Personally, the kindness and influence of the British Ambassador at St Petersburg procured for me every attention at the hands of the Russian authorities *en route*, and enabled me to travel at a speed which would not have been possible under other circumstances

Before leaving Zaisan I had given away the greater part of my camp kit, remaining stores and sundry other articles, having now no further need for them

I had two sledges, one for myself and Khatimski, the other for Giyani and the kit These sledges had been ordered from the postal authorities, and everything being ready we started on the long drive to the railway. The drivers were Kirghiz and the horses fresh and high spirited, so we glided swiftly along, doing the first stage of 17 versts in a little over two hours Here horses and sledges were changed and we sped on through the night and all the following day halting only to change at every stage Once or twice at the post-houses we indulged in a glass of tea and some ready cooked food, which I carried.

The cold was simply appalling, while during the night of the 7th the thermometer on the outside of the sledge sank to 46 degrees below zero.

At half-past seven on the morning of the 8th we arrived at one of the post-houses, literally stiff with the cold, despite innumerable fur coats, felt boots, felt socks, woollen "rizais," and blankets There had been a strong wind blowing through the night and this had added to our difficulties in keeping the merest semblance of warmth.

On arriving at the post-house above alluded to I felt my left foot numbed and lifeless, and when I pulled off the felt boots and stockings, it was quite white and insensible to several digs I gave it with Khatimski's knife The starosta, or man in charge of the post station, then came in and rubbed it vigorously with snow and vodka, the latter being considered an excellent remedy in such cases. Gradually he restored life to it though it was more than a month before resuming its normal condition, for the whole of the skin peeled, while in places where I had pricked it with the knife it festered badly, and later necessitated my halting three days in Ustkhamenogorsk to allay the swelling.

Siberia is a hard country to travel through in winter, and the starosta was much amused at my remarks on the climatic

KHATIMSKI AND MY ORDERLY.

rigours of his native land. He told me one might be the Czar of All the Russias but little King Frost cared not for that!

I was much astonished when the starosta and a Tartar merchant in the post-house at the time assured me the frost-bite was due to my being over-dressed, and that to avoid a repetition of it I must discard a few felt stockings and other articles of clothing, in order to give free play to the limbs. I followed this sage advice and had no further trouble, regretting I had not done so before leaving Zaisan, in accordance with Khatimski's advice. He wore only two pairs of thick stockings, whilst I had four.

The road here lay to the south of the great Zaisan Lake, on which small river steamers run in the summer months down the Irtish River to Omsk, a five-day journey and a pleasant one at that season of the year

The country around the Zaisan Lake is inhabited by Kirghiz, or Kazaks as they are known in the Chinese Empire, the sledge drivers on this portion of the road being recruited entirely from them. The land is a vast and desolate steppe, sparsely inhabited in winter, though a great grazing ground during the rest of the year, and affording fine pasturage to large herds of horses and cattle

In appearance, in their manners and customs, and in their mode of life, the Kirghiz of Russian territory closely resemble the Kazaks one encounters in Chinese Turkistan and Mongolia, with the exception that contact with the Russians has rendered them a trifle more civilised

In days gone by the steppe country throughout this region of Siberia was given over to the Kirghiz who roamed it unchecked, but with the advance of time they have become less independent than in former days.

Concerning the steppe country in the vicinity of Lake Zaisan the Kirghiz have an interesting legend to the effect that in days long before the Christian era the land was peopled by a high and mighty race, two individuals of which, a father and his son, with the object of damming the river, determined to remove one of the peaks of the Tarbagatai Range to the southward and transfer it to the banks of the Irtish River, hard by the town of Ustkhamenogorsk. As the distance was too great to be compassed in one day they decided to halt the night *en route*, and there the son desired to visit his *fiancée*, who lived in an aul by the lake The father granted permission but warned the son not to tarry the night there since the marriage portion had not been handed over, or the negotiations ratified. But the son, enamoured of the lady, paid no heed to his father's commands and remained there till dawn. When he returned and endeavoured to take up his portion of the load all his efforts proved futile, so the father divined the waywardness of his son He therefore directed him to stand beneath the mountain, and, once in that position, released his hold, with the result that the mountain fell and both were entombed The mother mourned many days for the lost ones, finally setting out in search of them, in the end discovering the mountain beneath which the two were buried She wept bitterly, shedding tears of blood in her anguish, and when these ceased to flow tears of crystal succeeded them The mountain in question, composed of argil, crystal, and quartz, stands to the south of the Zaisan Lake, and its appearance lends colour to this curious tradition of the nomad Kirghiz

Throughout the 8th I drove on at great speed, at 10 o'clock that night reaching the little town of Kokbekti, 240 versts from Zaisan The post-house was a fairly substantial one as they go in Siberia I had rather an interesting adventure there which deserves recording Wishing to change some photographic plates I entered one of the rooms and transformed it into an impromptu dark room by closing the door and drawing sundry curtains Whilst in the midst of operations I was startled by shrieks from the corner of the room, and then discovered I had penetrated the bedroom of an ancient dame, who, to judge from her protestations, must have thought I was on burglary bent or some other equally undesirable errand Photographic operations were consequently postponed indefinitely

The great feature of a post-house is the ever-prominent samovar, a brass urn with a chimney down the centre, the space beneath being filled with a charcoal fire The teapot contains a strong brew of tea, and a little poured into the glasses is diluted with hot water from the samovar   The tea is drunk from glasses, without milk, and is usually flavoured with a slice of lemon

The samovar is a popular institution in Russia, constantly in evidence, amongst rich and poor alike, so that although one can obtain little else in the post-houses along the line of route, this is ever to hand   Food in any shape is rarely obtainable, as travellers are expected to carry their own, though occasionally a few eggs are obtainable and a supply of the black bread, which forms the staple diet of the Siberian peasant

The post-houses are built of logs, the interstices being filled with mud and plaster   The interior is usually provided with benches, doing duty as beds, while a table, and one or two chairs, complete the furniture   In a corner is the brick stove, built into the wall, by which the apartment is heated   The front and edges of doors are heavily coated with felt to keep out the draught, and when one enters the rush of cold air from without mingling with the warmer air within creates a volume of dense mist, resembling that encountered on the mountain side   All windows are double and sealed in between and round the edges with paper and cotton wool, the result being the atmosphere is often so stale and heavy that one could almost cut it with a knife   Of washing arrangements there are none, for the Siberian does not regard the matter of ablutions in the same light as we do, and manages with quite a minimum amount of soap and water.

The men in charge of the post stations are usually moujiks, with shaggy beards, sheep-skin coats and caps, and wearing an air of savagery in keeping with their attire   The women one sees are distinctly plain and dull, having enormous waists and unduly large feet, which, if it does not add to their personal charm, enables them to keep a good hold on the country

All Russians are religious, or at any rate profess to be, and no room is complete without the familiar " ikon," or religious picture, standing on a bracket in one corner.   In front of it is suspended a lamp which is supposed to burn without intermission, though this rule is generally waived, especially by those possessed to only a limited extent of this world's goods. Portraits of the Czar and Czarina are also to be found in nearly every post-house, for the untutored moujik regards the Autocrat of All the Russias in the light of a being to whom all must bow in absolute submission.

None of the people are ever in a hurry except where officialdom is concerned, and then all are galvanised into activity, bustling

A HALT AT A SIBERIAN POST-HOUSE.

about to an extent that reveals the awe in which the ruling classes are held. To the energetic Britisher, accustomed to promptitude and despatch, the delays often met with and the lack of energy displayed are most exasperating.

If anything requires to be done the reply is " Séchas." Now the definition of this word as given in the dictionary is " within the hour," its idiomatic rendering being " immediately," but in practice it means " to-day " or " to-morrow," or within a lifetime if one is lucky. It is the first word one learns on entering the Russian Empire and the last heard on leaving it. There are other words in the language dear to the heart of the slothful Russian, but " Séchas " heads them all, and when he quits this mortal coil the last word breathed to the unwashed multitude around the bedside is " Séchas "

I left Kokbekti for Ustkhamenogorsk at 10 30 on the night of the 8th, the road being hilly and rough, and the thermometer dropping to 45 degrees below zero   Soon after midnight I arrived at one of the post-houses and found it full of soldiers sleeping on the benches, the table, and spread about in all positions over the floor   The starosta was asleep in the only other room in the house, and in no good humour at being disturbed at this unearthly hour of the night, grumbling loudly and declaring no horses were available   I allowed him to finish and then produced my papers, at the sight of which his face fell and horses were forthcoming without further delay   Though I rejoiced at the change thus brought about by the display of my credentials I inwardly sympathised with the man at being turned out at two in the morning to harness fresh horses, with nearly 80 degrees of frost and a cold wind that must have made him curse the " Angliski offitzier "

Throughout the 9th I drove hard, the horses at the different stages on the way being in excellent condition so that we literally tore over the snow-covered steppes, with never a sign of life save the post-houses situated at intervals of twenty and twenty-five versts.   These were the steppes over which in years gone by marched many a batch of prisoners doomed to perpetual exile in Siberia   Often the journey from Russia to the distant penal settlements occupied a full two years, during which the weaker amongst the detachments succumbed to the hardships of such a fearful ordeal   As one drives across the silent steppes one's thoughts travel back to those dark and gloomy days when every verst of the road was marked with such suffering as few have endured since sorrow first entered the world

Shortly before eleven that night I crossed the Irtish River and ran into Ustkhamenogorsk, driving first to the post-house with Giyani and the kit, and then to the house of Khatimski's elder brother. We succeeded with difficulty in rousing the latter who after cordial greetings produced a substantial supper.

This brother was engaged in the mining industry, of which Ustkhamenogorsk forms the principal centre, all the ore mined in the Altai and surrounding district being brought into the town, which thereby enjoys a considerable reputation.

Ustkhamenogorsk itself is situated on the Irtish River. The houses are constructed of wood, some two-storied, but the large

A SIBERIAN VILLAGE IN MID-WINTER.

majority single. It was a penal settlement in days gone by and old residents told me of the custom prevailing in those days to guard against the burglarious attacks of escaped convicts. With a view to obviating such possible eventualities from those endeavouring to evade the law and leave the horrors of this earthly hell behind them, bread and other provisions were placed upon the window sills of houses, more particularly those on the outskirts of a town; thus the fugitive might partake of them and not be forced to enter a house for food, a proceeding that might easily be accompanied by murder were the intruder disturbed

After supper and a long conversation I returned to the post-house to sleep, and had a good rest after the bumping of nearly three hundred miles from Zaisan

On the morning of the 10th my foot was still badly swollen and much inflamed, so I had perforce to halt here a few days pending its recovery to a condition enabling me to move with any degree of comfort and safety   I had it examined by a Russian doctor here and he was very dubious as to its state

Khatimski had three brothers in Ustkhamenogorsk, all married, and at their cordial and pressing invitations I divided my time between them, dining that day with the elder brother and supping at another's, all the ladies being dressed in the smartest of toilettes and particularly kind and gracious

With these good people I obtained further insight into Russian life, which varies considerably from our ideas, but though it is wanting in several essentials has much to recommend it

All Russians are gifted with voracious appetites and the care of the inner man has been reduced to a fine art. At dinner, which corresponds to our lunch, there is a formidable array of viands, commencing with the " zakouska," consisting of sardines, caviare, sliced tomatoes, raw fish and other delicacies In the afternoon there is tea, of which numerous glasses are consumed, and late at night, usually about 11 o'clock, supper is served, of dimensions warranted to give the untrained Anglo-Saxon nightmares for a month   At the close of this meal, music and singing supervenes until two or three in the morning, when it is considered time to retire!

Russians are very affectionate and spend much of their time in kissing each other, quite a popular pastime when indulged in with the ladies but apt to fall rather flat where it is confined to men

I dined and supped at a different place every day, and on arrival it was the custom for everyone to embrace, although twelve hours had not elapsed since they last saw each other. The Russian is, however, a hospitable soul and leaves no stone unturned in the service of his guest.

I spent an enjoyable three days in Ustkhamenogorsk, gathering much information on a variety of subjects so that the time was not altogether wasted.

CHAPTER XXV.

THROUGH THE SIBERIAN FORESTS TO THE TRANS-SIBERIAN RAILWAY.

SIBERIA is undoubtedly a country with a great future, and in this respect the mineral wealth it holds will play a prominent part. The latter is distributed throughout the country, the region east of the Baikal Lake being prolific in gold, whilst that

KAZAKS WATCHING OUR DEPARTURE FROM A POST-HOUSE.

portion of the Altai Range lying within the boundaries of the Russian Empire is known to contain the precious metal in large and payable quantities.

The Altai Mountains offer a favourable field for the gold miner, but the difficulty experienced in obtaining concessions has acted as a deterrent to mining enterprise, though there are at the present time a few companies engaged in the industry

It has not yet, however, assumed the proportions its importance and the amount of gold in the land demand.

Whilst in Ustkhamenogorsk I was shown nuggets and gold dust obtained from neighbouring districts, and from my own observations and enquiries made on the southern slopes of the Altai and in passing through Western Siberia, I gathered gold was to be found in considerable quantities, and more than sufficient to warrant its careful exploitation. Besides this,

AN AERIAL RAILWAY IN THE SIBERIAN ALTAI.

copper is also found in the country, as well as silver, platinum, galena, coal and numerous products which only need working on modern lines for them to develop into thriving industries.

Several million pounds' worth of gold are exported from Siberia annually, but this is no criterion as to the true output, since a large amount is stolen by the miners and others, and only a comparatively small part of what really issues from the mines finds its way to the proper destination.

Within recent years much progress has been made in the mining industry, and facilities, though meagre and by no means sufficient to meet up-to-date requirements, have been granted to parties of mining experts with a view to opening up the country and developing this most important part of its hidden wealth, though much yet remains to be done in this direction

Fresh orders had been received by the Chief of Police in Ustkhamenogorsk with regard to my onward journey, he having instructions to render any assistance of which I might stand in need   An officer of police was detailed to accompany me to make the necessary arrangements and ensure my reaching the railway without undue delay

On the day of my departure I dined with one of the Khatimski brothers and his dainty young wife, who spoke French, and in the morning I went to see the only Englishman in the place, he being in charge of a mine in the district , the first Englishman I had seen since leaving Kashgar eight months before

At seven in the evening the sledges drove into the courtyard, and having said good-bye to all and thanked them cordially for much hospitality experienced at their hands, I sped forth into the night   There were now three sledges, my own and Khatimski's, another for Giyani and the kit, and a third occupied by the police officer   We drove on all night, halting only to change horses and sledges at the post stations, fresh relays being instantly forthcoming, for the presence of the police officer and the previous receipt of orders to further the onward drive galvanised the natives into a state of activity that did one good to see.

At the second stage out from Ustkhamenogorsk we left the great road running to Semipalatinsk and Omsk, and branched off due north on the Barnaul route, entering a part of Western Siberia administered by the Governor of Tomsk

At the post-house on this stage I was met by the head man of the village, arrayed in his chain of office and official robes.

A Drunken Driver.

He was a big, shaggy-bearded individual and stood stiffly at attention when I addressed him through Khatimski, calling me "Your Exalted Excellency," and apparently regarding me as a second Czar. When I embarked in my sledge he wished me long life and happiness, and gave a salute as though I were the high and mighty Czar himself.

I enjoyed this part of the long sledge drive immensely, despite the terrific cold, as the horses were first rate and simply flew over the ground.

A PORTLY SIBERIAN.

At one or two of the post houses some difficulty was experienced in obtaining Government animals as the Imperial mails had but recently passed through, and all available horses had been taken for their conduct to the posts ahead. With the aid, however, of the officers who accompanied me I was able to engage others from the peasantry who showed no reluctance in complying with our requests, a state of affairs for which the appearance of my escort, booted and spurred, and adorned with clanking swords, was largely responsible.

This ready compliance was yet another proof of the awe in which officials are held in the Russian Empire, and the alacrity with which their behests are obeyed.

All the drivers were now Siberians, fine stalwart fellows, and they handled the teams of three horses in a manner that compelled my unqualified admiration. The roads were in good condition from the heavy snowfalls and hard frosts, so that the iron shod runners on the sledges glided over the surface at great speed They are hardy people, these dwellers of the steppes, inured to all the rigours of the Siberian winter and capable of undergoing much hardship Often during the night I would look round the side of the leather apron covering the front of the sledge to note the pace we were going, there sat the driver on the cross-board which does duty as a seat, muffled up in innumerable sheep-skins, a huge round figure having the appearance of a gigantic barrel Now and again he would brandish his long whip and the team would dash on in a mad gallop to the next post-house there they would be unharnessed, their coats a mass of icicles from the perspiration, fresh horses being put in for us to continue those exciting and breakneck drives which sledge driving in Siberia alone can give

On the morning of the 13th I reached the village of Vidrika, the Chief of Police meeting me at the post-house, in accordance with instructions received from the Governor of Tomsk, through whose district I was now passing

For the last stage into Zaminagorsk, a fair-sized town, I had a drunken yemshik on the box, and the way he handled the team, taking me over the plain at racing speed, was worthy of the chariot days of Rome

Just before reaching the town there was a long descent to make which we took at full speed, the yemshik yelling and flourishing his whip, the while I was busy preparing for the upset which seemed inevitable But nothing happened and we reached the bottom of the hill in safety and bowled on into Zaminagorsk, where I gave the yemshik a more than usually large tip, whereat he saluted me with much deference and promptly went off to invest it in the local saloon

Beyond Zaminagorsk the country is undulating, and it becomes more thickly populated, villages occurring at every fifteen or twenty versts When passing through a village a Siberian yemshik always does so at a pace calculated to maintain his reputation as a handler of the ribbons of a high order, and the sledge, bumping in and out of ruts and depressions in the street, almost throws one out. But the vehicles are probably the strongest of their class in the world and stand the bumping well. During the whole of my journey through Siberia I never had a sledge break down nor any delay through collision with others.

I held on all day during the 14th and arrived at the little village of Chistunika that night, being met there by two police officers, one of whom was to accompany me in relief of the Ustkhamenogorsk official as far as the railway.

CAMEL SLEDGES IN SIBERIA.

There was a fire in this village, a house and shop being a sheet of flame, against which all the efforts of the unfortunate inmates were unavailing, for the water being frozen solid, they could do nothing against the fierce blaze, the light from which threw a lurid glare over the white wilderness around. No one, however, seemed to worry much until the alarm bell 'from the church rang out summoning all hands to the scene. I stayed an hour there but could not do much in view of the utter lack of water, while all the rescue party could effect was the saving of the inmates and such goods and chattels as they could recover from the burning building.

After leaving Chistunika I pressed on with the utmost speed throughout the night, at dawn reaching Barnaul, a large town of 40,000 inhabitants on the left bank of the Ob River, some 200 miles south of the Trans-Siberian Railway. It is the chief centre of the mining industry of the Altai, and a rising place, mainly due to the trade with Mongolia, which is on the increase.

A SIBERIAN FISH MARKET.

Trade with Mongolia is carried on with Kosh Agach, on the frontier south-east of Barnaul, through Kobdo to Uliassutai, the route thither from Russian territory having in recent years been greatly improved, with the result that large quantities of Russian made goods are imported, and every facility afforded traders by the Government.

The larger villages in Siberia boast a market place, where fish all frozen stiff and hard are sold in solid blocks, the portions being cut up with an axe. Such scenes as these throw out in still stronger relief the rigours of the Siberian winter.

Barnaul, and Bisk, another town some forty miles to the south-east, is also the point of departure for the *Ovis ammon* ground in the Kosh Agach district and the Chinese Altai. To reach these hunting grounds one can leave the railway at Novo-Nicholaevsk and journey by boat to the above towns, where there is a post road to the Russo-Chinese frontier at Kosh Agach,

THROUGH THE SIBERIAN FORESTS.

whence it is only three or four days trekking to the haunts of the ammon.

In view of the great possibilities of trade with Mongolia the Russians are improving the communications and opening up the country ; steps that are progressing yearly.

I halted a few hours in Barnaul for a substantial meal and to snatch some much-needed rest, and then later with fresh horses and sledges continued the journey.

North of Barnaul there is much forest country, and wolves, creatures inseparably associated with sledge travelling in Siberia, were said to be common there, but on this occasion they failed to show themselves

All have heard of onslaughts committed by fierce and hungry wolves in the gloomy recesses of the Siberian forests, as they pursued the sledge of the traveller, the horses at a mad gallop born of despair, the occupants sitting grim and determined, striking down members of the howling pack, who nevertheless prosecuted the chase with that energy characteristic of this fierce denizen of the woods. I was not, however, troubled with their attentions, and thus the romances I had read in childhood days were not borne out in after years on that long drive through the vast and silent forests.

In the evening I reached a fairly large village where apparently everyone was out on the spree, so considerable difficulty was experienced in getting fresh horses at the post-house, as the man in charge could not be found. When finally he did appear he proved to be very drunk and impertinent. This sent the police officer into such a towering rage that it reduced the wretched man to a state of pitiable misery and dejection, the more so when he realised how gravely he had offended the power and majesty of the law. Horses and sledges were then forthcoming, and I was of opinion that a little clemency might be exercised, but the affront to the police officer could not apparently be overlooked and he condemned the man and his family to the care of the local gaol, where no doubt he had time to reflect on the indiscretion of falling foul of officialdom

The same police officer told me a story amply portraying the state of ignorance prevalent amongst the peasant classes It appears some Indian traders, with a view to opening up trade, had recently arrived in Barnaul from Russian Turkistan. With their advent a rumour spread abroad that they were there for the purpose of abducting children, and the result was the unfortunate men were mobbed and badly handled, one of them being killed and others injured. The police officer on duty told me he had only saved them with the utmost difficulty, breaking his "nagaika," or Cossack whip, in beating back the mob.

Between Barnaul and Novo Nicholaevsk I met large caravans of freight sledges engaged in trade with the district to the south towards Mongolia and the Altai. Each sledge was drawn by a single horse, about ten or twelve sledges being in charge of one driver, who slept most of the time, which, however, did not

"THE ROAD BECOMES WORN INTO A SUCCESSION OF
TRANSVERSE RIDGES."

seem to matter much, for the horses knew the way, plodding on with great sagacity.

From the number of these freight sledges, which are constantly passing, the road becomes worn into a succession of transverse ridges, caused by the animals treading in each other's footsteps, thus leaving a series of equi-distant and parallel lines as though sleepers had been laid across the roadway.

All night we pressed on, alternately cantering and galloping, but occasionally breaking into a furious run over some

specially favourable stretch, and pushing onward over the immense
steppes which had long since begun to pall in the monotony of
their desolation On the morning of the 16th we entered
an extensive forest country of fir and pine, sombre and forbidding
in their coats of snow and frost.

Northward of Barnaul there is a continual succession of
verst posts which mark the distances between towns and villages,
tall poles painted black and white, and as we glided past at
intervals I experienced a feeling of inward satisfaction at the
rapid approach to the railway

My story is now drawing to a close In the late afternoon of
February 16th I reached a small village, where, after an
hour's halt, I started out on the final stage which was to bring
me to the Siberian Railway, and the end of the trans-Asiatic
journey

From this point the winter road follows the Ob River, and
less than an hour's run revealed the lights of Novo Nicholaevsk.
Those twinkling lights in the distance were full of significance,
for they denoted the end of a long trek, of the close of
nearly a year's wanderings across the great Asiatic continent, a
journey to accomplish which many and varied forms of
transport had been utilised—"tongas," boats, coolies, ponies,
yaks, camels, oxen, mapas, Chinese carts, and sledges. The
long land journey of 3,500 miles was nearing its conclusion—the
great trek was drawing to a close.

Those lights, too, now momentarily becoming more distinct
as we glided swiftly onward over the silent steppe, brought
home to me the fact that I was approaching the Trans-Siberian
Railway, that greatest of modern engineering wonders

Further on we crossed to the left bank of the river, passing
the fine railway bridge which here spans it and over which runs
the line from Moscow to Vladivostok The construction of
this great railway, initiated by Czar Alexander III and constructed at a cost of one hundred millions sterling, was a task
involving big engineering problems by reason of the immense

natural difficulties which confronted the engineers, but which skill and foresight, coupled with untiring energy, brought into life and being—a work that will be handed down as one of the most gigantic enterprises of our time.

Siberia has ever been associated with gangs of convicts and bands of exiles doomed to perpetual banishment in the gloomy recesses of that land of ice and snow. It has also been regarded

NEARING THE END OF THE JOURNEY—THE LAST
POST-HOUSE.

as a land of misery and despair, and one unfit for the coloniser and the emigrant. The advent of the railway has, however, swept aside these terrors and opened up a country which possesses unlimited resources. The line runs for six thousand miles, linking east with west—a line that has brought in its wake momentous changes in the politics of the Far East.

As I have remarked, Siberia, along the line of its great

railway, is no longer the unhappy land of former days, and although convict settlements exist in the country, they are situated to the north of the railway, many hundreds of miles beyond civilisation, some of them within the Arctic circle, a land of desolation and solitude, and where for nine months in the year the sun never shines.

The inauguration of the Trans-Siberian Railway has rendered possible the journey from London to Pekin in fifteen days, whilst the assistance it afforded the Russians during the late campaign in Manchuria testifies to the great value its construction has conferred from a military standpoint alone.

I drove on into the town and up to the post-house, which was full of other travellers, so we had perforce to be content with the entrance hall which the proprietor transformed into a bedroom

I dined that night at a restaurant in company with the police officer and Khatimski, and the following day disposed of the remainder of my kit by presenting it to the latter   Later in the evening I drove down to take the overland express to Moscow

As I neared the station I realised the long journey was at an end   For nearly a year I had been marching across mountain ranges, over interminable plains, and across the mighty steppes of Mongolia and Siberia, lands of desolation, as they might well be in mid-winter   I mentally reviewed the results of such an undertaking, the regions I had traversed, the strange and interesting tribes I had encountered, the superb shooting I had enjoyed in the heart of Asia, the journey accomplished which no man had ever done before

We rattled into the courtyard and drew up at the station entrance, already my little orderly was busy bundling out our traps in readiness to place aboard the Moscow express   My thoughts travelled back across the weary wastes to the Roof of the World and the smiling valleys of the Thian Shan   I forgot the hardships and the toil of nigh 4,000 miles of trekking, forgot all I had endured, and wished only that I might some day return to see again the big ibex and hear the wapiti calling

But I was awakened from my musings by the clanging of the bell warning all to step aboard. The last good-byes were said, and the next moment the train rumbled out of the station over the silent snow-covered wilderness on the way to Moscow and—England. The long trek was over

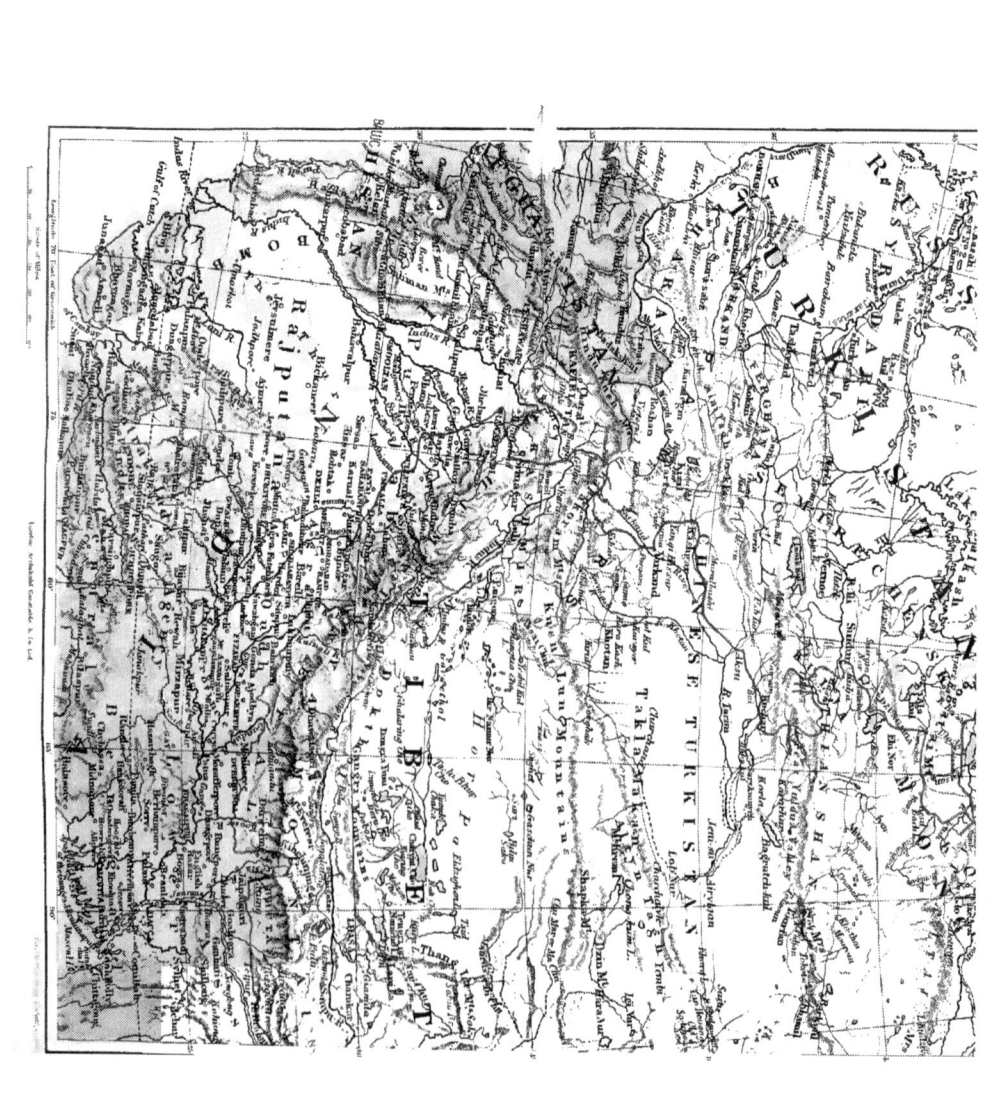

85°
90°
95°
60°
55°
Mikulina
Dubtchevsk
Sergieva
Katska
R. Sim
Kolmogorova
R. Pit
Dubinina
Pitsha
Yeniseisk
R. V. Tunguska
Ketsh
R. Ket
Notzka
R. Tchulim
Karginsk
Kemtchuga
Tasievsk
R. Kia
Turuntzeva
Atchinsk
KRASNOIARSK
TOMSK
Kansk
Uirska
Tomsk
Baraitsk
Karaulnoi
R. Tom
Novoselovo
Abakansk
Minusinsk
Kuznetzk
R I A
Yenisei
Tomsk
R. Obi
Bisk
R. Bia
Tashtinsk
Ibkansk
R. Us

Index

Index

Index.

2 F 2

Index

Index

LONDON
PRINTED BY HARRISON & SONS, ST MARTIN'S LANE, W C
PRINTERS IN ORDINARY TO HIS MAJESTY

Ingram Content Group UK Ltd.
Milton Keynes UK
UKHW022208240723
425713UK00005B/175